STEPHEN J. NICHOLS

A CULTURAL HISTORY FROM THE PURITANS
TO *THE PASSION OF THE CHRIST*

IVP Academic

An imprint of InterVarsity Press
Downers Grove, Illinois

InterVarsity Press
P.O. Box 1400, Downers Grove, IL 60515-1426
World Wide Web: www.ivpress.com
E-mail: email@ivpress.com

InterVarsity Press® is the book-publishing division of InterVarsity Christian Fellowship/USA®, a student movement active on campus at hundreds of universities, colleges and schools of nursing in the United States of America, and a member movement of the International Fellowship of Evangelical Students. For information about local and regional activities, write Public Relations Dept., InterVarsity Christian Fellowship/USA, 6400 Schroeder Rd., P.O. Box 7895, Madison, WI 53707-7895, or visit the IVCF website at <www.intervarsity.org>.

Scripture quotations, unless otherwise noted, are from The Holy Bible, English Standard Version, copyright © 2001 by Crossway Bibles, a division of Good News Publishers. Used by permission. All rights reserved.

Design: Cindy Kiple
Images: gold starburst: Nic Taylor/iStockphoto
    Jesus banner: Dynamic Graphics/Jupiter Images

ISBN 978-0-8308-2849-4

Printed in the United States of America ∞

Library of Congress Cataloging-in-Publication Data

Nichols, Stephen J., 1970-
  Jesus made in America: cultural history from the Puritans to the
  Passion of the Christ / Stephen J. Nichols.
     p. cm.
  Includes bibliographical references and indexes.
  ISBN 978-0-8308-2849-4 (pbk.: alk. paper)
  1. Christianity and culture—United States—History. 2. United
States—Church history. I. Title.
  BR517.N53 2008
  277.3—dc22

                                                              2008002177

| P | 21 | 20 | 19 | 18 | 17 | 16 | 15 | 14 | 13 | 12 | 11 | 10 | 9 | 8 | 7 | 6 | 5 | 4 | 3 | 2 | 1 |
| Y | 26 | 25 | 24 | 23 | 22 | 21 | 20 | 19 | 18 | 17 | 16 | 15 | 14 | 13 | 12 | 11 | 10 | 09 | 08 |

CONTENTS

ACKNOWLEDGMENTS

A number of friends and colleagues have given shape indirectly or directly to this book, including Darryl Hart, Lester Hicks, Mike Horton, Sean Lucas, Michael Rogers, Justin Taylor, Derek Thomas and Carl Trueman. Tim Larsen and Doug Sweeney, as well as an anonymous reader, also kept me from (most of my) errors. Those remaining errors, both in fact and in judgment, solely belong to me. My former student Eric Brandt helpfully uncovered song lyrics, websites and many more things too numerous to list. I am grateful for our friendship. I am also thankful for Megan Stripling (soon to be Brandt) for her help in preparing the index.

I am also grateful to the staffs at the Montgomery Library at Westminster Theological Seminary, the Phillip Schaff Library at Lancaster Theological Seminary and the library at Lancaster Bible College. The administrators at Lancaster Bible College have been most gracious to me. Peter Teague, Philip Dearborn, Ray Naugle, Gordon Gregory and Bob Spender have all offered unstinting support.

Writing this book has had an added bonus of affording the opportunity to forge a friendship with Joel Scandrett and his colleagues at InterVarsity Press. Joel has been encouraging and gracious at every step of the way. Thanks for having me in your fold.

Writing this book has also caused me to disappear at various times. I am grateful to my family for letting me do so. They graciously allowed me to inflict them with all sorts of Jesus talk, music, DVDs and trinkets over the last many months. I am especially grateful to Heidi, without whom I simply wouldn't be writing at all. This book is for you.

INTRODUCTION

Americans apparently want Christ, but they do not want him straight.

ROBERT DETWEILER

It was Billy Sunday who, in addition to saving thousands of souls and raising millions of dollars for the war effort in the late 1910s, snarled, "Turn Hell upside down and what do you find stamped on the bottom? Made in Germany!" What so enraged the revivalist and ordained Presbyterian minister about the Germans was that they had undermined biblical authority. They had exported higher criticism to the fine shores of America, dismantling the Mosaic authorship of the Pentateuch. Worse yet, the Germans had begun the hellish course of severing the Christ of faith from the Jesus of history. It was Adolf Harnack and Albert Schweitzer, and before them Ferdinand Christian Bauer and David Friedrich Strauss, and even before them H. E. G. Paulus and Herman Samuel Reimarus—Germans all—who had quested after the historical Jesus, leaving the Gospels churned up in the wake. Yes, Mr. Sunday thundered, Germany was to blame.

Sunday makes a fair point. One thesis to account for religious decline in twentieth-century America has Germany's higher criticism subtly eroding biblical authority until all manner of evil breaks loose in time for the 1920s and the Scopes Trial and the fundamentalist-modernist controversy. There might, after all, be credence to Sunday's argument. Yet something else lurks around the edges of Sunday's retort: a quite (un)healthy dose of patriotism pulses through it, a patriotism that blinds Sunday to the complicity of his own nation in the so-called making of hell. Stamped not too far away from "Made in Germany" one might see "Made in America," as well. Long before Bauer and Strauss and the Tübingen School set to work unraveling the Gospel narratives, Thomas Jefferson grabbed a pair of scissors and began cutting and pasting his own version of the Gospels, excised of those aspects odious to *Reason,* the Enlightenment's best friend. And as Tom Paine, the great pamphleteer of the Revolutionary War, lay on his deathbed, he mustered enough strength to write that Jesus and the disciples were a story copped from Eastern religions, "a parody on the sun and the twelve signs of the Zodiac." Whatever Jefferson and Paine lacked in scholarship (compared to the German efforts at textual criticism), they made up for in raw ingenuity. So it may be argued, with apologies to Sunday, that America has its own quest for Jesus, its own reshaping of the Son of God, fashioning him into something more palatable to American tastes and acceptable to American sensibilities. Only in America would you find such books as *Jesus, CEO* or its sequel, *Jesus in Blue Jeans.*

As historian Stephen Prothero puts it, "Jesus has an American history."[1] For some Americans, Jesus is the consummate best friend and lover. For others, he is strong and mighty, ready for the defense of the weak. For others still, he's a guru, a wise and enlightened sage. For American Roman Catholics, he is first the Savior on the cross, bloodied and suffering. For American Protestants, he is first, largely due to the prominence of Warner Sallman's *Head of Christ* (1941), nearly angelic, soft and beloved by children. For countercultural rebels, he's a crazed malcontent, hurling the establishment—in the form of money changers—from the temple. For the inimitable Johnny Cash, he's "The Greatest Cowboy of them all."

Jesus, like most cultural heroes, is malleable. And his given shape has much more to say about the shapers than it does of him. Christians in all cultures and ages have the tendency to impose their understandings and cultural expressions on Scripture or beliefs. The pictures in woodcuts prepared for Bibles during the Reformation era look remarkably similar to scenes prevalent in the sixteenth, not the first, century. Medieval theologians imbued their discussions of Christology with language and concepts that might surprise even the most knowledgeable and cosmopolitan of the twelve disciples. But there is something peculiar to the tendency to contemporize in American evangelicalism. This may be explained on four counts. First, American evangelicals reflexively harbor suspicions of tradition. In fact, most tend toward being (rabidly) antitradition. Consequently, the past is overlooked as a significant source of direction. This leaves

---

[1]Stephen Prothero, *American Jesus: How the Son of God Became a National Icon* (New York: Farrar, Straus & Giroux, 2003), p. 9.

American evangelicals more vulnerable than most when it comes to cultural pressures and influences. In the absence of tradition, we tend to make up a new one, one not tested by time and more or less constructed by individuals or by a limited community. This antitradition animus arises from what Sidney Mead once labeled *historylessness*, and what I have elsewhere called *ahistoricism*. This is the tendency of Americans in general to be not only amnesiacs of the past but to be amnesiacs who aren't necessarily looking to be cured.[2]

Second, American evangelicals, when they do dip into tradition, tend only to find Luther's *sola scriptura* principle. The use of this principle not only denigrates tradition but also results in a naive hermeneutic and theology. The mistaken conclusion is that because American evangelicals hold firmly and prize *sola scriptura*, it naturally follows that all of the beliefs of American evangelicals naturally flow from the pages of Scripture. "I'm a biblicist," as one might say, is tantamount to saying "My ideas and beliefs are biblical." Third, American evangelicals tend toward an objectivist or foundational epistemology. This is a particular way of understanding knowledge and how we come to accept certain things as knowledge. The objectivist or foundational approach posits that knowledge is fundamentally objective, even neutral. Putting the matter differently, when a tree falls in the woods, it does make a sound even if no one hears it. Recent work in epistemology has raised awareness of how much we as the subjects, the knowers, bring to the table when we talk about knowledge, or the object or thing known. In other words, we have biases and presuppositions and limited perspectives, all of which impact the way we acquire knowledge. Much of contemporary evangelicalism, or at least evangelicalism of the past decades, operates under the assumption that we are neutral in the acquisition of knowledge. The upshot of all this is that our ideas or beliefs are not held as *our* ideas or beliefs but as *the* ideas or beliefs.[3]

---

[2]See Jaroslav Pelikan's *The Illustrated Jesus Through the Centuries* (New Haven, Conn.: Yale University Press, 1997) for a comprehensive history of the appropriations of Jesus throughout history in various cultures and religions. For a helpful discussion of the value that tradition can play in the life of the church, especially for evangelicals, see D. H. Williams, *Evangelicals and Tradition: The Formative Influence of the Early Church* (Grand Rapids: Baker Academic, 2005). See also Sidney Mead, *The Lively Experiment: The Shaping of Christianity in America* (New York: Harper Collins, 1977).

[3]For Luther's intention of *sola scriptura* versus its use in contemporary American evangelicalism, see Stephen J. Nichols, *Martin Luther: A Guided Tour of His Life and Thought* (Phillipsburg, N.J.: P & R, 2002), pp. 76-82. For a discussion of the epistemological shift and its impact on theological methodology, see John R. Franke, *The Character of Theology: An Introduction to Its Nature, Task and Purpose* (Grand Rapids: Baker Academic, 2005).

Finally, American evangelicals are strongly influenced by pietism, which emphasizes personal religious experience, and values devotion and practice over doctrine. For example, pietism leads us to say that imitating Christ is far better than having a right set of beliefs about who Christ is. Pietism leads to viewing Christ primarily from the lens of personal experience rather than the lenses of the Gospel pericopes or of theological formulations. David Wells offers a fascinating example of this in his *No Place for Truth*. He contrasts two sets of articles in *Christianity Today* that appeared thirty years apart. The first, from 1959, dealt with Easter by lining up articles on the historicity of the event, apologetic discussions of the resurrection and theological reflections. The next set of articles appeared in 1989. This time prominent popular authors such as Walter Wangerin and Philip Yancey approached the event of the resurrection from the perspective of "What does the resurrection mean to me?" Once launched through that portal, "reflections of personal experience," using the words of Wells, filled the magazine's columns.[4]

These theological and philosophical impulses of ahistoricism, biblicism, foundationalism and pietism all conspire to make American evangelicals quite susceptible to culture in the shaping of beliefs and interpretation of Scripture. And perhaps nowhere is this more poignantly felt than in the area of Christology and the shape and identity of Jesus, the American Jesus.[5]

Certainly that has not always been, nor is it always presently, the case. The New England Puritans had a very high view of Christ. They would likely, if we could transport them forward to our time, blush at the contemporary overfamiliarity in our references to the second person of the Trinity. Further, the narrative of American Christology contains plenty of dissenters from the Jeffersonian trajectory. For every Harry Emerson Fosdick, there is a J. Gresham Machen. Nevertheless, there is something to be said for the notion that there is a distinctly American religious Christology, speaking more broadly, and an American evangelical Christology, speaking closer to home. This distinct American Christology is shaped in many ways by distinctly American ideals, such as rugged individualism or an ethic of consumption. This distinct Chris-

---

[4]David Wells, *No Place for Truth: Or, Whatever Happened to Evangelical Theology* (Grand Rapids: Eerdmans, 1993), p. 210.

[5]For a provocative discussion of American evangelicals' tortured relationship with culture, see D. G. Hart, *That Old-Time Religion in Modern America: Evangelical Protestantism in the Twentieth Century* (Chicago: Ivan R. Dee, 2002).

tology is also shaped by particular American experiences, such as the frontier or the experiment in democracy. Some of these ideals and experiences are perennial, while some shift as cultural moods and expressions wax and wane. They all influence the way we read the Gospels, adding distinctive color to the picture of Jesus that emerges. This book is an attempt to unveil these pictures of Jesus in American evangelicalism, to tell the story of his American evangelical incarnations.

Among the works that have treated this topic, R. Laurence Moore's *Touchdown Jesus*, Clint Willis and Nate Hardcastle's *Jesus Is Not a Republican* and Dan Gilgoff's *The Jesus Machine* get at the misappropriations, in the authors' views, of Jesus' conscription in American politics. Books on this topic keep coming. Two other studies have sketched this story of the American Jesus more programmatically, though both have dealt with American religion much more broadly than evangelicalism or even Christianity. Richard Wightman Fox's *Jesus in America: Personal Savior, Cultural Hero, National Obsession* carefully walks through American history from the time of its European settlement to the present day. Along the way Fox explores the impact of the cultural adaptations of Jesus for theology and religion, and also locates the historical and present depictions and depicters of Christ in the culture wars. Stephen Prothero's *American Jesus: How the Son of God Became a National Icon* takes a more thematic approach, looking at the appropriations of Jesus in American Christianity as well as within popular African American culture, Mormonism, Judaism and various forms of Hinduism and Buddhism. Writing nearly forty years before Fox and Prothero, Robert Detweiler, after surveying Christ in American fiction, had already reached the conclusion that "Americans apparently want Christ, but they do not want him straight."[6]

In this book I cover some of the same terrain as Fox and Prothero but also venture into texts not considered by either one. The scope of this book is more sharply focused. While issues and influences of American religion

---

[6]R. Laurence Moore, *Touchdown Jesus: Mixing Sacred and Secular in America* (Louisville, Ky.: Westminster John Knox Press, 2003); Clint Willis and Nate Hardcastle, eds., *Jesus Is Not a Republican: The Religious Right's War on America* (New York: Avalon, 2005); Dan Gilgoff, *The Jesus Machine: How James Dobson, Focus on the Family, and Evangelical America Are Winning the Culture War* (New York: St. Martin's Press, 2007); Richard Wightman Fox, *Jesus in America: Personal Savior, Cultural Hero, National Obsession* (New York: Harper San Francisco, 2004); Prothero, *American Jesus*; and Robert Detweiler, "Christ in American Religious Fiction," *Journal of Bible and Religion* 32, no. 1 (1964): 13.

more broadly speaking will come into play, the primary concern here centers
on American evangelicalism. Fox and Prothero have both accomplished
drawing attention to the explicit ways cultural forces have shaped the identity
of the American Jesus. This book attempts the same for the American evangelical Jesus.

Historians of American religion, from Sidney Mead to Mark Noll and
D. G. Hart, as well as American theologians, from H. Richard Niebuhr to
Michael Horton and David Wells, have uncovered a particular insight—that
theology, like nature, abhors a vacuum. Theologizing, in other words, is influenced by culture. One of the first books that got me thinking in this direction
was Michael Horton's *Made in America*. Reading that book was like pulling
back the curtain to see the wizard at the controls. If what Horton and company wrote is true, then what occurs in culture certainly affects the theology
and life of the church. And given the centrality of Christology, understanding
how culture affects our thinking of Jesus and his identity could not be more
important for the mission of the church. Pulling back this curtain might be
painful but nevertheless necessary.[7]

In trying to tell this story, I have chosen many "texts" that bear witness to
an American evangelical Christology. These texts, some lost to contemporary readers, all played a pivotal role in their time—or are at least reflective of
larger currents of their time—in one way or another. These texts include
books, essays, sermons, presidential inaugural speeches, songs, artwork and
film. They also include artifacts from material culture, ranging from Victorian
tree toppers to bracelets with a quartet of well-known initials. These artifacts
perhaps best get at the evangelical impulse, since this is where most evangelicals not only live out but literally wear their Christianity.

I have framed this story as a cultural history. While there is a chronological
flow, I'm more interested in the highlights of that flow than in a comprehensive treatment of the details. Consequently, this book is a series of "snapshots" or of "sightings" of the American Jesus—and, like UFOs or Elvis, he
shows up in the most interesting places. The first four chapters roam from the

---

[7]Michael Scott Horton, *Made in America: The Shaping of Modern American Evangelicalism* (Grand
Rapids: Baker, 1991); David Wells, *No Place for Truth*, and *Above All Earthly Pow'rs: Christ in a
Postmodern World* (Grand Rapids: Eerdmans, 2005); D. G. Hart, *That Old-Time Religion in Modern
America*, and *Deconstructing Evangelicalism: Conservative Protestantism in the Age of Billy Gra-
ham* (Grand Rapids: Baker Academic, 2004); and Mark Noll, *The Scandal of the Evangelical Mind*
(Grand Rapids: Eerdmans, 1994).

seventeenth to the early twentieth centuries. The next four camp out in the latter half of the twentieth and the dawn of the twenty-first centuries. Combined, these chapters reveal the making of the American Jesus.

We begin with New England Puritans, the theological heavyweights. Edward Taylor was little known until his cache of poetry hidden in Yale's Beinecke Library was discovered in the early twentieth century. He once preached a tour-de-force sermon series on two-nature Christology. Not only did Taylor stretch the series into fourteen sermon units, which would have been preached for far more than fourteen Sundays, but he even went so far as to embellish the series with a Latin title: *Christographia* (1701-1703). Taylor also spent most of his Saturday evenings composing poems as he contemplated the person of Christ, prompted by the Lord's Supper he would be administering the next day. These poems, collected as *Preparatory Meditations,* span from the 1680s through the 1720s, though existing in virtual obscurity for over two centuries.

One cannot talk about New England Puritans without mentioning Jonathan Edwards, whose work has been anything but obscure. Edwards had not only the foresight to see the perennial value of a robust Christology for the church—and so devoted much of his preaching to it—but he also had the prescience to see age-old Arianism washing ashore in New England. What Edwards suspected would happen did happen in the 1810s, when William Ellery Channing led the old Puritan Congregational churches into the tall grass of Unitarianism. In the Puritans, one sees the triumph of the word over image. Cultural historians attribute the word's victory to the Puritan's iconophobia, owing to their view of the Second Commandment, which they inherited from John Calvin. Eventually, however, the image would come to overtake the word.

After the Puritans we'll look at the formative decades of the emerging and early Republic. Jefferson, Franklin, Washington, Adams, Paine: all had a great deal (or very little, depending on how you judge it) to say about Christ. Much attention has been turned on the founders and their religion, attention that has resulted in deeply heated debates. One thing can be said for certain, however: the founders did set many significant trajectories for the American Jesus. In fact they are of such prominence that they have essentially obscured the Puritan view of Jesus. Once the Republic was established, America pushed westward with vengeance, introducing the ethos of the frontier to mass American culture, symbolized in Andrew Jackson and the Jacksonian era of politics, culture and religion. The rugged frontier ethos sparked a reaction in the opposite direction, ushering the more refined and genteel Victorian era. Jesus was retooled to fit both frontier and Victorian cultures, morphing from a rough and tumble scion of true grit to Jesus as gentle, meek and mild. Chapter three explores these pendulum swings, while taking a glance at Jesus in the Civil War.

The story that dominates American religion from the close of the nineteenth century to the early decades of the twentieth is that of the fundamentalist-modernist controversy, the subject of chapter four. Christology took center stage in this debate. Here Harry Emerson Fosdick provides the perfect foil for J. Gresham Machen, as close to a theological prize fight as one might ever find. While these four chapters trace the evolution of the American evangelical Jesus from the seventeenth century to the early twentieth, the next four chapters turn the spotlight on events and occasions more closely related to our times. These chapters wade in the waters of popular culture, which Andrew Greeley has described as the *locus theologicus* of our age; that is, pop culture is not only where people live, it's also the place where we moderns like to do theology. And in this respect, American evangelicals seem ideally suited to the climates of pop culture.

Chapter five begins this quest with the story of the Jesus Movement and the founding era of Contemporary Christian Music (CCM). A billion dollar business, CCM is a network of recording companies, radio stations, retail outlets and megagroups and fans, all topped off by its own awards show. CCM represents for many contemporary evangelicals the sum of their theological training and discipleship.

Evangelicals, as well as the general public, have also learned of Jesus through his many portrayals on the silver screen. Consequently, film, stretching back from old black-and-white silents right up to the present box office offerings, is the subject of chapter six. Chapter seven explores the evangelical consumer culture. The marketing of Jesus has been quite successful, at least in terms of sales. This phenomenon, perhaps, reached a zenith with the remarkably successful WWJD—What Would Jesus Do?—cottage industry. The case of WWJD is an intriguing one. On the one hand, it so reflects the tendencies of the twentieth and now twenty-first centuries, the era of consumerism and the revolving doors of passing fads. On the other hand, there is something perennial about it. In the late 1800s Charles Monroe Sheldon's *In His Steps* (1897) advanced a WWJD-styled approach to the life of Christ. Many centuries prior to that, it was Thomas à Kempis's *Imitation of Christ* (1393). Contemporary audiences have simply reduced such book-length treatments down to four little initials that fetch big profits.

Chapter eight steps into the currently troubled waters of religion and politics. The last several presidents have claimed to be born again. But with George W. Bush such political God talk has become remarkably Jesus centered. When then Governor Bush told an audience of the Republican presidential candidates' debate that the political philosopher who influenced him the most was Jesus, he signaled this new era. Since then, Jesus has been a prominent part of both evangelicalism's right and left wings of political engagement. Evangelicals are clearly influencing politics in America, perhaps like never before. This chapter turns the tables, exploring how all of this political engagement has affected evangelicalism and the evangelical Jesus.

This survey of the American evangelical Jesus intends to do more than inform. It intends to raise significant questions about the state of Christology in American evangelicalism. Consequently, the epilogue holds up the American evangelical Jesus as a mirror for our own self-examination. This self-examination becomes all the more important when we realize that Christology has everything to do with the church's task of proclaiming the gospel.

Some, such as David Wells, have argued rather persuasively that contemporary American evangelicalism lacks a robust theological center and, what's worse, the skill and the moral will to construct one. Such judgments don't bode well for the future of evangelicalism, especially in terms of Christology. A rigorous and detailed and even fought-for Christology was the lifeblood of the early church. Early Christians recognized that Christianity would indeed stand or fall based on how it settled the question of Christ's identity. So they debated. They debated the subtle distinctions between the terms *nature* and *person*, and on the issue of the Trinity, *person* and *substance*. They agonized over the biblical data. Getting it right on Christology meant everything to the early church. The church fathers labored over Christology not because they enjoyed splitting theological hairs and relished a good debate, but because if they didn't, there would not be much of a Christianity at all. In the words of the Nicene and Chalcedonian creeds, Christ is the God-man, two natures conjoined in one person, "for us and for our salvation."[8]

The history of the American evangelical Jesus reveals that such complexities as the two natures of Christ have often been brushed aside, either on purpose or out of expediency. Too often his deity has been eclipsed by his humanity, and occasionally the reverse is true. Too often American evangelicals have settled for a Christology that can be reduced to a bumper sticker. Too often devotion to Jesus has eclipsed theologizing about Jesus. Today's American evangelicals may be quick to speak of their love for Jesus, even wearing their devotion on their sleeve, literally in the case of WWJD bracelets. But they may not be so quick to articulate an orthodox view of the object of their devotion. Their devotion is commendable, but the lack of a rigorous theology behind it means that a generation of contemporary evangelicals is living off of borrowed capital. This quest for the historical Jesus of American evangelicalism is not just a story of the past; it perhaps will help us understand the present, and it might even be a parable for the future. This parable teaches us that Jesus is not actually *made* in America. He is made and remade and remade again. What will next year's model look like?

---

[8]See Stephen J. Nichols, *For Us and for Our Salvation: The Doctrine of Christ in the Early Church* (Wheaton, Ill.: Crossway, 2007).

THE PURITAN CHRIST

Image and Word in Early New England

What Love is this of thine, that Cannot bee
In thine Infinity, O Lord, Confinde,
Unless it in thy very Person see,
Infinity and Finity Conjoyn'd? . . .
Oh, Matchless Love! filling heaven to the Brim.

EDWARD TAYLOR

The Incarnation shows man the greatness of his wretchedness
through the greatness of the remedy required.

BLAISE PASCAL

The identity of Jesus has been the center of attention through the centuries. Not surprisingly, the question of his identity dominates the pages of the New Testament. At one particularly crucial moment in the narrative of the life of Christ found in the Synoptic Gospels, the disciples, huddled together after a time of separation from their Master, have the question put to them by Christ himself: "Who do people say that the Son of Man is?" (Mt 16:13). Christ was leading his original disciples to see that the right answer to this question is essential to the church and to the gospel. Answers from the first century on, however, have not always been right. Americans and even American evangelicals have also had a variety of answers to this question. Those answers stretch back to the beginnings of Protestantism in America, back to the Puritans.

The Puritans have been the recipients of mixed reviews. To the intelligentsia of the nineteenth century the Puritans embodied the shackles of Old World thinking. The Puritan insistence on original sin did not sit well with the absolute belief in the innocence and purity of childhood held by nineteenth-century Victorians. New England's nineteenth-century religious establishment was more than ready to walk away from the rigid Calvinism of their forebears. Some evangelicals love the Puritans, stocking up on shelf loads of reprints as evidence of their affection, while others stumble over their alleged prudishness, or simply find them disagreeable.

As for the academy, a great deal of the negative publicity has trailed off in the recent decades, thanks in no small part to the heroic efforts in rescuing the Puritans by the late Harvard literary scholar Perry Miller and those who have followed him. But there are still those in the academy who are haunted by what they perceive as the narrow and sanctimonious Puritan outlook.

Popular evangelical authors, such as J. I. Packer, Leland Ryken and John Piper, have done the same for the Puritans in the evangelical church as Perry Miller did for them in the academy. But, as with the holdouts in the academy, many in the church remain less than convinced that the Puritans are worth any recovery efforts. Indeed, overall the reviews of the Puritans are mixed. People love them. People hate them.[1]

When it comes to the American Jesus, the Puritans are targeted for their overzealousness in their quest for a pure theology and a pure church. They are also held guilty for revering Jesus too much, for failing to see him, as so many evangelicals do today, as the friend of sinners. To be sure, the Puritan Jesus is incarnate; he is the God-man. Yet he's just a bit too far out of reach for the personal touch. Working independently, two scholars of American religious history have recently drawn significant attention to the Puritan contribution to the American Jesus. Stephen Prothero traces the development from the more pristine and uniform Jesus of the Puritans to the more fluid and multiform Jesus of the contemporary American religious land-

---

[1]See Perry Miller, *The New England Mind: The Seventeenth Century* (1939; reprint, Cambridge, Mass.: Harvard University Press, 1959); and Murray G. Murphey, "Perry Miller and American Studies," *American Studies* 42, no. 2 (2001): 5-18. For a discussion of the historiography of Puritan studies, see David D. Hall, "Narrating Puritanism," *New Directions in American Religious History,* ed. Harry S. Stout and D. G. Hart (New York: Oxford University Press, 1997), pp. 51-83; and Darren Staloff, *The Making of an American Thinking Class: Intellectuals and Intelligentsia in Puritan Massachusetts* (New York: Oxford University Press, 1998), pp. 192-205. For the Puritans in evangelical thought, see J. I. Packer, *A Quest for Godliness: The Puritan Vision of the Christian Life* (Wheaton, Ill.: Crossway Books, 1991); Leland Ryken, *Worldly Saints: The Puritans as They Really Were* (Grand Rapids: Zondervan, 1990); and John Piper, *Desiring God* (Eugene, Ore.: Multnomah Press, 2003).

scape, noting three stages of declension. American religion crossed the first threshold when, in the early nineteenth century, "evangelicals liberated Jesus first from Calvinism and then from creeds." Second, following America's Civil War, "they disentangled Jesus from the Bible, replacing the *sola scriptura* ('Bible Alone') rallying cry of the Reformation with *solus Jesus:* Jesus alone." The final stage came when, in fulfillment of Thomas Jefferson's seminal dream of religious diversity, Jesus was liberated from Christianity itself, which came into "fruition in the midst of the post-1965 immigration boom."[2]

Prothero's story of declension from the Puritan-dominated theology of early American Christianity to the present day has much to commend it. But Prothero overplays his hand. He states, "In Puritan theology, Christ had a limited role to play, Jesus had almost none." Consequently, the American quest for a cultural Jesus, which necessarily meant liberating him from orthodox theology and the Bible, all began because the Puritans had no time for the human face of Jesus. The Puritans' focus on the distance between God and humanity, their tendency to see Christ as sovereign Lord but not as a friend of sinners, goes Prothero's argument, served as a catalyst for the current multifarious American Jesus.

Richard Wightman Fox, the other scholar drawing our attention to the Puritan contribution to the American Jesus, tempers Prothero's thesis with a far more nuanced treatment. Fox notes how the New England Puritan clergy vigorously staked out orthodox Christology, but he sees them motivated by what David Hall has referred to as the Puritan "world of wonders," a world of superstition and spirits. Darren Staloff argues similarly that establishing orthodoxy was the clergy's "primary task," especially in the face of the controversies and heresies of the deists and the superstitions of the folk religions. The clerical establishment countered this world of wonders and the concurrent heterodoxy, thundering from their pulpits that the Trinity reigned supreme and sovereign over the supernatural world, the world filled with devils—and angels. Further, the clergy wanted orthodox theology to trump superstition and heresy, which further sent sound Christology reverberating from these New England pulpits. But, Fox argues contrary to Prothero, amidst

---

[2]Stephen Prothero, *American Jesus: How the Son of God Became a National Icon* (New York: Farrar, Straus, & Giroux, 2003), pp. 10-14. It should be noted that Prothero's study is more descriptive in nature than prescriptive.

all of their theologizing, the Puritans had plenty to say about Christ and about Jesus on the personal level.

In fact, Fox cites numerous sermons by such Puritan stalwarts as Thomas Hooker (1586-1647) and John Cotton (1584-1652) that poetically express the "believer's intimate tie to Christ." Hooker's son-in-law and a Harvard founder, Thomas Shepard (1605-1649), went so far as to close "one of his sermons at his Cambridge meetinghouse by officiating at a mock marriage ceremony between Christ and each of the members of his congregation." The Puritans, Fox concludes, spoke with "intense passion of the union with the Lord." Nevertheless, Fox concedes that in general the Puritans more often took the doctrines of the Trinity and Christology as propositional creeds, not as personal experiences. Such an admission reveals Fox's failure to see the full picture of Puritan devotion to Christ. Notwithstanding, Fox offers his own narrative of the declension of American Christology. He focuses on the Puritan view of conversion. The Puritan view was heavy on theology, too heavy in fact. Eventually it gave way to the overwhelming emphasis stemming from the revivals of the nineteenth century. This new emphasis was heavy on experience, the experience of a personal relationship with Christ begun by answering the altar call. As the decades rolled on, Fox concludes, the American Jesus became more and more known by direct personal experience while becoming less and less hemmed in by the orthodox theology of the creeds. Jesus' portrait took on the contours of this shift in understanding conversion, but the increasingly multiplex portrait also took on the contours of America's broadening religious identity beyond the confines of Protestant Christianity.[3]

Fox's telling of the story reveals that Prothero's argument concerning the Puritans having limited space for Christ and almost none for Jesus is wide of the mark. But both Fox and Prothero may be on to something when it comes to the move from the orthodox Christology of the Puritan era to more fast and loose Christologies of later American theology. In fact, the oft-told story

---

[3]Richard Wightman Fox, *Jesus in America: Personal Savior, Cultural Hero, National Obsession* (New York: Harper, 2004), pp. 95-96; see also pp. 86-119 for his narrative of the declension from the Puritans to the nineteenth century. See also David D. Hall, *Worlds of Wonder, Days of Judgment: Popular Religion in Early New England* (New York: Knopf, 1989); and Darren Staloff, *The Making of an American Thinking Class* (New York: Oxford University Press, 1998), pp. 91-113. The American Puritans were following suit of their Old World counterparts. For an insightful study of English Puritanism and the treatment of heresy, see Leo Damrosch, *The Sorrows of the Quaker Jesus: James Naylor and the Puritan Crackdown on the Free Spirit* (Cambridge, Mass.: Harvard University Press, 1996). Naylor's 1656 trial was due in no small part to his unorthodox Christology.

of theological declension from creedal confines to the more open spaces of experience takes place on a grander stage than in America alone. Jaroslav Pelikan narrates this grander story, taking place in Britain and on the continent, in his recent work on the church's creeds. Pelikan draws attention to Hinrich Stoevesandt's observation of "the discomfort with creed caused by the conscience of modernity." Pelikan unpacks modernity's consciousness, outlining how emphases on personal faith, the historical-critical method—applied both to Scripture and to the history of theological development—the disestablishment of religion in politics and culture, and even the rise in biblical theology have all led to the marginalization of creeds both inside and outside the modern church. All of these factors come into play with the American Jesus, as the following chapters will show.[4]

We need, however, a starting point for the story of the American Jesus, and one is agreeably provided for in these premodern Puritans. The story told of the shift away from the orthodox Christology by Prothero, Fox, Pelikan and others serves as a parable for contemporary American evangelicals. We can, in other words, learn a great deal by looking at Puritan views of Christ. Most of what Americans know about the Puritans has come to them by three mediators: Nathaniel Hawthorne's *The Scarlet Letter* (1850), Arthur Miller's *The Crucible* (1953), and the infamous and oft-anthologized "Sinners in the Hands of an Angry God" (1741) by Jonathan Edwards—all of which offer limited glimpses, and some of which offer outright distortions, into the complex world and thought of the Puritans. Most American evangelicals, despite the efforts of J. I. Packer and company, would not be that much more conversant with the Puritans either. The Puritans, however, merit a deeper and longer look. Holding up the portrait of Christ drawn by the Puritans to those drawn of Christ today might very well be a revealing and beneficial, maybe even painful, exercise. Two Puritan portraits, in particular, worth examining are those of Edward Taylor and Jonathan Edwards.

---

[4]Jaroslav Pelikan, *Credo: Historical and Theological Guide to Creeds and Confessions in the Christian Tradition* (New Haven, Conn.: Yale University Press, 2003), pp. 488-504. The citation is from Hinrich Stoevesandt, *Die Bedeutung des Symbolums in Theologie und Kirche: Versuch einer Dogmatisch-Kritischen Ortsbestimmung aus Evangelischer Sicht* (Munich: Christian Kaiser Verlag, 1970), p. 12.

POETIC PURITANS

Edward Taylor's life (c. 1642-1729) would have remained in relative obscurity were it not for a doctoral student in literature looking for a dissertation subject in Yale's Beinecke Rare Book and Manuscript Library. The felicitous discovery by Thomas H. Johnson ended Taylor's anonymity, introducing him as America's great colonial poet, rivaled only by Anne Bradstreet. A pastor by profession, Taylor dedicated the late hours in the evening to writing poetry, reams and reams of it. His *Gods Determinations* runs 2,102 lines, far outdone, however, by his creative *Metrical History of Christianity*, a staggering 19,864 lines. In addition, he wrote numerous occasional pieces, as well as *Preparatory Meditations*. Like his contemporaries, he also left behind a literary legacy of sermons, not the least of which is his meticulously prepared series on two-nature Christology, to which he appended the auspicious title *Christographia.*

Taylor scholar Daniel Patterson sums up the statistics, noting that Taylor "had delivered several thousand sermons, written more than 2,000 manuscript pages of original prose, and composed some 40,000 lines of poetry." In addition, he served as the town doctor, having also studied medicine at Harvard. When he died, after fifty-eight years of ministry at Westfield, Massachusetts, he left a will forbidding the publishing of his poetry. The material eventually ended up in the care of his grandson, Ezra Stiles. Stiles, during his tenure as Yale's president, deposited the material inconspicuously in the library. Some time later the material migrated to the Beinecke's basement, lying unnoticed until Johnson's discovery. Johnson not only pulled a dissertation from the find, he made a career out of it. Taylor's works, while read among literature scholars, never seemed to make many inroads among theologians. Though obscure in the theological world, Taylor's work nevertheless offers a significant contribution to understanding the Puritan Christ.[5]

Edward Taylor had the consummate Puritan résumé. Born in 1642, 1643 or 1644 in Leicestershire, England, Taylor left for Boston on July 5, 1668. Taylor was part of a wave of immigration as many nonconformists,

---

[5]One exception to the lack of interest among theologians is the work of Charles Hambrick-Stowe, *Early New England Meditative Poetry: Anne Bradstreet and Edward Taylor* (New York: Paulist Press, 1988). Daniel Patterson, *Edward Taylor's Gods Determinations and Preparatory Meditations: A Critical Edition* (Kent, Ohio: Kent State University Press, 2003), p. 1.

hounded by Charles II's program of Restoration and the Act of Uniformity (1662), sought the freer environs of the Puritan colony. He records in his diary that he passed the time on the voyage reading his Greek New Testament and conducting worship services for the other passengers. Presumably with letters of introduction, he was welcomed into the home of Increase Mather (1639-1723), one of the last defenders of the old Puritan way. Mather also was president of Harvard, and three weeks after Taylor landed in the New World, Taylor found himself under Mather's tutelage and as Samuel Sewall's (1652-1730) roommate at Harvard. He studied divinity and medicine, leaving Harvard after his graduation in 1671 for the town of Westfield, Massachusetts. Westfield was about one hundred miles from Boston, on the far side of the Connecticut River in Massachusetts' frontier. Taylor's frontier ministry was not a romanticized, charmed existence. His first wife died, and he buried five of his eight children, sadly not uncommon for the era. His would be a parish ministry filled with fires and deaths and Indian skirmishes. Every Sunday for over fifty years, he would give the sermon in Westfield's Congregational Church. And there he wrote his poetry.[6]

The Puritans have a long history, contrary to popular opinion, as patrons of the arts. While they boycotted the contemporary theater—they could not countenance the bawdy elements—they drank deeply of classical and Renaissance culture and art. All students at Harvard, and later at Yale, as well as the Puritan-dominated colleges of Cambridge University in old England read the great poets and writers, in the original and not in translation. Taylor was no exception and his poetry bears the marks of classical influences. Taylor was also not alone as poet. His colleagues include John Milton and John Donne in old England and Michael Wigglesworth and Anne Bradstreet in New England. The Puritans applied such poetic artistry to their sermonizing, as Puritan scholar Lisa M. Gordis has recently argued. She notes, "Puritan writers, readers, and auditors found not only piety, but also aesthetic pleasure, in the manipulation of the biblical text." She then confesses her own enjoyment of reading John Cotton and Michael Wigglesworth, noting that Puritan scholars

[6]Francis Murphy, ed., *The Diary of Edward Taylor* (Springfield: Connecticut Valley Historical Museum, 1964), pp. 25-36. For a discussion of the impact of these crises on Taylor's life and thought, see Stephen J. Nichols, "An Early Response to Open Theism: Edward Taylor's *Gods Determinations* and the Puritan View of History," *Reformation & Revival Journal* 12, no. 2 (2003): 111-29.

are too reticent to admit such, colored as they are by former judgments of the likes of H. L. Mencken.[7]

INFINITY AND FINITY CONJOYN'D

The significance of the *Preparatory Meditations* and *Christographia* lies in Taylor's ability to wed theological precision, even using orthodox terminology, with heartfelt piety. Further, Taylor could write both intensely personal poetry and meticulously and logically constructed sermons on two-nature Christology. He brought together, in other words, what so often typically gets torn asunder. In this way he very much follows the path of two very significant figures in the early church, Athanasius (c. 296-373) and Leo the Great, who was bishop of Rome from 440 until his death in 461. These two stand out among the church fathers who guided the church in the theological development and creedal formulation of the biblical teaching on Christ. The result of the combined efforts of Athanasius and Leo the Great is what theologians refer to as the Nicene-Chalcedonian two-nature Christology, the marker of orthodoxy for the church through the centuries. The Nicene (325) and Chalcedonian (451) creeds bring the whole swath of the biblical data regarding Christ into concise formulation, stressing in sum that Jesus is very God of very God, very man of very man; two natures, human and divine, conjoined in one person.[8]

These formulas are drawn from various biblical texts. Significant texts include John's prologue (Jn 1:1-18) and various "I am" statements (Jn 8:48-59), Romans 10:9-10, 1 Corinthians 8:4-6 and Hebrews 1:1-4, among many others. Paul offers a paragraph-length statement of two-nature Christology in Philippians 2:1-11, and he puts forth perhaps the most succinct biblical statement in Colossians 2:9, noting that in Christ "the whole fullness of deity dwells bodily."

What the biblical authors originally wrote of and the church fathers summarized into creeds, Edward Taylor put poetically:

---

[7]Lisa M. Gordis, *Opening Scripture: Bible Reading and Interpretive Authority in Puritan New England* (Chicago: University of Chicago Press, 2003), p. 6. Harry Stout, for one, has made the case that the Puritans have been unduly maligned as naysayers of the arts. See his interview on the Puritans in *Christian History* 13, no. 1 (2001): 38. See also the helpful, though dated, work of Samuel Eliot Morison, *The Intellectual Life of Colonial New England* (Ithaca, N.Y.: Cornell University Press, 1960), pp. 3-26, 210-40. For a discussion of Puritan poetry see Heidi L. Nichols, *Anne Bradstreet: A Guided Tour of Her Life and Poetry* (Phillipsburg, N.J.: P & R, 2006).

[8]For a discussion of early developments in Christology, see Stephen J. Nichols, *For Us and for Our Salvation: The Doctrine of Christ in the Early Church* (Wheaton, Ill.: Crossway, 2007).

What Love is this of thine, that Cannot bee
In thine Infinity, O Lord, Confinde,
Unless it in thy very Person See,
Infinity and Finity conjoyn'd?
What hath thy Godhead, as not satisfide,
Marri'de our Manhood, making it its Bride?[9]

This poem comes from Taylor's "First Series" of *Preparatory Meditations*, which Taylor wrote for his own, private preparations for the Lord's Supper. Taylor, of course, did not believe such theologizing to be restricted to personal reflection; he thought it belonged in the church. Consequently, in addition to poetically ruminating on two-nature Christology, Taylor also preached a rather lengthy sermon series on it. *Christographia* consists of fourteen sermons preached on the occasion of the monthly Lord's Supper at Westfield from 1701-1703. This sermon series corresponds to Taylor's poetic "Second Series" of *Preparatory Meditations*, begun in 1693. When he started preaching the sermons, he composed a poem for each one. Taylor once wrote, "This rich banquet," referring to the Lord's Supper, "makes me thus a Poet." John Gatta finds further motivation for Taylor's poetry and sermons when he notes Taylor's "devotional fixation on Christ." The result in both poems and sermons is a theologically rich and heartfelt Christology, which according to Taylor, speaks to the very essence of life.[10]

In the introduction to his edition of Taylor's *Christographia* and the corresponding poems, Norman Grabo connects Taylor's aim in these particular

---

[9]Edward Taylor, *Preparatory Meditations*, in Daniel Patterson, *Edward Taylor's Gods Determinations and Preparatory Meditations: A Critical Edition* (Kent, Ohio: Kent State University Press, 2003), p. 127. For discussion of the biblical data, see James D. G. Dunn, *Christology In the Making: A New Testament Inquiry into the Origins of the Doctrine of the Incarnation*, 2nd ed. (Grand Rapids: Eerdmans, 1996); and Darrell Bock, *Jesus According to Scripture: Restoring the Portrait from the Gospels* (Grand Rapids: Baker Academic, 2002).

[10]The first series consists of forty-five poems, or as Taylor termed them, meditations, written from 1682-1692, while the second series consists of 165 poems written from 1693-1725. Taylor's citation is from series two, meditation 110, in Patterson, *Edward Taylor's Gods Determinations and Preparatory Meditations*, p. 410. John Gatta, *Gracious Laughter: The Meditative Wit of Edward Taylor* (Columbia: University of Missouri Press, 1989), p. 187. Karen E. Rowe adds that the Lord's Supper functioned for Taylor as a type of the eschatological and heavenly wedding feast with Christ (*Saint and Singer: Edward Taylor's Typology and the Poetics of Meditation* [Cambridge: Cambridge University Press, 1986], pp. 196-228). The psalms also made Taylor a poet. See Rosemary Fithian Guruswamy, "A Farewell to David: Edward Taylor's *Valediction* and Psalm 19," in *The Tayloring Shop: Essays on the Poetry of Edward Taylor*, ed. Michael Schuldiner (Newark: University of Delaware Press, 1997), pp. 193-216. Guruswamy specifically refers to the psalmists' Christology as a model for Taylor (p. 194).

works to that of the heart of New England Puritanism, the covenants of redemption, of grace and of the church. Grabo then notes, "All three [covenants] also depended on the fundamental acceptance of Christ the mediator; therefore Taylor directs his energies, as both preacher and teacher, to unfolding this crucial conception—the nature of Christ as redeemer." Like the Nicene and Chalcedonian creeds, Taylor's Christology finds impetus in Christ's work. As that memorable line from the Nicene Creed resounds, Christ is the God-man *"for us and for our salvation."* Taylor begins with the incarnation, moving on in the second sermon to discuss Christ's divine nature. The third sermon is a statement of the Chalcedonian Creed, engaging a rather heady and intricate discourse. He follows up in the fourth sermon with a more meditative treatment, drawing from Colossians 2:3, which declares all the treasures of wisdom and knowledge are hidden in Christ. The fifth sermon summarizes the matter so far, elaborating on Paul's succinct christological pronouncement in Colossians 2:9. The next eight sermons look to Christ in the fullness of his humanity, culminating in the thirteenth sermon, extolling him as the possessor of "all Mediatory Power in Heaven and Earth" through his function of Prophet, Priest and King, the *munis triplex*. The typical Puritan sermon, known as the "Plain Style," consisted of the text, doctrine and application, or what they termed "use" or "improvement." While Taylor makes application from the various texts he cites and the doctrines he develops throughout the sermons, the final sermon may be seen as one grand application of the series. Here words fail him as he expresses the excellence of Christ in his person and his work, at one point saying that Christ is "the most Beautifulst," before resorting to the Latin, which allows for such grammatical superlatives, "*Supremum Excellentiae.*"[11]

Taylor knew all too well the limitation of words. In *Christographia* he warns his audience of such a limitation when it comes to the work of Christ, summed up in the theological word *grace:* "Grace excels all metaphors. The varnish laid upon it doth but darken, and not decorate it: its own colours are too glorious to be made more glorious." As a poet he puts it this way, "What,

---

[11]Norman Grabo, *Edward Taylor's* Christographia (New Haven, Conn.: Yale University Press, 1962), pp. xvi-xix, 404, 447-55. The sermon series was left by Taylor in folio manuscript form. The manuscript, as Grabo observes, evidences that while the sermons were written at different times, Taylor made corrections and a unified revision (pp. xlv-xlvii). Like his poetry, however, Taylor intended that this work not see publication.

Can I ever tune those melodies / Who have no tune at all?" How will he ever, he laments, learn the gamut of singing praises to God?[12]

Despite Taylor's awareness of the limitation of the word, he found himself bound to the word nevertheless. His Greek Orthodox, Roman Catholic or even Anglican contemporaries might have been more comfortable supporting the word with the image, but not so for Taylor and his fellow Puritans. Even though words may have failed in terms of full expression, Taylor used them. In fact, he used them again and again. He used them by the tens of thousands. Neither did Taylor find these words inhibiting his devotion to God or the expression of praise. These words, with all of their limitations, actually served him quite well. He might have confessed to have a stammering tongue, but with his stammering tongue he spoke elegantly.

Literary scholar William J. Scheick was one of the first scholars to refer to this tendency in Taylor and the other Puritans as *logocentrism*. More recently, William A. Dyrness has argued persuasively that such logocentrism was not a counter to art or imagination, but it was the Puritan art form—the expression of imagination and creativity. Dyrness looks past the mere visual austerity of the Puritans to their artful use of the word. Dyrness even finds Edward Taylor and Jonathan Edwards to be, in addition to being first-rate theologians and pastors, creative and imaginative artists whose medium of choice was the word.[13]

Taylor's artistry of words in these fourteen sermons and corresponding poems, and elsewhere, express fully the orthodox teaching of the person and work of Christ. Taylor engages discussions of Nicaea and Chalcedon, walking his congregation through the tricky waters of the Arian controversy and other heresies such as Sabellianism and Apollonarianism. What he presented as sermons would pass for lectures in a theological seminary today. This is not to detract from their value or nature as sermons. Consider, for example, the third sermon on "the Personal Union" of Christ—meaning the hypostatic union. Here he declares, "[The Personal Union] is a joining of the Godhead,

---

[12]Grabo, *Edwards Taylor's* Christographia, p. 253. The poetic citation is from Taylor's *Gods Determinations*, "The Soul's Admiration Hereupon," in Daniel Patterson, *Edward Taylor's Gods Determinations and Preparatory Meditations: A Critical Edition* (Kent, Ohio: Kent State University Press, 2003).

[13]See William J. Scheick, "Anonymity and Art in *The Life and Death of that Reverend Man of God Richard Mather,*" *American Literature* 42 (1971): 457-67; William A. Dyrness, *Reformed Theology and Visual Culture: The Protestant Imagination from Calvin to Edwards* (Cambridge: Cambridge University Press, 2004), pp. 240-99.

and the Manhood so together into an Oneness in the Person of Christ, as that they remain essentially the Same in Nature, united inseparably forever." It was important to Taylor that his congregation understood this, despite the intellectual and logical challenges it presents. He lays out the logical problems with the hypostatic union in the first part of the sermon. Despite its problems, the truth of it holds and demands to be held. As he told them, "Deny this Personall Union, and you destroy the Efficacy of Christ's Mediatory Works, and the means of Grace." He continued, noting that because of the union of Christ's two natures, humanity receives "highest advancement that ever God gave, giveth, or can give," that of union and peace with God. Then Taylor exclaims, "And that this Should be granted to Sinfull Human nature. What grace is here? Oh! It is not only such as carries along with it eternall Glory, and Happiness to all the Elect, but advanceth . . . also our nature . . . out of the most wretched State, into the most transcendent preferment that is possible." He proceeds to note, "That of all things in the World, Sin is the most mischievous," most mischievous because there is "no reliefe to be found." But because of the personal union with Christ, there is relief found in grace. Taylor describes such grace as "the Wonderfull Grace of God," noting that it is unrivaled, "unheard of" and "unparalleled." Taylor ends by imploring his audience and himself to display their union with Christ, made possible by the union of his two natures, "in every branch of our lives."[14]

The poem corresponding to the sermon has similar themes. Here he writes of the incompatibility of the divine and human natures, before declaring their union in Christ:

> In Essence two, in Properties each are
> Unlike, as unlike can be. One All-Might,
> A Mite the other; One Imortall Fair:
> One mortall, This all Glory, that all night:
> One Infinite, One finite. So forever:
> Yet ONED are in Person. Part'd never.

Taylor then connects the person of Christ to his work, noting how grace overtakes sin:

---

[14]Grabo, *Edward Taylor's Christographia*, pp. 77, 91-92, 93-95, 105. When Taylor refers to "essentially the same," he does not use essentially as we might use it to mean "mostly." Instead, he intends a technical meaning, following Nicaea and Chalcedon, that Christ is the same essence (*substantia* in Latin) with humanity and the same essence with deity.

Oh! Dignifide Humanity indeed:

Divinely Person'd, almost Deifide.

Nameing one Godhead person, in our Creed,

The Word-made-Flesh. Here's Grace's 'maizing stride.

The vilst design, the villany e're hatcht

Hath tap't Such Grace in God, that can't be matcht.[15]

Taylor's poems and sermons form an interesting alliance. On the one hand, his poems were private, whereas he obviously made public his sermons. Karl Keller has criticized Taylor the preacher for using language that "seldom soar[ed]" vis-à-vis the language of Taylor the poet that tended to live in the stratosphere. Grabo reaches an altogether different conclusion, noting that Taylor's poetry was "a restricted poetry," hemmed in a bit due to his self-imposed theological constraints. Despite their criticisms, both Keller and Grabo concede the artistry of Taylor's poems and sermons alike. In both sermon and poem, Taylor reflects on the rich legacy of the scriptural teaching of Christ, as succinctly stated in the Nicene and Chalcedonian creeds. Karen Rowe situates this approach of Taylor in what she terms the "worship mould" of the Puritans, a mold focused on Christ's mediatorial and sacerdotal roles, a mold that demanded the two-nature view of Christ—one of Puritanism's "unshakeable tenets."[16]

Taylor's work, however, is not merely one of theological precision; it is also deeply pious. He was not concerned merely to teach of Jesus. Taylor desired to worship and to use his words to lead his congregation into worship. In this, Taylor was in no way the lone Puritan voice. Samuel Sewall, the infamous judge over the Salem witchcraft trials, could proclaim in his private diary, "I had a sweet and very affectionate meditation concerning the Lord Jesus."[17] One assumes that he was not having the sweet meditation while he was condemning people to death (and let's not forget the dogs he also condemned). More on this glaring inconsistency later, but for now it suffices that if a Puritan wanted to wax rhapsodic, then he or she certainly could. No less an auspicious figure than Harvard President Samuel Willard could write in a theology textbook, "Here [Christ] comes to give us the caresses of his love, and lay us

---

[15]Ibid., pp. 73-74. Both the poem and the third sermon are on John 1:14.

[16]Karl Keller, *The Example of Edward Taylor* (Amherst: University of Massachusetts Press, 1975), p. 117; Grabo, *Edward Taylor's Christographia*, p. xliii; and Karen Rowe, *Saint and Singer*, p. 98.

[17]M. Halsey Thomas, ed., *The Diary of Samuel Sewall*, vol. 2 (New York: Farrar, Straus, & Giroux, 1973), p. 882.

in his bosom and embraces. And now, oh my soul! Hast thou ever experienced the love of a saviour?" The Puritans, while committed to the word, seemed unfettered by it when it came to expressing their devotion to Christ. They could be carried away in flights of spiritual ecstasy just as easily as they could be lost in the intricacies of logical syllogisms.[18]

In his interpretation of Edward Taylor, Daniel Patterson draws attention to the first sermon Taylor preached at Westfield. Taylor chose Matthew 3:2 as his text, likely seeing himself as a seventeenth-century embodiment of John the Baptist, preparing the way for Christ in the Massachusetts wilderness. Beyond Taylor's wilderness connection, there lies the confraternity with John the Baptist on message. Taylor's ministry was one of declaring Christ as the God-man and preparing his own heart and the hearts of his parishioners for Christ's kingdom. Fellow Puritan Jonathan Edwards would do the same.[19]

WWJED?

What Would Jonathan Edwards Do? Even if one only reads Jonathan Edwards's "Sinners in the Hands of an Angry God," the caricature of him that too often abounds in the popular consensus would have to go. To be sure he pulls out all rhetorical stops to stress the plight of humanity in sin. The bow of God's wrath is bent; one foot is already on the slippery precipice; and sinners are adrift in a troubled sea. Most famously, sinners are seen dangling from a mere spider's string over the pit of hell. But there is also the rich imagery of Christ who has flung the great "door of mercy wide open and stands in the way calling and crying with a loud voice to poor sinners." If one were to look to the broader, rather copious writings of Edwards, then the caricature of him would not be so narrow. His lexicon overflowed with the words *sweetness* and *beauty, harmony* and *excellence, joy* and *delight.* And nowhere do these words appear more conspicuously than when Edwards refers to Christ. This is not to imply that Edwards never talked about sin and hell, judgment and wrath. He did, vehemently. But in order to appreciate Edwards we must see the full dimension of his teaching.[20]

---

[18]Samuel Willard, *A Complete Body of Divinity* (Boston: 1726), p. 879.

[19]Patterson, *Edward Taylor's Gods Determinations*, pp. 4-5.

[20]Jonathan Edwards, "Sinners in the Hands of an Angry God," in *The Works of Jonathan Edwards,* vol. 22, *Sermons and Discourses, 1739-1742,* ed. Harry Stout and Nathan O. Hatch, with Kyle P. Farley (New Haven, Conn.: Yale University Press, 2003), p. 416. For recent biographies on Edwards, see George M. Marsden, *Jonathan Edwards: A Life* (New Haven, Conn.: Yale University Press, 2003); and Philip Gura, *Jonathan Edwards: America's Evangelical* (New York: Hill & Wang, 2005).

Like Taylor before him, a great deal of Edwards's Christology stems from Christ's mediatorial role. Edwards filled page after page of his *Miscellanies* notebooks with entries on Christ as mediator. Because Christ took upon himself a fully human nature, he could stand in relation to the elect as "their representative, their brother, and the husband of the church," the latter image, according to Edwards, "intimat[ing] an admittance to the greatest nearness, intimacy and communion of good." Edwards continues discussing the union of Christ with his church, predicated on the union of the human and divine natures in his person, noting that "Christ will conform his people to himself: he'll give them his glory, the glory of his person; their souls shall be made like his soul, their bodies like to his glorious body, they shall partake with him in his riches, as co-heirs in his pleasures. He shall bring them in to his banqueting house, and they shall drink new wine with him." Without the God-man, humanity would remain at "an infinite distance from the father." Both natures make Christ the fit mediator who purchases both "our holiness and happiness." Blaise Pascal draws a further implication when he observes, "The incarnation shows man the greatness of his wretchedness through the greatness of the remedy required."[21]

Edwards's *Miscellanies* functioned somewhat like Taylor's poems and meditations. In them we find the more private reflecting and ruminating that eventually comes visible in sermons. Unlike Taylor's poems, however, Edwards's *Miscellanies,* given the nature of the genre, allow him not only to rhapsodize on Christology but also to engage in polemics. In the specific case of Christology, Edwards directed his polemics toward what he saw as a burgeoning Arianism in such writers as Isaac Watts, the famed hymn writer. Edwards recorded an extensive entry in response to Watts's argument that Christ had a preexisting human soul. Engaging in christological polemics also meant encounters with the deists. Edwards did not, however, reserve his polemics for the *Miscellanies,* he also brought them into his sermons. As Gerald McDermott notes, Edwards had detected drifts in the thinking of his colonial colleagues. He saw such drifts leaving his beloved New England Congregationalism susceptible to the damning waves of Arianism and deism. At the time,

---

[21]Jonathan Edwards, *The Works of Jonathan Edwards,* vol. 18, *The "Miscellanies" (Entry Nos. 501-832),* ed. Ava Chamberlain (New Haven, Conn.: Yale University Press, 2000), pp. 108, 111, 419-21. Blaise Pascal is cited in David F. Wells, *Losing Our Virtue: Why the Church Must Recover Its Moral Vision* (Grand Rapids: Eerdmans, 1998), p. 179.

Edwards knew, deism confined itself to the tight circles of the English Enlightenment, including such figures as David Hume and John Locke. Edwards
equally knew, or at least suspected, that the coming generations of Americans, and even American Christians, could easily be drawn into the circle.
Consequently, Edwards responded by writing treatises and thundering sermons. These works had a double edge. In them Edwards offered polemics to
tear down and efforts toward the more constructive task of extolling the virtues of orthodox theology.[22]

The doctrine of the Trinity long fascinated Edwards. In 1730, as a busy
pastor of New England's second largest church and as a twenty-six-year-old,
Edwards began a manuscript he titled "Discourse on the Trinity." As Sang
Hyun Lee observes, Edwards returned to the manuscript in the mid-1730s
and again in the 1740s. By the time of his death, he was likely intending to in-
corporate it into what would have been his magnum opus. But we'll never
know. Lee is of the opinion that Edwards abandoned the pursuit of it as a sep-
arate manuscript, seeing Edwards instead resort to "cannibalize it" for sermon material. That Edwards began such a discourse so young, returned to it
so often and found it convenient for his sermons points to the centrality of
this doctrine in the thought of Edwards. Edwards was a profoundly trinitarian
theologian and pastor, which means that he had a high place for the Father,
the Son and the Holy Spirit. For our purposes, we'll focus on his high view of
Christ, his christocentrism.[23]

Edwards's thoughts on Christ stem from both his awe of God and his sense
of sin. Like his fellow Puritans, Edwards took the grandeur, holiness and glory
of God to underscore the magnitude of humanity's plight as sinners. Christ in
his mediatorial role as the God-man closed the gap, so much so that Edwards
at one time preached a sermon titled "The Sweet Harmony of Christ," in

---

[22]Jonathan Edwards, *The Works of Jonathan Edwards*, vol. 23, *The "Miscellanies" (Entry Nos 1153-
1360)*, ed. Douglas A. Sweeney (New Haven, Conn.: Yale University Press, 2004), pp. 89-92. See
also Donald MacLeod, "God or god? Arianism, Ancient and Modern," *The Evangelical Quarterly*
46 (1996): 121-38. Sweeney notes that MacLeod "compares Watts's view to that of Philip Dodd-
ridge, another of J[onathan] E[dwards]'s sources" (*"Miscellanies,"* p. 89). For Edwards and deism, see
Gerald R. McDermott, *Jonathan Edwards Confronts the Gods: Christian Theology, Enlightenment
Religion, and Non-Christian Faiths* (New York: Oxford University Press, 2000). As McDermott
points out, most of Edwards's polemical engagement with the deists involved views of revelation.
[23]See Jonathan Edwards, *The Works of Jonathan Edwards*, vol. 21, *Writings on the Trinity, Grace, and
Faith* (New Haven, Conn.: Yale University Press, 2003), p. 109. For a discussion of Edwards's trini-
tarianism, see Amy Plantinga Pauw, *The Supreme Harmony of All: The Trinitarian Theology of
Jonathan Edwards* (Grand Rapids: Eerdmans, 2002).

which he expounded the doctrine that "there is a sweet harmony between Christ and the soul of a true Christian." There is, he continued, a mutual love between Christ and the Christian, noting that "Christ is altogether lovely in the eyes of a Christian," adding, "Such is Christ's love to a true Christian that nothing is esteemed too good, too great an happiness or honor to be bestowed, or too much to do or to suffer to procure it"—not what one might expect of the Edwards of "Sinners in the Hands of an Angry God." Christ was, for Edwards, the object of devotion for the Christian, and, like Edward Taylor, he didn't shrink from saying or preaching so.[24]

Neither did Edwards shrink from preaching on Christ as judge. His vision of heaven included the necessary corollary of hell. As Harry Stout observes of Edwards, "With relentless logic he would insist that because God hates sin, 'it is suitable that he should execute an infinite punishment.' " So Edwards states in "Sinners," "And you children that are unconverted, don't you know that you are going down to hell, to bear the dreadful wrath of that God that is now angry with you every day, and every night?" In addition to his famous "Sinners" sermon, numerous sermons contain visceral treatments of hell and the judgment to come. Edwards would not allow his Northampton or, later, his Stockbridge congregations to be lulled into complacency over their eternal destiny should they neglect Christ. It's not that he sought a balance between preaching on hell and heaven or the sweetness and love of Christ with his judgment and wrath. Rather, the picture of Christ that Edwards drew from the Bible was complex and multidimensional. And Edwards would not reduce what he saw.[25]

Edwards's ministry to the Native Americans at Stockbridge bears this out. When he first arrived, he declared that the Indians had been in darkness, without the light of the gospel, and consequently stood outside of God's grace. But now, he tells them, the gospel is in their midst. "Christ," he informs them, "is the original [*sic*] and fountain of all spiritual life and nourishment."

---

[24]Jonathan Edwards, "The Sweet Harmony of Christ," *The Works of Jonathan Edwards*, vol. 19, *Sermons and Discourses, 1734-1738*, ed. M. X. Lesser (New Haven, Conn.: Yale University Press, 2001), pp. 439-41.

[25]Harry S. Stout, "Jonathan Edwards' Tri-World Vision," *The Legacy of Jonathan Edwards: American Religion and the Evangelical Tradition*, ed. D. G. Hart, Sean Michael Lucas and Stephen J. Nichols (Grand Rapids: Baker Academic, 2003), p. 37; Edwards, "Sinners in the Hands of an Angry God," p. 417. Edwards's talk of judgment for sin focused more on the relational implications of separation from God than on the physical torments of hell.

Edwards scholarship of previous decades paid little attention to his actual ministry to the natives there, focusing instead on his work on his great treatises. Recently, through the documentary evidence that has come to light, this is changing. Edwards's letters and sermons from the period all reflect a deep engagement on his part in the lives of his Native American congregation. Two curious manuscripts also survive: statements of faith that Edwards had written for communicant members. In one, he begins by noting the Fall and the doctrine of original sin before he has the communicant declare, "But God in mercy sent his Son in our Nature to redeem & save us." The profession continues:

> Having been made Sensible of Christ's glorious Excellency & sufficiency as a
> saviour and the Excellency of the way of Salvation by free grace through his
> Blood & Righteousness . . . I profess to receive Him as my Saviour; my heart
> cleaving to Him and acquiescing in Him as the Refuge and rest of my soul &
> fountain of my Comfort and removing all ways of Sin to accept Christ as my
> great King and Example resolving & promising to follow him and obey him in
> All things as long as I live.[26]

Whether at Northampton or at Stockbridge, Jonathan Edwards could not find capacity large enough for Christ. In his sermon series on the "history of the work of redemption," Christ is both the center of and the meaning of all of human history. He is not far off, but in his human nature Christ is near, or rather, in Edwards's view, has brought us who were far off near to God. Edwards had a deep sense of humanity's sinfulness and the consequence of judgment. He had an equally profound sense of the beauty and sweetness of Christ, as did Edward Taylor and other New England Puritans. In fact, precisely the sourness of sin led him to the sweetness of Christ, resulting in a compelling portrait of the person of Christ. And his belief in hell and judgment led him precisely to his understanding of the necessity of Christ's atoning sacrifice, resulting in a compelling story of Christ's work. Preaching to the children of Northampton in 1739, Edwards could say, "There is no love so great and so wonderful as that which is in the heart of Christ. He is one that delights in mercy; he is ready to pity those that [are] in suffering and sorrowful

---

[26]For the sermon citation and professions of faith as well as a discussion of Edwards's ministry at Stockbridge, see Stephen J. Nichols, "Last of the Mohican Missionaries: Jonathan Edwards at Stockbridge," in *The Legacy of Jonathan Edwards,* ed. D. G. Hart, Sean Michael Lucas and Stephen J. Nichols (Grand Rapids: Baker Academic, 2003), pp. 47-63.

circumstances. . . . Parents are often full of kindness towards their children, but that is no kindness like Jesus Christ." So Edwards concludes, "Children ought to love the Lord Jesus Christ above all things in this world." But what he and the other Puritans worked so hard to construct would soon splinter off into a number of directions as America came of theological age.[27]

BEFRIENDING INWARD PIETY

The drifts from the centrally placed and highly prized orthodox Christology of the Puritans to the lesser christologies of successive generations is not only seen in the arguments offered here or in the previously mentioned works by Prothero, Fox and Pelikan. Mark Noll's magisterial treatment of American theology from the Puritans to the Civil War also argues for these drifts. Noll notes of his own work, "The book's main narrative describes a shift away from the European theological traditions, descended directly from the Protestant Reformation, toward a protestant evangelical theology decisively shaped by its engagement with Revolutionary and post-Revolutionary America." Noll proceeds to observe that "it is not an exaggeration" to liken this shift to that which occurred from later medieval Roman Catholicism to the Reformation itself. This shift, as he fine tunes his thesis, involves the synthesis of specifically American ideals and philosophies with religious belief. The Christianization of the United States, occurring from 1790-1865, was a two-way street: religion informed the Republic and the Republic shaped religion. Noll further outlines shifts in specific theological beliefs, including the notion that "God was perceived less often as transcendent and self-contained, more often as immanent and relational." Other shifts included biblical interpretation and the doctrine of salvation. Noll draws attention to how the conversionism of nineteenth-century revivalism overtook the more creedal and ecclesiastical sensibilities of the seventeenth and early eighteenth centuries. A pivotal event in Noll's narrative, "the transition that mattered most for the future United States," is the dismissal of Edwards from his Northampton congregation, a local event that Noll takes as a symbol of things occurring on a larger

---

[27]See *The Works of Jonathan Edwards*, vol. 9, *A History of the Work of Redemption*, ed. John F. Wilson (New Haven, Conn.: Yale University Press, 1989); Jonathan Edwards, "Children Ought to Love the Lord Jesus Christ Above All," in *The Works of Jonathan Edwards*, vol. 22, *Sermons and Discourses, 1739-1742*, ed. Harry Stout and Nathan O. Hatch, with Kyle P. Farley (New Haven, Conn.: Yale University Press, 2003), p. 171.

stage. From then on, American theology moved out from under, in his words, the "protective theological canopy" of the Puritans.[28]

Joining Noll in a similar reading of American theology, Brooks Holifield draws attention to the shift from the creedal Puritans to the successive generations of later evangelicals and Protestants. Holifield's narrative, however, stresses something often overlooked. The Puritans were stalwarts of logic and exegesis and the so-called encyclopedia. Any given Puritan minister "would know Hebrew, Latin, Greek, history, the Bible." Holifield adds, that in addition to these achievements, the Puritans also greatly emphasized the practical side of theology. Thomas Hooker represented a "consensus," argues Holifield, "when he explained that theology was a discipline of 'godliness,' which produced not only insight into the 'nature of things,' but also 'practicall wisdom.' " The Puritans, to put it another way, were stout of mind *and* heart, stalwarts of theory *and* practice. Jonathan Edwards, like his forebears, said that both speculative or notional knowledge (the rational or cognitive domain) and spiritual knowledge (the affective domain) are necessary in order to know truly. One without the other simply won't suffice. In the next century, as Holifield plays out his thesis, the union dissolved in favor of the practical emphasis. The heart overtook the head.[29]

Even before the onset of the eighteenth century, the tremors of a theological plate shift were noticed. Edwards anticipated that Arianism, burgeoning in old England, would indeed wash up on the shores of New England. What he expected came to pass, and it only took a generation or two. The climax of Arianism in American theology came in the early decades of the nineteenth century with the work of William Ellery Channing (1780-1842). Channing gets the credit for taking New England Congregationalists into the brave new

---

[28]Mark A. Noll, *America's God: From Jonathan Edwards to Abraham Lincoln* (New York: Oxford University Press, 2002), pp. 3-11, 31.

[29]E. Brooks Holifield, *Theology in America: Christian Thought from the Age of the Puritans to the Civil War* (New Haven, Conn.: Yale University Press, 2003), pp. 25-28. The citations of Hooker are from *The Paterne of Perfection* (London: F. Clinton, 1640), pp. 43-46. Holifield's narrative differs slightly from Noll's as Holifield is more prone to see the quest for theological rationality more contiguously from the Puritan theologians through the nineteenth-century commonsense realists than Noll. See Edwards's sermon, "A Divine and Supernatural Light," *The Works of Jonathan Edwards*, vol. 17, *Sermons and Discourses, 1730-1733*, ed. Mark Valeri (New Haven, Conn.: Yale University Press, 1999), pp. 83-102. I have argued that Edwards distinguishes between speculative and spiritual knowledge, not to present types of knowledge but to show the full dimensionality of true knowledge. See Stephen J. Nichols, *An Absolute Sort of Certainty: The Holy Spirit and the Apologetics of Jonathan Edwards* (Phillipsburg, N.J.: P & R, 2003), pp. 21-45.

world of Unitarianism. He did so by recasting Christ's person and work. Christ remained one substance with humanity, but no longer one substance with the Father. Christ did, however, possess uniquely and strikingly a divine self-consciousness, an awareness that he was a son of God. Channing wished to extend Christ's vision of the self to all of humanity. His *Likeness to God* (1828) underscores humanity's potential to reach such divine heights, freed, as he argued, from the weight of original sin and spurred on by the example of Christ. Edwards's view of humanity as "sinners in the hands of an angry God" became Channing's view of humanity as underdeveloped selves in the hands of an ever-benign and most-benevolent deity. Channing's most definitive statement of departure comes in the infamous ordination sermon for the Reverend Jared Sparks in Baltimore in 1819, titled "Unitarian Christianity." He rejects the "irrational and unscriptural" doctrine of the Trinity. Its irrationality leads to a rather unanticipated practical consequence: the Trinity causes us to be divided in our devotion, whereas devotion to an undivided deity possesses "a chasteness, a singleness, most favorable to religious awe and love." He further rejects Chalcedon's two-nature Christology on the grounds that it is too confusing. Jesus, he concludes, is exactly "as we are." No less than we are and no more than we are too. Consequently, like humanity, Christ "is equally distinct from the one God"—Arianism reborn. With Christ's person and work remixed, Channing exchanges the "protective canopy" of Puritan theology that Mark Noll talks about for the unprotected wide open spaces of Unitarian Universalism.[50]

Brooks Holifield points out that Channing's methodology led to his faulty theological conclusions. Channing, above all, stressed the "practical" side of theology, "detested systems" and, according to Holifield, "believed that all the doctrines of Christianity were 'designed to teach the supreme worth of Christian virtue.' " Channing had company when it came to the distaste for "speculation." Frontier churchmen Alexander Campbell and Barton Stone, a host of Victorian thinkers, and even the twentieth century's Harry Emerson Fosdick would later argue that Christianity's reasonableness lies not in its truthfulness or in its doctrines, but in its practical application, in its virtue and practice— words that even Ralph Waldo Emerson could take a liking to. Some elements

---

[50]William Ellery Channing, "Unitarian Christianity," *The Works of William E. Channing, D.D.* (Boston: American Unitarian Association, 1875), p. 373. Channing's "Likeness to God" is also reprinted in ibid., pp. 291-302.

of biblical teaching and orthodox theology may be found in Channing. He does talk of Christ's resurrection as providing hope for immortality, for instance. But in his hands all of these and more become distorted beyond recognition, resulting in a distorted picture of Jesus. It cannot be missed, however, that Channing's Unitarian heterodoxy stems from his underlying commitment to be practical, from his reduction of theology to sentiment. In yet another ordination sermon titled "Unitarian Christianity Most Favorable to Piety" (1826), Channing remarks, "We regard Unitarianism as peculiarly the friend of inward, living, practical religion." It has a sterling quality, being uniquely fit to promote "true, deep, and living piety."[31]

A few decades later, after Unitarianism was firmly established in many of the old Puritan Congregational churches, Joseph Henry Allen claimed that the early church took Jesus to Christ over a period of four centuries. In one generation, the Unitarians took him back. The Unitarians thought the old orthodoxy too constraining, too restrictive, too mean-spirited, too confusing and, above all, too speculative and theoretical—all the while the poetry of Edward Taylor lay unnoticed in their very midst at Yale's library. Jonathan Edwards's work, however, lay fully exposed in the noonday sun. Channing and others used it to construct a convenient, though incorrect, straw man of a confining orthodoxy as unfit for the times as the Geneva bands and the powdered wig that Edwards wore. Channing's failure to appreciate the Puritans is a sort of parable, functioning to remind evangelicals not to allow the impulse to be practical to win out.[32]

HEAD, HEART AND HANDS

But alas, amidst all of this appreciation of the Puritans, a criticism is in order. Given their dexterity in articulating both an orthodox, creedal Christology

---

[31]Holifield, *Theology in America*, p. 203; and William Ellery Channing, "Unitarian Christianity Most Favorable to Piety," *The Works of William E. Channing* (Boston: American Unitarian Association, 1875), p. 385.

[32]Joseph Henry Allen, *Unitarianism: Its Origin and History, A Course of Sixteen Lectures Delivered in Channing Hall, Boston,* 2nd ed. (Boston: American Unitarian Association, 1889), pp. 1-25. Interestingly, Paula Fredrickson has argued for the same development from Jesus to Christ, though in this case the development occurred from the teachings of Jesus to Paul, or the Pauline community (see *From Jesus to Christ: The Origins of the New Testament Images of Jesus* [New Haven, Conn.: Yale University Press, 1988]). Fredrickson specifically locates "the church's experience of the resurrection," and not the resurrection itself, as the catalyst for the Christology of the New Testament (pp. xii, 133-76).

and a heartfelt piety, they didn't always follow through with Christlike action. A fully biblical Christology is capacious enough for not only theology and devotion but also morality. Not just, if I can extend the metaphor, a Christology of head and heart, but also one of hands. The lack of a Christlike morality may be evidenced in certain Puritan treatments of Native Americans, in the Puritan attitude toward slavery and in the infamous Salem witch trials. Not all Puritans exploited the Native Americans; Jonathan Edwards, for one, stands as a notable exception. But many did abuse and exploit them. Eventually the Indians were forced from their native lands, ever moving westward from home. Allan Dwight Callahan offers a stinging criticism of the Puritan ownership of slaves and complicity in the slave trade when he writes, "The land that the Puritan founders called the Promised Land has been Pharaoh's Egypt for African Americans." Reflecting back on the period of America's slavery, Frederick Douglas concluded that there are two religions, each calling itself Christianity. Douglas called the first the Christianity of "this land," referring to the United States, while he called the other "the Christianity of Christ." The first was the Christianity of the master; the second was that of the slave. The difference between the two, Douglas argued, has everything to do with morality, with how an adherent to either Christianity treats fellow human beings. Admittedly, Douglas was speaking of nineteenth-century southern slavery, but what he had to say applies to the earlier New England slaveholders as well.[33]

Finally, how well the Puritans measured up to a holistic biblical Christology can also be seen in the ill-fated Salem witch trials. This event stands out in historical memory of the Puritans, right alongside of Nathaniel Hawthorne's *The Scarlet Letter*. Together these cultural artifacts, one from fact and one from fiction, symbolize both the self-righteousness and hypocrisy that many attribute to the Puritans. In the Gospels Christ tends to reserve his condemnations for the elites of the religious establishment, while extending mercy to those on the margins. In the Salem witch trials and in the fictional characters of Hawthorne, the reverse seems to have been at work. Again, for all of the appreciation of the Puritans' ability to wed theological precision with intense devotion, they can still be criticized for not always applying their Christology deeply or widely enough.

[33]Allan Dwight Callahan, *The Talking Book: African Americans and the Bible* (New Haven, Conn.: Yale University Press, 2006), pp. 240-41. Frederick Douglas, *Narrative of the Life of Frederick Douglas* (New York: Signet, 1968), p. 120.

CONCLUSION

The lessons for contemporary evangelicals to learn from the rise and fall of the Puritans come on two levels. First, concerning method, the Puritans brought together theological precision and piety. They stressed both conversion and the Bible, but both within the confines of creedal and ecclesiastical traditions, viewing themselves as participants within the Reformation traditions and the Augustinian and creedal lineage of the early church. They made room for personal spiritual experience, but grounded such experience in Scripture and theology, and in the covenant community. Further, they viewed theology as incomplete unless it led to "practicall wisdome." They all read, and some even memorized, William Ames's *Marrow of Theology* (1623), with the opening lines declaring that theology is no less than the art of living to God. Nineteenth-century theological developments reveal the difficulty in maintaining such unions. Finally, the Puritans, especially as seen in the examples of Taylor and Edwards, stressed devotion and meditation as equally as rational exercise when it came to the task of theology. They equally valued theological precision and personal piety.[34]

Beyond methodology, the Puritans also have a great deal to teach about how the church should think about Christ. First, the church needs to safeguard against the humanity of Jesus overtaking his deity or overtaking a precisely stated two-nature Christology. Second, the church needs to safeguard against distorting or downplaying Jesus' teaching on hell and judgment, thus only allowing the Jesus who is the friend of sinners and who reserves his ire for the religious establishment only, to win out over the complex biblical portrayal of Jesus as both friend and judge of sinners. Any portrait of Christ needs to accommodate the full complexity of Jesus' person and work, not relaxing the uncomfortable tensions that may be encountered. That teaching of Christ's work must be extended to Christ's interaction with those on the margins of society, a teaching that the Puritans didn't always follow in their interactions with Native Americans and with the slaves they owned. Finally, the Puritans located their Christology within a sound framework of trinitarianism and a biblically informed view of the human condition. In the interpretations of Fox and especially Pro-

---

[34]William Ames, *The Marrow of Theology*, ed. John Dykstra Eusden (Grand Rapids: Baker, 1997), pp. 77-78.

thero, the Puritans are seen as focusing more on God than on Christ and more on the distance between humanity and God than on any closeness. Such a view, however, betrays the Puritans. It's not true of Taylor or of Edwards, nor is it true of Increase Mather and Cotton Mather or of Samuel Sewall or Samuel Willard.

Aligning theological precision and piety without making a Faustian bargain is the legacy of Edward Taylor and Jonathan Edwards and these other Puritans. Moving back in time, it is also the legacy of Athanasius, Leo the Great, Augustine, Anselm and the Reformers. All of these parties applied that method to their Christology in particular, resulting in not only the orthodox statements of the person and work of Christ as handed down in the creeds, but also in a rich legacy of sermons and meditations—and even poems—of the beauty of Christ, the wonders of Christ's work, and the rapturous nature of our union with Christ. But in the hands of these Puritans and church fathers, such devotion to and meditation on Christ did not serve as a substitute for right thinking about Christ. Instead, their devotion stemmed from right thinking. Christ demands devotion precisely because he is, in the words of Taylor, "infinity and finity conjoyn'd."

If Prothero and Fox are right in their story of the drift from the creedal Christology of the Puritans, and they are joined by others from the ranks of American religious historians, including Mark Noll and Brooks Holifield, then Puritan thought on the person and work of Christ sets a benchmark for the Christology of successive generations of American evangelicals. Curiously, though, they may have unwittingly contributed to deviations from that standard. Puritan emphases on reason and logic on the one hand and on deeply pious rhetoric on the other, without the tethers of biblical orthodoxy or without the counterbalancing effect of each one on the other, could and did trail off into dangerous territories. This is not to lay the blame on the Puritans for the sins of their (step)children. It's simply to point out that the Puritans laid the foundation for and played a significant role in the making of the American Jesus.

In some instances the story told of the movement from the Puritans to later forms of American theology is one of decline, a downward slide away from creedal and biblical fidelity. There is likely some truth to the declension thesis. But it is also true that at points along that downward slide there are bright spots. The story, in other words, isn't exactly one of a straight line of

declension from point A down to points B and C and beyond. Perhaps a better model might be to think of a wheel with the Puritans at the center, trying
to hold together these elements that normally stand in tension. From that
center extends many spokes going off in a variety of directions. Some trajectories do quite well in maintaining that tension, of holding the center. Others
lop off one of those elements, and being freed from the tension they strike
out in reckless abandon.

The ensuing chapters will see how the successive generations fare, teasing
out these various trajectories. As for the present, the rhetoric of contemporary American evangelicals overflows with such statements as "Jesus is the
friend of sinners." It overflows to the point where it may very well crowd out
other equally biblical and necessary statements and views of Christ. The
tameness of Jesus in most children's books is but one example. To highlight
such tameness, consider the Brick Testament, a retelling of the Bible in Legos
on the Web and in print. Rarely, do children's books on the Christmas narrative include Herod's slaughter of the infants (Mt 2:16-18). But such an episode is included in the Brick Testament. While prone to taking artistic license, the Brick Testament, using the medium of a child's toy, Lego blocks,
tells the biblical story, including many scenes from the life of Christ, in a very
adult fashion. Even a quick glance through it will reveal, however, the extent
to which Christian children's books censor and tame the biblical texts.[35]

The Puritans worked with words, not Legos. The Puritan rhetoric, when
examined below the surface and beyond the caricature, reveals the full complexity and dimensionality of the person and teaching of Christ. Liberating
Jesus from his own complexity results in a distorted image of his person. It
also easily leads to distorting his work. Contemporary evangelicals can be re-
luctant to speak of what some have termed "the other side of the good news."
Jesus, however, did not reserve his doomsday sayings for the religious establishment, embodied in the Pharisees, only; he also directed them to the
crowds.[36]

Jesus is both friend of sinners, the human face of God on the one hand, and

---

[35]See Brendan Powell Smith, *The Brick Testament* <thebricktestament.com> or his *The Brick Testament: Stories from the Book of Genesis* (2003), *The Brick Testament: The Story of Christmas*
(2004) and *The Brick Testament: The Ten Commandments* (2005), published by Quirk Books.
[36]Larry Dixon, *The Other Side of the Good News: Contemporary Challenges to Jesus' Teaching on
Hell* (Ross-shire, U.K.: Christian Focus Publications, 2003).

the sovereign Lord on the other. He is at once weeping over Jerusalem and hurling judgment on those who do not follow him. The reductionist tendencies of contemporary American evangelicals lead to lopping off part of these equations, resulting in distorted pictures of Jesus. The Puritans also remind us—we who are all-too-often dizzied by the power of the image—of the power of the word. In fact, they remind us of the necessity of the word. Perry Miller, J. I. Packer and others have resuscitated the Puritans for the academy and for the church. Bringing the Puritans, with some corrections, back into the contemporary discussion of the American evangelical Jesus wouldn't hurt either.

JESUS FOR A NEW REPUBLIC

The Politics and Piety of Franklin, Jefferson, Washington and Paine

There they laid Jesus.
And rolled a great stone to the door
of the sepulcher, and departed.
Finis.

THE JEFFERSON BIBLE

My Mother grieves that one of her Sons is an Arian,
another an Arminian.

BENJAMIN FRANKLIN

In a letter to his parents, no less a figure than Benjamin Franklin· wandered warily into theological territory. He never flinched when it came to talking about religion or especially what he saw as the essence of religion, *virtue*—what has been reduced these days to the more insipid substitute, *character*. But theology, requiring precision and dogma, was another story for Franklin. So he tread lightly as he tried to assuage his parents' fears of his having "imbib'd some erroneous Opinions" in the manner of theology. He first sets the stage, "I imagine a Man must have a good deal of Vanity who believes, and a good deal of Boldness who affirms, that all the Doctrines he holds, are true; and all he rejects, are false." "Opinions should be judg'd of," he continues, "by their Influences and Effects." If the doctrines a person holds do not "tend to make him less Virtuous"—there is the word—then "he holds none that are dangerous." With that as a preamble, he makes his case:

My Mother grieves that one of her Sons is an Arian, another an Arminian. What an Arminian or an Arian is, I cannot say that I very well know; the Truth is, I make such Distinctions very little my Study; I think vital Religion has always suffer'd, when Orthodoxy is more regarded than Virtue."

Then he punctuates it:

And the Scripture assures me, that at the last Day, we shall not be examin'd what we *thought*, but what we *did;* and our Recommendation will not be that we said *Lord, Lord,* but that we did GOOD to our Fellow Creatures. See Matth. 2[5]."[1]

Though written while Franklin was a young adult and long before he became swept up in the ferment of independence, the letter's sentiments on religion, theology and Christ go a long way in explaining the role of Jesus in the new Republic. Franklin put the matter more directly later in his life, again in a letter, and this time as an American citizen and not a British colonial. Ezra Stiles, fellow revolutionary zealot and president of Yale, not to mention Jonathan Edwards's grandson, wanted to put the matter of Franklin's religion to rest. Stiles knew Franklin to be religious, so he particularly asked Franklin what he believed about Jesus of Nazareth. Franklin, as typical, built up to the question by affirming his belief in "one God" and in virtue—"The most acceptable service we render to [God] is doing good to his other children." Then, drawing a deep breath, he proceeds:

As to Jesus of Nazareth, my opinion of who you particularly desire, I think the system of morals, and his religion, as he left them to us, the best the world ever saw, or is likely to see; but I apprehend it has received various corrupting changes, and I have, with most of the present dissenters in England some doubts as to his divinity.

Knowing he has crossed the line, he adds, "Tho' it is a question I do not dogmatize upon, having never studied it, and," continuing with a signature touch of humor, "think it needless to busy myself with it now, when I expect soon an opportunity of knowing the truth with less trouble." Knowing he has transgressed even further, Franklin, ever mindful of his posterity, appends a postscript appealing to Stiles to keep the contents of the letter private. He of-

---

[1]Benjamin Franklin, "Benjamin Franklin to Josiah and Abiah Franklin, April 13, 1738," in *The Autobiography and Other Writings*, ed. L. Jesse Lemisch (New York: Signet Classic, 1961), pp. 316-17, and in *The Papers of Benjamin Franklin*, vol. 2, *January 1, 1735 Through December 13, 1744*, ed. Leonard W. Labaree (New Haven, Conn.: Yale University Press, 1960), pp. 202-4.

fers up one final defense, noting that he always advocated religious freedom, expressed "good will" in donating to the building of churches of all sects in Philadelphia and, having "never opposed any of their doctrines," hoped "to go out of the world in peace with them all." Five weeks later, on April 17, 1790, Franklin died, never doubting that God loved him, as he once said in a letter to his longtime friend George Whitefield.[2]

Posterity, especially in the nineteenth century, was kind to Franklin. Historian Gordon S. Wood looks to the work of the nineteenth-century biographer of the founding fathers Mason Locke Weems as evidence. Franklin had already been redeemed as a businessman and educator, but, Wood contends, if Franklin were to be a national icon for the nineteenth century, he would have to be turned into a true Christian. So Weems stepped up to the plate, having all of Franklin's virtue and benevolence stemming "even unconsciously from the gospel." Weems continues, "For whence but from the luminous and sublime doctrines of that blessed book could he have gained such pure and worthy ideas of God." And for the grand finale, Weems has a dying Franklin gaining comfort by looking on a picture of Christ on the cross: "O it was a *noble picture*, sure enough! It was the picture of our Saviour on the cross." So "Happy Franklin" died "blest in death, with his closing eyes piously fixed upon [Jesus]." Artists too rose to the occasion. Most notably, amidst a bevy of French portraits nearly deifying their adopted American son, American painter Benjamin West's *Franklin Drawing Electricity from the Sky* secured him iconic status. On the effect of the painting, Edwin Gaustad notes, "Franklin, no longer mortal, was like Elijah translated by the hand of God." These artistic and literary tributes to Franklin lead Gaustad to conclude that in the generation of the early republic "Franklin had himself become a cult object" of the new civil religion. Twentieth-century and more recent scholarship has overturned Weems's interpretation. Franklin was religious, no doubt. But his being a Christian is another story. Suspending the question of Christ's di-

---

[2]Benjamin Franklin, "Benjamin Franklin to Ezra Stiles, March 9, 1790," *The Autobiography and Other Writings*, ed. L. Jesse Lemisch (New York: Signet Classic, 1961), pp. 334-35. Material from this era has not yet been published in the scholarly edition of Franklin's writings, *The Papers of Benjamin Franklin*. For a full discussion of Franklin's view of God, see Kerry S. Walters, *Benjamin Franklin and His Gods* (Urbana: University of Illinois Press, 1999). For a religious interpretation of Franklin's *Autobiography* see Melvin H. Buxbaum, *Benjamin Franklin and the Zealous Presbyterians* (University Park: Pennsylvania State University Press, 1975). Franklin's letter to George Whitefield was written June 19, 1764.

vinity, as Franklin did, cannot be as easily brushed aside as Franklin would have liked.[3]

Franklin's biography, however, is not what made Weems famous. That honor would go to his biography of George Washington, which contains one of the most enduring pieces of American mythology, the famous incident of the ax and the cherry tree. Weems calls it "an anecdote too valuable to be lost, and too true to be doubted"; above all it is a true testimony of Washington's piety. But Weems, as he did for Franklin, reserves his best defense of Washington's Christianity for the deathbed scene. Washington, according to Weems, dismissed those who were attending him in his final hours so that he could be alone "with his God." Weems then transforms Washington into Moses, depicting Washington as "alone on the top of Pisgah[, seeking] the face of God." Weems wasn't the first to liken Washington to Moses. Timothy Dwight did so in his sermonic eulogy for the fallen leader, taking Deuteronomy 34:10-12 as his text: "And there has not arisen a prophet since in Israel like Moses, whom the LORD knew face to face, none like him for all the signs and wonders that the LORD sent him to do in Egypt"—from Moses to Washington, from Israel to the new Promised Land, all under the guiding hand of God. Dwight and all of Washington's other eulogists may have been outdone by Henry Holcombe, former Revolutionary soldier/chaplain and Georgian Baptist minister. Holcombe explains that not only has a "great man fallen," using David's lament over Abner in 2 Samuel 3:38 as his text, but "the greatest of men." Washington's fear of the Lord kept both his mouth from profanity, Holcombe reveals, and his heart "from pollution." His piety "was genuine and exalted," and his "high Christianity" was plain enough that "every one may see." Then Holcombe notches it up. Washington "was eyes to the blind, and feet to the lame; he was father to the poor . . . and he brake the jaws of the wicked and pluckt the spoil out of his teeth." Having granted Washington Christlike status as a sinless miracle-worker, Holcombe ends with a rousing

---

[3]Gordon S. Wood, *The Americanization of Benjamin Franklin* (New York: Penguin, 2004), pp. 239-40. Mason L. Weems, *The Life of Benjamin Franklin with Many Choice Anecdotes and Admirable Sayings of the Great Man* (Philadelphia: Uriah Hunt, 1835), pp. 221, 237-38. First published in 1825, Weems's biography enjoyed numerous reprints, even into the twentieth century. Edwin S. Gaustad, *Neither King Nor Prelate: Religion and the New Nation, 1776-1826* (Grand Rapids: Eerdmans, 1993), pp. 69-73. H. W. Brands points out how Franklin wore the label of deist reluctantly. Brands notes that Franklin's ultimate religion might be best termed, in Franklin's own words, "pragmatic moralism" (*The First American: The Life and Times of Benjamin Franklin* [New York: Anchor, 2000], pp. 95-100).

admonition to "imitate his virtuous and pious example." What Would Washington Do?[4]

Weems also stresses the personal piety of Washington, observing, "With what angelic fervor did he adore that Almighty Love." Then, after God called Washington to his eternal home, Weems crescendos that Washington "resign[ed] his departing spirit into the arms of his Redeemer God." Finally, Weems contemplates Washington's legacy, taking up the question of the secret to Washington's success, the question most surely to come in succeeding generations: " 'What was it that raised Washington to such a height of glory?' let them be told that it was HIS GREAT TALENTS, CONSTANTLY GUIDED AND GUARDED BY RELIGION." Indeed, "there never was a truly great man without religion." Weems, an Episcopalian minister, was writing more than a biography; he was drafting a template for the role of religion in the early republic. For this, fiction proved more useful than fact.[5]

Again artists also rose to the occasion, aiding and abetting Weems and other literary and sermonic efforts. Versions of the "Apotheosis of Washington" were wildly popular in the years immediately following Washington's death, making their way from canvas to engravings to transfer-printed creamware—a virtual cottage industry. In the depiction, Washington, like Horatio wished for Hamlet, makes his way to heaven on flights of angels' wings. Edwin Gaustad notes of J. J. Barrelet's engraving, one of the most popular, that "Classical virtues here joined with the Christian virtues of faith, hope, and charity to raise a leader, an American Moses, to sainthood. To this icon one re-

---

[4]Mason L. Weems, *The Life of George Washington: Together with Curious Anecdotes, Equally Honourable to Himself and Exemplary to His Young Countrymen* (Philadelphia: J. B. Lippincott, 1860), pp. 15, 183-84. Timothy Dwight, cited in James H. Smylie, "The President as Republican Prophet and King: Clerical Reflections on the Death of Washington," *Journal of Church and State*, 18 (spring 1978): 233-53. Henry Holcombe, "A Sermon Occasioned by the Death of Washington," in *Political Sermons of the American Founding Era, 1730-1805*, vol. 2, ed. Ellis Sandoz, second ed. (1800; reprint, Indianapolis: Liberty Fund, 1998), pp. 1409-12. For more examples of Washington as a Christlike example, see Catherine L. Albanese's chapter "Our Father, Our Washington," in *Sons of the Fathers: The Civil Religion of the American Revolution* (Philadelphia: Temple University Press, 1976), pp. 143-81.
[5]Weems, *Life of Washington*, pp. 188-89. For a biographical and historiographical discussion of Weems and his work, see Marcus Cunliffe's introduction to the John Harvard Library reprint of Weems's *Life of Washington* (Cambridge, Mass.: Harvard University Press, 1962), pp. ix-lxii. Weems is outdone by William J. Johnson, *George Washington, the Christian* (Nashville: Abingdon Press, 1919), reprinted as recently as 2003.

sponded with veneration. America now had a saint to intercede on its behalf."
Washington's role as icon is not without irony. Gaustad notes that of all the
founders, Washington "had the least to say about religion." At least, that's
what Gaustad argues.[6]

The works of Weems and others on Franklin and Washington have staying
power in popular opinion, and especially among many American evangelicals
desirous of having their nation's founders on their side. Franklin, Washington,
Adams, Jefferson—the founding fathers all—are seen to be "true Christians,"
or as Jefferson called himself, "a *real Christian*," founding a Christian nation
on Christian principles, leaving a Christian heritage. The founders were
deeply religious but, with an exception here or there, not Christian in any orthodox sense—precisely because they answered the question of the identity
of Jesus of Nazareth wrongly. Further, as many have argued, they did not es-
tablish a Christian nation but a religious one imbued with a great deal of
Christian principles, what scholars refer to as America's "civil religion." While
many evangelicals persist in the Weems trajectory of interpreting Franklin,
Washington and the other founders, other historians are more apt to see the
founders as they really were, so to speak. For instance, Gary Wills, himself no
stranger to religion, finds depicting Washington as Cincinnatus more fitting
than as Moses. Washington's closest contemporaries also chose Cincinnatus,
while the clergy and more distant onlookers opted for Moses and even
Christ.[7]

Jean-Jacques Rousseau coined the term *civil religion*, which to him en-
tailed belief in "the existence of a powerful, intelligent, beneficent, fore-
sighted, and providential divinity; the afterlife; the happiness of the just; the
punishment of the wicked"; and, the clincher for Rousseau, belief in "the sanc-
tity of the social contract." In America's case, each of these elements plays a
vital role, and they collectively need to be set against the Puritan backdrop.
A secular state simply would not suffice for the founders, not only due to their
own personal convictions but also due to their sense of a need for a just sys-

---

[6]Gaustad, *Neither King Nor Prelate*, pp. 80-83; Gaustad, "Disciples of Reason: What Did the Founding Fathers Really Believe," *Christian History* 15, no. 2 (1996): 29. For a challenge to Gaustad's view,
see Peter A. Lillback, *George Washington's Sacred Fire* (Bryn Mawr, Penn.: Providence Forum Press,
2006).
[7]Garry Wills, *Cincinnatus: George Washington & the Enlightenment* (New York: St. Martin's Press,
1984). After conquering Rome's enemies and briefly governing, Cincinnatus (519-438 B.C.) returned to his farm, modeling the citizen-politician.

tem of law and ethics, their acute sense of one's "duty" to the world. But neither could the founders countenance the Puritan God or Christ. Civil religion
provided a way through the impasse. Franklin's plundering of the Puritans for
a work ethic, a useful virtue, a generic God and a convenient doctrine of providence, while discarding the core and essence of their theology, represents
the dynamic well. As John Updike cleverly put it, Franklin liberated Puritan
energies from Puritan doom, thus creating the distinctive "American Religion." There was a necessary place for religion and even for Christ in the new
republic, just not the Christ of the Puritans, of orthodoxy and of the Bible.
Many historians and scholars have engaged these broader themes of American civil religion and Christianity. The question taken up here concerns the
immediate impact of the founders' picture of Christ in the formative decades
of the young republic, as well as its residual effects on the American evangelical Jesus. Before that can be done, the founders' picture of Jesus needs to be
drawn in the first place.[8]

CUTTING AND PASTING IN THE WHITE HOUSE

The most well-known and most-often-turned-to case in the discussion of
the American founders and Christ is Thomas Jefferson and his popularly
called "Jefferson Bible." Jefferson's agrarianism belies his rather cosmopolitan education and proclivities. He could converse with the best of Europe's Enlightenment thinkers, and he even presaged what would come to
be a rather intense program of higher criticism and Gospels scholarship,
the so-called quest of the historical Jesus, a quest with a long history in Germany that ironically has been felt in earnest recently in America. While
Robert Funk, Marcus Borg and John Dominick Crossan—Americans all
and fellows of the infamous Jesus Seminar—have wooed popular audiences

---

[8]Jean-Jacques Rousseau, *On the Social Contract,* trans. Judith R. Masters, ed. Roger D. Masters (New
York: St. Martin's Press 1978), p. 131 (see bk. four, chap. 8 for the full discussion). The classic statement on American civil religion is Robert N. Bellah, "Civil Religion in America," *Daedalus* 96, no. 1
(1967): 1-19. John Updike, "Many Bens," *New Yorker,* February 22, 1985, p. 115. For more on Franklin's plundering of the Puritans see Edwin S. Gaustad, "The Nature of True—and Useful—Virtue:
From Edwards to Franklin," *Benjamin Franklin, Jonathan Edwards, and the Representation of American Culture,* ed. Barbara B. Oberg and Harry S. Stout (New York: Oxford University Press, 1993),
pp. 42-57. For American civil religion and Christianity, see Mark A. Noll, Nathan O. Hatch and
George M. Marsden, *The Search for Christian America* (Westchester, Ill.: Crossway Books, 1983).
One quote sums it up well: the founders "were at once genuinely religious but not specifically Christian" (*Search for Christian America,* p. 72).

and perturbed evangelicals with such products as *The Five Gospels,* the reality is that Jefferson beat them all to the punch. History doesn't repeat itself, it echoes.

Jefferson first embarked on his textual criticism project while president. In but a few hours during two winter nights in 1804, Jefferson, having procured two copies of the New Testament, cut and pasted passages he deemed authentic onto octavo leaves. Jefferson confessed that he "found the work obvious and easy." The result was a forty-six page book he titled *The Philosophy of Jesus.* After getting a cool reception for the project by people like Benjamin Rush, he decided to shelve it. That work is actually lost to history. But Jefferson repeated his efforts later in 1819 or 1820. This time he not only used the English text but also compiled a parallel text with Latin, Greek and even French. This he titled *The Life and Morals of Jesus of Nazareth.* It has become popularly known as the Jefferson Bible.[9]

Jefferson kept this work private, passing it around his inner circle of friends and family. Gaustad notes how it became public when it made its way into the possession of the Smithsonian in 1895. Shortly thereafter, Congress published an edition in 1904, with the intent of giving each new member a copy on their swearing into office. Forrest Church, who put out his own edition of the Jefferson Bible, recalls how his father, Senator Frank Church, received a copy in 1956. During the twentieth century, numerous editions were printed. Richard Wightman Fox astutely notes the irony in the reception of these twentieth-century editions. He writes, "The great irony of 'The Life and Morals of Jesus,' Jefferson's secularization of the gospels, is that in the twentieth century it was lauded as evidence of Jefferson's firm commitment to religion and to Christ." Fox continues, "[Jefferson's] desire to save Jesus from the churches, and from Christ's own apparent misconception about his divinity, was transmuted into a desire to champion Christian values in the face of rampant secularism." It is indeed ironic because, in sum, Jefferson took Jesus from his position of Lord and

---

[9]See E. M. Halliday, *Understanding Thomas Jefferson* (New York: Harper, 2001), pp. 202-10; and Edwin Gaustad, *Sworn on the Altar of God: A Religious Biography of Thomas Jefferson* (Grand Rapids: Eerdmans, 1996), pp. 118-31. Gaustad notes that Dickinson Adams, the editor of the *Jefferson Papers,* "has, in a remarkable feat of literary skill, essentially reconstructed the text [of *The Philosophy of Jesus*] as well as the process of its compilation" (p. 118). For that reconstruction see Dickinson W. Adams, *The Papers of Thomas Jefferson,* 2nd series, *Jefferson's Extracts from the Gospels, "The Philosophy of Jesus" and "The Life and Morals of Jesus"* (Princeton, N.J.: Princeton University Press, 1983).

Savior to that of mere sage and moral exemplar.[10]

There's a fine Anglo tradition of textual criticism to complement the German one that gets all of the attention. And Thomas Jefferson knew that Anglo tradition quite well. Accordingly, Stephen Prothero points out that while Jefferson was creative in his efforts, he wasn't original. The chief influence was Joseph Priestly, who had published *The Corruptions of Christianity* (1782) and *An History of Early Opinions Concerning Jesus Christ* (1786). Jefferson showed his flattery in imitation. Prothero misses that Priestly was not the only influence, however. Both Thomas Hobbes and John Locke, the latter much appreciated by Jefferson and his fellow patriots, had their own thoughts on the Bible's textual difficulties. In *Leviathan* (1651), Hobbes asserted reason as judge over Scripture, questioned the face value of Scripture's authorial claims and drew attention to the inherent textual problems in the Bible's transmission, all three tenets finding a home in Jefferson's thought. Locke, while disagreeing with Hobbes on politics, followed him on these counts. Locke writes, "*Reason* must be our last Judge and Guide in everything." We must then submit divine revelation to reason, and "by [Reason] examine whether it be a *Revelation* from God or no: And if *Reason* finds it to be revealed from God, *Reason* then declares for it, as much as for any other Truth, and makes it one of her Dictates." Jefferson liked just about everything he read in Locke, such as Locke's notion of the inalienable rights to life, liberty and the ownership of property—Jefferson tweaked the last one a bit. But he especially liked Locke's exaltation of *Reason,* always capitalized by both paragons of the Enlightenment.[11]

With reason as his guide and scissors in hand, Jefferson set to his task. Jefferson's rendition of the birth narratives would be disappointing for a Christmas pageant: no angelic visitations, no wise men and no virgin birth. When

---

[10]Forrest Church, preface to *The Jefferson Bible: The Life and Morals of Jesus of Nazareth* (Boston: Beacon Press, 1989), p. vii. Richard Wightman Fox, *Jesus in America: Personal Savior, Cultural Hero, National Obsession* (New York: Harper, 2004), p. 172.

[11]Stephen Prothero, *American Jesus: How the Son of God Became a National Icon* (New York: Farrar, Straus, & Giroux, 2003), p. 22. Thomas Hobbes, *Leviathan,* ed. Richard Tuck (Cambridge: Cambridge University Press, 1994), pp. 245-69. John Locke, *An Essay Concerning Human Understanding,* ed. Peter Nidditch (Oxford: Oxford University Press, 1975), p. 704. See also Locke's *The Reasonableness of Christianity,* ed. I. T. Ramsey (Stanford, Calif.: Stanford University Press, 1958). Jonathan Edwards presciently saw the potential maleffect Hobbes and Locke would have once their ideas gained currency in America. See Stephen J. Nichols, *An Absolute Sort of Certainty: The Holy Spirit and the Apologetics of Jonathan Edwards* (Phillipsburg, N.J.: P & R, 2003), pp. 135-38.

Jesus starts his public ministry, he cleanses the temple in Jerusalem of the money-changers, but there's no changing of water into wine at the wedding. In fact, there are no miracles in Jefferson's Gospels. There are, however, plenty of moral teachings. The example of Jesus's pristine and virtuous character shines through. But no sign of or claim to divinity survived the cut. The Sermon on the Mount, of course, made it—Jefferson saw it as the contents of "genuine Christianity." After Jefferson meandered through Christ's public ministry, he came to the trial and the cross. Nicodemus came to provide a proper burial, then Jefferson closed his account, "Now in the place where he was crucified there was a garden; and in the garden a new sepulchre, wherein was never man yet laid. There they laid Jesus. And rolled a great stone to the door of the sepulchre, and departed." There is no resurrection; Jefferson's Easter observance never got beyond Good Friday. Despite his truncated ending, Jefferson wrote to a friend that his Gospels work "is a document in proof that *I* am a *Real Christian*." He used to simply say he was a Christian. Now, he added bravado.[12]

Jaroslav Pelikan notes that Jefferson did not embark on this task "as an exercise in historical investigation" as other questers after the historical Jesus have done. Instead, Jefferson was after "the essence of true religion in the gospels, an essence whose basic content he had already formulated for himself." In other words, Jefferson's Jesus, arrived at through the cool processes of reason, ended up looking remarkably similar to what Jefferson wanted him to look like. In fact, Thomas Jefferson's redrawing of Christ set the stage for what would come in the vagaries of the American Jesus. Once Jesus is liberated from the confines of revelation, he ends up looking a lot like the ideals of his reinterpreters. Jefferson wanted and felt that his country needed, in the words of Prothero, an "enlightened sage," who we might add stood at the center of an enlightened religion. A religion fit for public consumption. Curiously, that's exactly what Jefferson found.[13]

Jefferson may also have been politically motivated in his efforts, at least initially. Biographer Joseph J. Ellis notes that the attack on Jefferson by the Fed-

[12]Thomas Jefferson to Charles Thomson, January 9, 1816, reprinted in *Thomas Jefferson, Writings,* ed. Merrill D. Peterson (New York: Library of America, 1984), p. 1373. The authoritative edition of Jefferson's writings, *The Papers of Thomas Jefferson,* ed. Barbara B. Oberg (Princeton, N.J.: Princeton University Press, 1950-), includes material up to 1801, as of 2006.

[13]Jaroslav Pelikan, "Jefferson and His Contemporaries," in *The Jefferson Bible* (Boston: Beacon Press, 1989), p. 153. Prothero, *American Jesus,* pp. 28-32.

eralist clergy of New England lay behind his writings on Jesus. They saw their "Christian nation" captained by an atheist and heretic. Jefferson sought to show he was anything but an atheist, and indeed he clearly wasn't. While in the White House, he appealed to Benjamin Rush to broker his defense. He sent Rush a "Syllabus of an Estimate of the Merit of the Doctrines of Jesus, Compared with those of Others," a work inspired by similar efforts of Joseph Priestly. The syllabus was written in 1803, prior to his first work in cutting and pasting the Gospels. In fact, it provides the philosophy underlying his textual criticism. Jefferson prefaces the syllabus with a letter in which he fondly regards the Christian religion and states that his religious views "are very different from that of the anti-Christian system imputed to me by those who know nothing of my opinions." Then Jefferson gets to the heart of the matter:

> To the corruptions of Christianity I am indeed opposed; but not to the genuine
> precepts of Jesus himself. I am a Christian, in the only sense he wished any one
> to be; sincerely attached to his doctrines, in preference to all others; ascribing
> to himself every *human* excellence; & believing he never claimed any other.

Jefferson's self-claim to being a Christian, which often gets quoted by evangelicals, comes in the very sentence he denies the deity of Christ. In fact, Jefferson goes so far as to claim that being a Christian demands that one see Jesus as Jesus sees himself, which, according to Jefferson, was as human, never claiming divinity. Rush didn't take the bait, letting Jefferson know that anyone who denied the deity of Christ could not lay claim to the label Christian. Jefferson's Federalist detractors were half-wrong and half-right. He was no atheist, but on the grounds of the Nicene and Chalcedonian Creeds he was a heretic.[14]

Of course, in Jefferson's eyes, Athanasius was the heretic. He, along with Paul and John Calvin, were all esteemed by Jefferson as the enemies of the pure religion; "impious dogmatists," he called them. Jefferson rejoiced to see the trinitarianism of the Platonizing dogmatists waning—he liked to call

---

[14]Joseph J. Ellis, *American Sphinx: The Character of Thomas Jefferson* (New York: Vintage, 1998), p. 256. For a thorough discussion of Jefferson's fray with the clerical Federalists, see Jonathan D. Sassi, "Jeffersonian Disillusions and Dreams, 1799-1818," in *A Republic of Righteousness: The Public Christianity of the Post-Revolutionary New England Clergy* (New York: Oxford University Press, 2001), pp. 84-120. Thomas Jefferson's letter to Benjamin Rush, April 21, 1803, cited in Jefferson, *Writings*, p. 1122. See also Jefferson's letter to Joseph Priestly on the latter's comparison of Jesus and Socrates, April 9, 1803, cited in Jefferson, *Writings*, pp. 1120-22. For Benjamin Rush's reply, see Halliday, *Understanding Thomas Jefferson*, p. 202.

the doctrine of the Trinity "mere abracadabra"—while "the genuine doctrine of one only true God is reviving." Then he prophesied, "I trust that
there is not a *young man* now living in the United States who will not die
an Unitarian." What he liked best about Unitarianism, however, was not its
doctrine, but that it presented a simple and clear morality. What mattered
most to Jefferson, especially for the new republic, was that Jesus was a virtuous man. Charles Sanford speaks of two main religious beliefs guiding Jefferson's political philosophy: the belief in a God of justice, and the belief
"that the moral code taught by Jesus was the best one by which a person
could guide his personal life and that its teachings should be applied to the
life of the community."[15]

FILTHY LITTLE ATHEIST

While Thomas Jefferson endeavored to keep his true religious sentiments
private, Thomas Paine promulgated his to the four corners of the earth. At
the time of the Revolutionary War, Americans were reading Paine more than
any other author. He had roused the whole country in his pamphlets during
the Revolutionary War with such rhetorical flair as the well-known first line of
The Crisis, "These are the times that try men's Souls." His *Common Sense*
(1776), in merely forty-seven pages, crystallized what the colonists were fighting for. It was something unprecedented, a free and democratic republic,
which, as Paine biographer Harvey Kaye puts it, was nothing short of "a new
age in human history." Paine's much longer *Rights of Man* (1791), inspired by
America's successful effort at independence and fueled by a desire to vindi-
cate the French Revolution, was a manifesto for universal political liberty and
democracy. For his literary efforts, Paine's fellow citizens rewarded him well,
granting him a firm and secure place among the founders. Until, that is, he
went too far. As Paine, in his political writings, sought to liberate humanity
from the tyranny of monarchs and oppressive governments, his *The Age of
Reason* (1794) attempted to liberate faith and, above all, Jesus, from the
chains of biblical, institutional and creedal religion. Paine's book was a world-
wide success and the most talked about book of the day, but not in the way he
had envisioned. Kaye points out that "*The Age of Reason* shocked and of-

---

[15]Thomas Jefferson to Benjamin Waterhouse, June 26, 1822, in Jefferson, *Writings*, pp. 1458-59.
Charles B. Sanford, *The Religious Life of Thomas Jefferson* (Charlottesville: University Press of Virginia, 1984), p. 133.

fended far more people than those it inspired and 'converted.' " Kaye further points to the irony of Paine's dedication of the book "To my Fellow Citizens of The United States of America." Americans were the ones shocked and offended the most. As E. Brooks Holifield puts it, in a classic stroke of understatement, "Paine touched a nerve."[16]

Kaye explains the reason for all the fuss. Paine, Kaye points out, "mount[ed] a direct assault on organized religion and biblical scripture," going so far as to call Christianity a "species of atheism." Just as Kant, in his efforts for the Enlightenment cause, set out to "rescue" belief by severing it from knowledge, Paine wanted to "rescue" God and Jesus by severing them from the Bible and religion—any form thereof. Paine, not surprisingly, had little time for creeds or for confessional communities. "I do not believe," Paine writes in the early pages of the book, "in the creed professed by the Jewish church, by the Roman church, by the Greek Church, by the Turkish [Islamic] church, by the Protestant church, nor by any church that I know of. My own mind is my own church." Paine was a pluralist of a different sort. To him, all religions are equally wrong and equally invalid. The book proceeds to show Paine's skills at textual criticism, resulting in a Bible that's even slimmer than Jefferson's.[17]

As for Jesus, Paine explains, "It is, however, not difficult to account for the credit that was given to the story of Jesus Christ being the son of God. He was born when the heathen mythology had still some fashion and repute in the world, and that mythology had prepared the people for the belief of such a story." Paine continues, "The Christian theory [of Christ] is little else than the idolatry of the ancient Mythologists," which unfortunately masks "the *real* character of Jesus Christ." Christ, for Paine, is "a virtuous and an amiable man," who "preached and practiced" a morality "of the most benevolent kind."

---

[16]Harvey J. Kaye, *Thomas Paine and the Promise of America* (New York: Hill & Wang, 2005), pp. 15, 84. E. Brooks Holifield, *Theology in America: Christian Thought from the Age of the Puritans to the Civil War* (New Haven, Conn.: Yale University Press, 2003), p. 159. As Paine wrote, American Christians were just recovering from Ethan Allen's similar attack on the Bible and Christianity in his *The Only Oracle of Man* (1784).

[17]Kaye, *Thomas Paine and the Promise of America*, pp. 82-83. Thomas Paine, *The Age of Reason*, in *Thomas Paine's Theological Works* (New York: William Carver, 1831), p. 12. He, like Jefferson, was following Locke in his approach. Paine argued that revelation can only be firsthand, "something communicated *immediately* from God to man" (*Age of Reason*, p. 13). For everyone else, it's "hearsay." Locke argues similarly in *An Essay Concerning Human Understanding*, noting that inspiration is an immediate impression, thus counting for Locke as knowledge for the prophet only, not for a later reader.

The Gospel accounts, Paine concludes, are but a "wretched contrivance."[18]

Writing a few years later in 1806, Paine maintained his course. He notes first of the Bible, "As to the people called Christians, they have no evidence that their religion is true. There is no more proof that the Bible is the Word of God, than that the Koran of Mahomet is the Word of God." Then he turns to "the fable of Christ and his twelve apostles." This, Paine argues, "is a parody on the sun and the twelve signs of the Zodiac, copied from the ancient religions of the eastern world." Paine further renounces creeds that are filled with "imaginary things," among which he lists "the pretended resurrection and ascension" of Christ. Paine ends the letter by asking its recipient to make his thoughts "as publicly known as you find opportunities of doing." Paine would have been better had he been more discreet. He died in ignominy, with no fanfare at his funeral and no oil portraits of flights of angels singing him to his heavenly rest. Even as late as the 1880s, Theodore Roosevelt could score points by calling Paine a "filthy little atheist." In the twentieth-century, however, Paine made a comeback. Kaye notes how since the time of Reagan, the first of presidents, conservative or otherwise, to cite Paine approvingly, Paine has been enjoying respect and favorable attention.[19]

In his own day the shock and offense he made could scarcely be assuaged. John Adams put it directly, "He [Paine] understood neither government nor religion." The clergy chimed in with their discontent as well. From sermons to book-length salvos, clergy on both sides of the Atlantic lined up to refute Paine and his "vicious" and "viral"—those were the kind words people used attacks on Christianity, Scripture and Christ. Most critics noticed Paine's own predilections at work. As Thomas Scott noted in 1797, "Mr. P[aine]'s objections" to the doctrine of redemption stem from Paine's ability to see such a doctrine requiring one to think of humanity as, citing Paine, "out-law and out cast"—a view of human nature that Paine could not countenance. Scott also challenged Paine's lack of scholarship, sardonically noting that Paine "would have availed himself of other weapons, if he had known where to have procured them." Vicesimus Knox hesitated to reply to Paine, only because "animadverting upon the writings of infidels" only tends in most cases to draw

---

[18]Paine, *Age of Reason*, pp. 14-15.
[19]Thomas Paine to Andrew A. Dean, August 1806, in *Thomas Paine's Theological Works*, pp. 330-31. For the vagaries of Paine's legacy, see Kaye, *Thomas Paine and the Promise of America*, pp. 3-14, 222-57.

more attention to them. But Paine's work was so egregious as to bring Knox into the ring. David Simpson shared a similar hesitancy, but "the danger young and inexperienced people are in of being seduced into the paths of ir-religion" because of Paine, demanded his response.[20]

These works, as well as most other replies, however, veered toward the sentimental. Simpson's work represents this well. His book contains page after page of the dying remarks of peaceful saints. Strong on sentiment and short on argument, Simpson's apologetic amounts to little more than calling on his readers to ignore Paine and give Jesus and Christianity a try. Indeed, Paine wrote from the perspective of a learned man who had pulled back the veil and was now among the initiated. All of his learning, not to mention his rhetorical skill, however, did not seem to advance him very near the truth but further from it. He stood as an example of infidelity, and his commitment to *Reason* was the signpost along the way. This caused a reaction in the other direction. As will be seen in chapter three, a strong fervor for sentiment and for personal experience among American evangelicals would set in. On the other hand Paine, with his attack on institutional and creedal religion, makes a most ironic and strange bedfellow with many of the leaders of the new Christianity on the frontier, who were similarly disenchanted with creeds and denominations and who sought a simpler, purer Jesus.

One further note on Paine is in order. Theodore Roosevelt's assessment of Paine as a "filthy little atheist" is off the mark. Paine believed in God, and for that matter he was rather tall and quite gentlemanly. It can't be missed, either, that Paine wrote *The Age of Reason* from his conviction of the absolutely essential role of religion in public and private life. He was spurred to write in light of "the circumstance that has now taken place in France of the total abolition of the whole national order of priesthood." He feared that the secular wave would cross the Atlantic, wiping away religion in America. He feared that he and his fellow Americans would lose "sight of morality, of hu-

---

[20]John Adams to Benjamin Rush, January 21, 1810, in *The Works of John Adams, 2nd President of the United States,* ed. Charles Francis Adams (Boston: Little, Brown, 1854), 9:627. Thomas Scott, *A Vindication of the Divine Inspiration of the Holy Scriptures, and of the Doctrines Contained Therein: Being an Answer to the Two Parts of Mr. T. Paine's Age of Reason* (New York: G. Forman, 1797); Vicesimus Knox, *Christian Philosophy . . . with an Appendix on Mr. Paine's Pamphlet* (Philadelphia: Emmor Kimber, 1804); and David Simpson, *A Plea for Religion and the Sacred Writings: Addressed to the Disciples of Thomas Paine, and Wavering Christians of Every Persuasion* (1799; reprint, Philadelphia: McCarty & Davis, 1825). These are but a sampling of the rebuttals to Paine.

manity, and of theology that is true." This somewhat charitable reading of Paine may be giving him too much the benefit of the doubt. His initial commendatory remarks on rational religion may have been disingenuous. One must be careful, after all, in venturing to disagree with Teddy Roosevelt. Regardless, what can be said with certainty is that Paine accommodated religion to the sensibilities of the time, just like the modernists would do in early twentieth-century America. Curiously, the modernists too were fearful of European secularizing developments washing up on America's shores. In reality, Jefferson and Franklin were doing the exact same thing, just not as offensively or as indiscreetly as Tom Paine.[21]

A FAMILY OF "RAKES, FOPS, SOTS"

This is not to suggest utter homogeneity among the founders on being deeply religious without being particularly Christian. There were exceptions, most notably John Witherspoon, Benjamin Rush and, pushing beyond the founders a bit, John Quincy Adams. John Quincy Adams is helpful in revealing the religion of yet another founder, his father John Adams. John Adams once wrote to Benjamin Rush that the posterity of the Adams clan was owing to none other than religion: "I believe it is religion, without which they would have been rakes, fops, sots, gamblers, starved with hunger, or frozen with cold, scalped by Indians, etc., etc., etc." But the same Adams also once said, in a letter to his daughter-in-law, "I do not however attach much importance to creeds because I believe he cannot be wrong whose life is right." Like his friend Jefferson, Adams focused on virtue, not theology, when it came to defining and understanding Christianity. He, convinced by Jefferson, viewed the Gospels as corrupted texts heaping Platonist speculations on the nature and being of Christ. He sought the real and unadorned Jesus of virtue. And he, along with his wife, Abigail, made sure that their son, John Quincy Adams, also understood the value and necessity of religion for life. Both father and son read the Bible an hour most mornings. But John Quincy Adams couldn't see religion the same way his father did. John Quincy Adams's biographer Paul Nagel draws attention to a curious exchange of letters between father and son concerning deism, Scripture and, most importantly, the person of Christ. In the letters, John

---

[21]See Paine, *Age of Reason*, p. 11.

Adams pushed his Unitarianism, while John Quincy Adams responded by "conced[ing] that he cautiously followed the doctrines of Trinitarianism and Calvinism." He further viewed the work of Joseph Priestly, which his father applauded, as absurd. Priestly's Jesus may be compared to the real thing, the younger exclaimed to the older, as "a farthing candle with the Sun!" John Quincy Adams then recommended some reading to his father, noting, "after which be a Socinian if you can." John Quincy Adams then appended good-naturedly, "I hope you will not think me in danger of perishing everlastingly for believing too much."[22]

In his diary, John Quincy Adams fumed over preachers who viewed Genesis as an ancient fable and over Emerson's celebrated "Divinity School Address" at Harvard. Throughout his life John Quincy Adams acknowledged the intellectual challenges in trinitarianism. And at the end of his life he wrestled with the doctrine of the atonement. "It is not true. It is hateful," he said, before he added, "But how shall I contradict St. Paul?" So he resigned himself, "I reverence God as my creator. . . . I venerate Jesus Christ as my redeemer." Such struggles may show John Quincy Adams to be less than 100 percent pure in his orthodoxy. They do reveal, however, that he understood Christianity to be more than a generic belief in God and in the moral teachings of Christ. To John Quincy Adams, deism or Unitarianism, even if held by his honored father, was not Christianity.[23]

John Adams met similar challenges to his own religion by his fellow revolutionary Benjamin Rush. Though a physician and scientist by profession, Rush knew his theology. As a student first under Samuel Finley—Rush's uncle and the protégé of the Great Awakening's William Tennent—and then under Samuel Davies at Princeton, Rush became fully immersed in New School Presbyterianism. Rush would later complete his education in "physic" by taking his doctorate at Edinburgh. But religion always occupied

[22]John Adams to Benjamin Rush, July 19, 1812, cited in David McCullough, *John Adams* (New York: Simon & Schuster, 2001), p. 30. John Adams on creeds, cited in Gaustad, *Neither King Nor Prelate*, p. 94. For the exercise of Bible reading, see Robert V. Remini, *John Quincy Adams* (New York: Henry Holt, 2002), p. 4. Paul C. Nagel, *John Quincy Adams: A Public Life, a Private Life* (Cambridge, Mass.: Harvard University Press, 1997), pp. 230-31.

[23]The final religious commitment of both elder and younger Adams is a complicated manner. John Adams was more of a Unitarian than a rank deist, and by the end of his life John Quincy Adams likely had migrated from his trinitarianism to Unitarianism. But at least at one time in his life, John Quincy Adams was trinitarian. For further discussion see Nagel, *John Quincy Adams*, and James Grant, *John Adams: Party of One* (New York: Farrar, Straus & Giroux, 2005), pp. 113-24.

his mind. Even as an eighteen-year-old he lamented that "religion is at a low ebb among us," adding the plea, "May the Son of God arise and shine upon our souls. May we be made to feel our vileness and undone situations and earnestly cry aloud to Jesus till he opens our eyes to behold his all-sufficiency and fitness to be our Redeemer." Politics too occupied him. Avoiding the old adage, he readily mixed politics and religion just about as much as he could. At first, it wasn't a generic religion that interested him. He once wrote, "Christianity is the only true and perfect religion; and that in proportion as mankind adopt its principles and obey its precepts they will be wise and happy." As time moved on, Rush veered into universalism, disenchanted as he was with Calvinism's predestinarian teachings. Alyn Brodsky reveals some of Rush's thinking behind the move, "The doctrine of predestination hardly seemed fitting for a republic based on the incontrovertible thesis that all men are created equal." Rush also moved away from his desire for Christianity to be the national religion to a position of religious liberty. On that count, he sided with Jefferson.[24]

By the time of Jefferson's presidency, Rush had turned his energies away from politics, mostly to humanitarian efforts. Rush's reputation suffered a bit as he was dubbed "Dr. Vampire" for his defense of bloodletting as treatment for illness—a practice that contributed to the death of Washington. But Rush wasn't out of the picture entirely. He actively corresponded with most of his fellow patriots, most notably Adams and Jefferson, both of whom had a rather complicated relationship and were, for many reasons—not the least of which was the election of 1800—on the outs with each other. Rush negotiated a truce and set the two corresponding with one another again. Rush further poked and prodded each one on the question of religion and of Christ. It was to Rush that Jefferson offered his great line, "I have sworn upon the altar of God, eternal hostility against every form of tyranny over the mind of man." Rush would not go along with Jefferson's view of Christ. When Jefferson offered to send Rush a copy of his cut-and-pasted Gospels, Rush retorted that he would only be interested in the "little volume" if it "renders [Christ's] *death* as well as his *life* neces-

---

[24]Benjamin Rush to Ebenezer Hazard, August 2, 1764, in Lyman H. Butterfield, ed., *Letters of Benjamin Rush* (Princeton, N.J.: Princeton University Press, 1951); Benjamin Rush cited in Alyn Brodsky, *Benjamin Rush: Patriot and Physician* (New York: St. Martin's Press, 2004), pp. 349, 270. Rush once wrote a piece that would be reprinted by the American Tract Society in 1830 titled "A Defense of the Bible in Schools."

sary for the restoration of mankind" and if it, as summarized by Gaustad, "advanced the divinity of Christ." Rush may have abandoned his Presbyterianism and Calvinism for universalism, but he couldn't give up what he saw as the Christian view of God and Christ for Jefferson's deism.[25]

Finally, one cannot discuss Christianity and the fathers without mentioning Princeton's John Witherspoon (1723-1794), the only cleric to sign the Declaration of Independence—something anyone who writes anything about Witherspoon quickly points out (next to the curiosity that actress Reese Witherspoon is indeed a distant relative). Witherspoon was enticed to Princeton from Scotland to serve as president. His belief in the sovereignty of God probably helped him accept the invitation. A string of predecessors, Jonathan Edwards and Samuel Davies among them, didn't live long at all once they took the post. Witherspoon broke the streak, serving almost thirty years. He left his mark, not only on Princeton but also on America. Scottish born and bred, he disliked the British crown, perhaps even more than the colonials, and he did not waver in the Revolutionary cause. Beyond his own contribution, as a signer and member of the Continental Congress, he had immense influence on one of his star pupils, James Madison. Scholars like to attribute Madison's "checks and balances" of the three branches of government to Madison's belief in total depravity inbred in him by his mentor Witherspoon.[26]

Witherspoon had a great deal to say about God, or better, Christ and country, and he used arguably the most significant mouthpiece of eighteenth-century America to say it, the pulpit. Witherspoon advocated Christianity in all of its particulars. He could not talk about "providence" in a generic fashion, as his compatriots so often did. To him, providence must relate "to Christian life and conduct." Neither could he talk about Christianity without speaking of orthodox views of Christ's person and work. He would work alongside of deists in the Continental Congress, but that was as far as he would go. With-

---

[25]For Rush as the go-between with Jefferson and Adams, see McCullough, *John Adams,* pp. 600-605, and Brodsky, *Benjamin Rush,* pp. 348-56. Thomas Jefferson to Benjamin Rush, September 23, 1800, in Jefferson, *Writings,* p. 1082. For Rush's reply to Jefferson's edited Gospels account, see Gaustad, *Sworn on the Altar of God,* p. 120.

[26]For Witherspoon at Princeton, see Mark A. Noll, *Princeton and the Republic, 1768-1822: The Search for Enlightenment in the Era of Samuel Stanhope Smith* (Princeton, N.J.: Princeton University Press, 1989), pp. 16-58. For Witherspoon's influence on Madison, see Garry Wills, *James Madison* (New York: Henry Holt, 2002).

erspoon counseled his Princeton students not to bother even reading the deists, instead pointing them to sound, orthodox writers who refuted them. Further, Witherspoon saw deism as more of a threat than atheism, a true wolf in sheep's clothing. He hammered his students with round after round of apologetic argument against deism in favor of revealed religion, the rationality of Christianity, the fact of miracles and above all the divinity of Christ. Then he sent them out to do the same.[27]

Witherspoon labored for two things to prevail in his adopted country, "true religion and civil liberty." These were in his mind conjoined, supporting and establishing each other. He preached on the eve of the Declaration of Independence that "your duty to God, to your country, to your families, and to yourselves, is the same." Then he added, "peace with God and conformity to him, adds to the sweetness of created comforts while we possess them, so in times of difficulty and trial, it is the man of piety and inward principle, that we may expect to find the uncorrupted patriot, the useful citizen, and the invincible soldier." As other founders looked to deism and its system of virtue as the backbone for the revolutionary cause and the formation of the new republic, Witherspoon looked to Christianity. While Witherspoon may have been the only pastor to sign the Declaration, he was certainly not alone in employing the pulpit in the service of his country. Leading up to, throughout, and in the aftermath of the revolution, piety and patriotism, Christianity and citizenship flowed mingled down from America's pulpits.[28]

REVOLUTIONARY AND REPUBLICAN PULPITS

When President Washington declared a day of national thanksgiving and prayer on February 19, 1795, Bishop James Madison, an Anglican bishop of the same name as his cousin who would become president, took advantage of the occasion to preach on the "Manifestation of the Beneficence of Divine Providence Towards America." God had favored America with its recent victory, but America "should not rest contented." Why "halt at the threshold of

---

[27]For the prominence of the pulpit in eighteenth-century America, see Harry S. Stout, *The New England Soul: Preaching and Religious Culture in Colonial New England* (Oxford: Oxford University Press, 1986). For Witherspoon on providence, see his sermon "The Dominion of Providence over the Passions of Men," May 17, 1776, reprinted in Sandoz, *Political Sermons of the American Founding Era*, 1:529-58. For Witherspoon on deism, see L. Gordon Tait, *The Piety of John Witherspoon: Pew, Pulpit, and Public Forum* (Louisville, Ky.: Geneva Press, 2001), pp. 128-39.

[28]John Witherspoon, "Dominion of Providence over the Passions of Men," pp. 557-58.

the temple of God," he inquired, when America could walk into its very chambers? But great privilege begets great responsibility. Consequently, Bishop Madison exhorted his audience to live good Christian lives, reminding them that an irreligious nation lives precariously. Madison proceeded, as did Witherspoon, to link good citizenship with good Christian living: "Certainly, my brethren, it is a fundamental maxim, that virtue is the soul of a republic." Madison did not mean a vague sense of virtue or religion, either. He meant "the religion which our Saviour himself declared." The "first and last duty" of "genuine patriotism" is "to fear the Lord and serve him."[29]

Jonathan Edwards Jr. also preached on the role that should be afforded to Christianity in the new republic. Addressing Connecticut's governor and General Assembly, he titled his sermon, "The Necessity of the Belief in Christianity by the Citizens of the State, in Order to Our Political Prosperity," taking as his text Psalm 144:15: "Yea, happy is that people whose God is the LORD." In the sermon, he contends that religion is necessary for the state, but then probes, "But what religion shall we adopt?" In his final analysis only Christianity fits the bill for the public welfare. Along the way, he does not resist the urge to take on the insufficiencies of deism, "the philosophical religion." Connecticut can be a "happy people," he admonishes its governor, assemblymen and citizens, if "they unite to practice virtue and Christianity." By preaching sermons like these, Jon Butler notes how ministers "sought to sacralize the Revolution and American society through a Christian rhetoric that pulled secular optimism within a Christian orbit." These were good days, and better days awaited the Christian nation.[30]

In many of these sermons, we hear mostly rings of triumph, but sometimes we also hear peals of fear, fear lest America get away from its Christian commitments. And nothing could amount to the fears of Christians when it looked as though Jefferson was headed to the White House. Timothy Dwight mounted the pulpit in New Haven, Connecticut, to sound the alarm. In fact, he sounded an apocalyptic alarm, taking Revelation 16:15 as his text. Amer-

---

[29]James Madison, "Manifestations of the Beneficence of Divine Providence," reprinted in Ellis Sandoz, ed., *Political Sermons of the Founding Era, 1730-1805*, vol. 2, 2nd ed. (1800; reprint, Indianapolis: Liberty Fund, 1998), pp. 1319-20.

[30]Jonathan Edwards Jr., "The Necessity of the Belief of Christianity," (1794), in Ellis Sandoz, ed., *Political Sermons of the Founding Era, 1730-1805*, vol. 2, 2nd ed. (1800; reprint, Indianapolis: Liberty Fund, 1998), pp. 1191, 1215-16. Jon Butler, *Awash in a Sea of Faith: Christianizing the American People* (Cambridge, Mass.: Harvard University Press, 1990), p. 223.

ica stood poised on the brink of an "Antichristian empire," where "we may see our wives and daughters the victims of legal prostitution" should the Jacobins, with Jeffersonian Republicans leading the way, take ascendancy. While Dwight makes the impending danger clear, even vivid, he does not exactly make clear how atheism is necessarily linked to the Jeffersonian Republicans, and God-fearing Christianity is inextricably linked with the Federalists. The enlisting of Christianity in the service of the nation was quickly becoming a political tool. It had already served such a purpose quite well in the cause of the Revolutionary War. Gordon S. Wood represents a host of historians when he writes, "Protestant ministers were in the forefront of the Revolutionary movement. In fact, it was the clergy who made the Revolution meaningful for most common people." The forces of evil were aligned with King George III and his troops; God backed the Colonials. That was the 1770s. In the decades of the 1790s and 1800s it would be Jefferson and the Republicans on the dark side and the Federalists on the side of light. Biographer Joseph J. Ellis notes how the Federalist clergy of New England would seize various remarks made by Jefferson "as conclusive evidence that Jefferson was some combination of pagan, infidel, atheist, and heretic." When he invited Paine to the White House, after Paine had published *The Age of Reason*, the Federalist newspapers had a field day. Once demonized, Jefferson had to go on the defensive.[31]

Reeling from such attacks, Jefferson was bent on establishing disestablishment when it came to religion in America's public arena. While he was out of favor with Dwight and other New England Congregationalists, as well as the Presbyterians and Anglicans, Jefferson found allies among the liberty-loving Baptists. While many of these aforementioned sermons are lost to today's audiences, buried deep somewhere in the nation's collective conscious, one phrase spurned on by a group of Baptists from Danbury, Connecticut, lives on. These Baptists, finding themselves in the minority when it came to denominational influences in the founding era, were nervous about their place in society. In the ensuing decades they would flourish, but at the time they could not see

---

[31]Timothy Dwight, "The Duty of Americans, at the Present Crisis," (1798), reprinted in Ellis Sandoz, ed., *Political Sermons of the American Founding Era, 1730-1805*, vol. 2, 2nd ed. (1800; reprint, Indianapolis: Liberty Fund, 1998), pp. 1382-83. For more on Dwight see John R. Fitzmier, *New England's Moral Legislator: Timothy Dwight, 1752-1817* (Bloomington: Indiana University Press, 1998). Gordon S. Wood, *The American Revolution: A History* (New York: Modern Library, 2002), p. 129. Ellis, *American Sphinx*, p. 256.

what triumphs awaited. So with such fears, however misplaced they may have been, they approached Thomas Jefferson for help. This was not the first time the Baptists took preemptive measures. When the first Continental Congress assembled in 1774, the Baptist Warren Association sent Isaac Backus (1724-1806) as a lobbyist, with the hopes that religious liberty could ride the coat-tails of political liberty. Once the nation was established, the Danbury Baptist Association pled a similar case. Jefferson returned with one of the most fought over phrases in American politics, religion and culture.

In his reply, Jefferson, while sitting president, both quotes the First Amendment and adds his famous commentary, "I contemplate with sovereign reverence the act of the whole American people which declared that their legislature should 'make no law respecting an establishment of religion, or prohibiting the free exercise thereof,' thus building a wall of separation between church and State." With that short, final phrase, Jefferson bequeathed what is arguably the basis of the American experiment, religious freedom and religious disestablishment. What is often overlooked is the other phrase in Jefferson's letter that leads up to the quote. "Religion," Jefferson contends, "is a matter which lies solely between man and his God." So he bequeaths yet another American original, the privatization of faith, which necessarily results in a pluralistic religious culture. This same impetus lies behind the famous quip of John Leland, another Baptist: whether "a man worships one God, three Gods, twenty Gods, or no God" was not the concern of the state and of no consequence to one's citizenship. We might paraphrase Leland, noting that whatever one believes about Jesus is also a matter of private discretion. And as the early republic came of age Leland's hyperbole of twenty gods was far outdone by the many Jesuses of the religiously disestablished American public.[32]

---

[32]Thomas Jefferson to "Messrs. Nehemiah Dodge and Others, a Committee of the Danbury Baptist Association, in the State of Connecticut," January 1, 1802, in Jefferson, *Writings*, p. 510. John Leland, writing under the pen name Jack Nipps for *The Yankee Spy*, 1794. For his nonpseudonymous thoughts see his sermon, "The Rights of Conscience Inalienable," (1791), reprinted in Ellis Sandoz, ed., *Political Sermons of the Founding Era, 1730-1805*, vol. 2, 2nd ed. (1800; reprint, Indianapolis: Liberty Fund, 1998), pp. 1079-99. Writing a few decades later as one who saw the dangers of inherent pluralism in America's disestablishment is Jasper Adams, an Episcopal minister from South Carolina. For a full discussion on him and his widely read 1833 sermon "The Relation of Christianity to Civil Government in the United States," see *Religion and Politics in the Early Republic: Jasper Adams and the Church-State Debate,* ed. Daniel L. Dreisbach (Lexington: University Press of Kentucky, 1996).

AMERICA'S CIVIL RELIGION AND THE AMERICAN
EVANGELICAL JESUS

I found my copy of *The Jefferson Bible* rummaging the shelves of a used book-store. Nicely bound in a slip case, the edition, published by David McKay Company in 1948, has woodcuts and a biographical sketch. Inside the slip case, however, I found the real bonus. A previous owner had clipped an ad from *Moody Monthly* magazine, April 1978, for an edition of the Jefferson Bible published by Jubilee Press. The ad copy notes, "Most historians know that Thomas Jefferson took a pair of scissors and cut the words of Christ out of his Bible." It continues, disparagingly using quotes, "And many modern 'historians' are all too happy to conclude that Jefferson, therefore, was not a real Christian." "Such a conclusion," the ad remarks, "does a great injustice to American history . . . and to Thomas Jefferson." Bent on restoring his image, the ad asserts, "The real truth is that Jefferson cut the words from two Bibles"—no one ever accused advertisers of overplaying logic. Having made its case, refuting the modern "historians," next comes the pitch for the product: "The Jefferson Bible can never replace the complete Bible; but what better way to spend those miscellaneous free moments during the day than in the study of the very essence of Christianity—the words of Christ." This is not an ad that appeared in *American Heritage*. It appeared in the evangelical if not fundamentalist *Moody Monthly*. Most damning, however, is that a Bible that avoids the virgin birth and Christ's claims to deity, that denies Christ performed miracles, and that ends with Christ still in the tomb is hailed, in the ad copy, as espousing the "essence of Christianity."[33]

With equal irony, the Christian Coalition's Ralph Reed once lauded how Thomas Paine extensively used the Bible in arguing for the Revolutionary War, despite the fact that Paine thought less of the Bible than the Fellows of the Jesus Seminar do.[34] If Paine liked something he saw in Scripture, it was because it accorded with human reason, not because it was in Scripture. Numerous reproductions of George Washington kneeling in prayer in the win-

[33]Jubilee Press advertisement for *The Jefferson Bible* in *Moody Monthly*, April 1978, p. 25. The introduction to the edition published by the David McKay Company, in which I found the ad, notes that Jefferson's "religion has been questioned, and yet he was a member of the Episcopal Church in Charlottesville, VA"—of course, the introduction neglects to mention that you could count on one hand the number of times Jefferson actually attended services.
[34]Ralph Reed, cited in Harvey J. Kaye, *Thomas Paine and the Promise of America* (New York: Hill & Wang, 2005), p. 9.

ter snow at Valley Forge have graced pieces of evangelical literature, almost assuming iconic status for the belief in Christian America. The "Prayer at Valley Forge" has been captured many times by artists, most famously by H. Brueckner in the nineteenth century and more recently by Arnold Friberg, commissioned for the bicentennial in 1976. An advertisement for a Friberg reproduction boasts, "Based on the accounts of many eyewitnesses, *'The Prayer at Valley Forge'* actually happened and Mr. Friberg's painting is accurate in all historical detail." In 1928, a version of the Valley Forge prayer made it onto a postage stamp. Not surprisingly, Mason Weems affords the prayer a prominent place in his biography. This portrait of the praying Washington is yet another irony on a number of levels. First, Washington may have often spoken of the "Grand Architect," but he had little time for Christ. Second, Washington preferred to stand rather than kneel when praying—reflecting that he preferred taking action rather than waiting on God; he may have kneeled at Valley Forge, but it wasn't his usual practice. Further, Washington may very well have prayed at Valley Forge. Given the dire straits he and the Continental Army were in at the time, it is highly likely that he did. The historical evidence for the prayer, however, is not conclusive, sourced in the testimony of Isaac Potts, the owner of the actual forge at Valley Forge, and made prominent by Weems. The truth is that praying doesn't make anyone a Christian any more than, as singer Keith Green used to put it, going to McDonald's makes one a hamburger. It's true even if you do happen to be George Washington.[35]

It isn't just a question of accurate history. All of these (mis)appropriations fail to realize that unduly Christianizing America's past is a two-way street. It's one thing to say America and its founders were religious, even in a Judeo-Christian vein; it's another to claim that they were orthodox in their theology. Not only does it do injustice to the past and to the true thought of the founders, it does injustice to Christianity and the true picture of Jesus.

---

[35]Joseph J. Ellis, *His Excellency: George Washington* (New York: Knopf, 2004), p. 45. Ellis refers to Washington as "a lukewarm Episcopalian." Church records show that Washington rarely attended services, averaging approximately ten attendances per year. Gordon Wood similarly argues, noting that "in all his voluminous papers [Washington] never mentioned Jesus Christ" (*American Revolution*, p. 130). For more discussion of Washington on Christianity and religion, see Gaustad, *Neither King Nor Prelate*, pp. 71-84. The advertisement appeared in *Christian History* 15, no. 2 (1996): 7. The literature on the "Prayer" is immense, especially on the Web. Interacting with the "Prayer," or with Washington's Christianity for that matter, is like stumbling into a minefield. Those zealous on the left and on the right have quite a bit to say on the topic.

To put the matter differently, America's civil religion cuts two ways, adversely affecting American civility and adversely affecting American Christianity, especially American evangelicalism. Franklin and Jefferson's moralizing, as well as Paine's rationalizing, have a direct impact on the early nineteenth-century evangelical Jesus. Paine, as mentioned earlier, set off a reaction. Franklin, Jefferson and Washington, once touched-up, set off a zealous following of those who saw the essence of Christianity in the life and morals of Jesus of Nazareth. It was not what Jesus taught, and certainly not what was taught about him, that mattered, but instead what Jesus did. In a culture so deeply imbibing civil religion, Christian living became merged with good citizenship and vice versa. This seed germinates and flowers throughout the antebellum period. Civil religion and Christianity are not, however, cut from the same cloth. Christianity, in any orthodox sense, demands that Jesus is more than a teacher of morals and an exemplar of virtue, that the Bible is more than a helpful resource, and that God is more than a benevolent deity. John Quincy Adams got it right—the Jesus of his father and most of the other founders compares to the real thing as "a farthing candle to the sun!"

CONCLUSION

Colonial historian Frank Lambert has a knack for setting the record straight, navigating extremist views and interpretations and landing quite near the truth. He has accomplished as much for the First Great Awakening and more recently for the role of religion and Christianity in America's founding and early life as a nation. Contrary to those who argue that the founders were bent on establishing a secular nation, Lambert shows how deeply religion mattered to the founders and to the early republic, especially for morality. Religion, he argues, "thrived in the early republic." But it was by and large a "free, expanding religious marketplace" that thrived, not a particularly Christian one. Lambert further notes that especially during times of national crises "Some people express the view that the country's woes are linked to spiritual decline, and advocate measures designed to reestablish the country's Christian foundation." Such an attempt occurred in 1862 during America's Civil War with the demand for a "Christian Amendment" to the Constitution of the United States. Attempts reemerged during the fundamentalist-modernist era and, almost with a vengeance, in the recent years closing out the twentieth century and now beginning the new one. But, as Lambert argues, the model for the Christian heritage lies not in the founders or in the early republic. Rather, it lies a few generations previous in the Puritans. Lambert continues, "The Founding Fathers rejected the Puritan model. Instead they ensured the free exchange of competing faiths without government support of or opposition to any faith," a free and pluralistic religious marketplace. The Puritans set one trajectory for the American Jesus; the founders set another, altogether different one.[36]

One cannot underestimate the celebrity status afforded the founders by their fellow citizens. They were originally icons of liberty. They quickly became icons of religious and even Christian virtue. As the founders were seen as imitators of Christ, they themselves became the examples that American Christians were called on to follow. Jesus, at least in the Protestant Bible, had a sketchy childhood. But American boys and girls could all follow the example of never telling a lie, even when confronted with chopping down their fathers' trees. Memory can be tricky. The collective historical memory, shaped as it was by the writings of Mason Weems and the paintings of Benjamin West, transformed soldiers, politicians and statesmen—such as the modern world rarely sees, to be sure—into priests of a civil religion. They were not, however, theologians, nor were they orthodox in their theology. Mark Noll categorically states, "Most of the important founding fathers were not evangelicals." But that didn't seem to stop their appropriation by evangelicals in the nineteenth century, nor does it seem to stop the appropriation of them by evangelicals in the twenty-first. Such appropriations, however, should come with a warning label.[37]

The Jesus of America's founders compares to Jesus throughout the rest of America's history like a prelude to a symphony: we hear in brief the melodies and motifs to come. Jesus is a fine purveyor of morality and virtue. He is humble and meek, industrious and honest. The Gospels are a fine companion for life, especially for the young who are making their way in the world. Both Jesus and the Gospels are indispensable to both public welfare and private devotion and piety. Jesus is needed in life, to be sure, but he is also needed at

[36]Frank Lambert, *The Founding Fathers and the Place of Religion in America* (Princeton, N.J.: Princeton University Press, 2003), pp. 288-96. See also his *Inventing the "Great Awakening"* (Princeton, N.J.: Princeton University Press, 1999).

[37]Noll, *America's God*, p. 15. For contemporary evangelical appropriations of the founders see the CDs, DVDs and books of David Barton, D. James Kennedy, Gary Demar and Pat Robertson.

death, where he welcomes departed saints into heaven's bosom. But he is less than divine. He is amiable and loving, but not judge. All of these motifs reverberate throughout nineteenth- and twentieth-century treatments of Jesus, all too often drowning out the still, small voices of the Puritans.

If Lambert and Noll are right, then their analyses raise a significant question concerning the American Jesus. In the religious marketplace, Jesus will fare as well as the Bible, God and any of the doctrines of Christianity—they will all need to be retooled for pluralistic environs. Jefferson and Franklin and Adams compared Jesus to Socrates. Thomas Paine likened Jesus and the twelve disciples to the Zodiac. Marcus Borg of the Jesus Seminar has recently published a work simply placing the quotes of Jesus side by side with quotes from the Buddha, his attempt at showing the perfect harmony of their respective teaching. Evangelicals are not as susceptible to such traps. Nevertheless, they are at risk when it comes to seeking cultural capital by trading on the religious sentiments of the founders. It's one thing to honor Jesus as a moral teacher, even the supreme moral teacher of the supreme system of morality. It's quite another to kneel before him as Lord and Savior. With modest apologies to the opinion of Thomas Jefferson, only the latter, according to the Bible, is what makes for "a real Christian."[38]

---

[38]Marcus Borg, ed., *Jesus and Buddha* (Berkeley, Calif.: Ulysses Press, 2002).

GENTLE JESUS, MEEK AND MILD

Nineteenth-Century Makeovers
from the Frontier to Victorian Culture

For He is our childhood's pattern;
Day by day, like us He grew;
He was little, weak, and helpless,
Tears and smiles like us He knew;
And He feeleth for our sadness,
And He shareth in our gladness.

C. F. ALEXANDER, "ONCE IN DAVID'S ROYAL CITY" (1848)

With what high rapture beat the matron heart,
When those fair infants in His sheltering arms
Were folded, and amid their lustrous curls
His hand benignant laid.

L. H. SIGOURNEY, "CHRIST BLESSING THE CHILDREN" (1850)

It might be truly impossible to capture an entire century with merely a few icons. But, with all apologies to my historian friends, perhaps we can come close if we pick the right two icons and if we have the good fortune of considering the right century. In looking at nineteenth-century American culture, two icons vie for the honor. The first is the image of Andrew Jackson, flamboyant yet a "noble and impressive figure." Virile and vigorous, Jackson strikes the pose of the alpha male. His frontier past signaled the end of the hegemony of the Atlantic coast establishment, exemplified in his trouncing of John Quincy Adams for the presidency in 1828. Adams had accompanied his father to Europe, was speaking Russian as a twelve-year-old and listening in on conversations between heads of state. He had served as a senator from Massachusetts, U.S. Secretary of State and was finishing his first term in the White House. He returned to Congress, serving for another seventeen years right up until his death. Adams revealed his moral fiber when, after his presidency, he would take on and win the Amistad case. Jackson's resumé? He had killed a number of Seminoles in defending American interests in the swamps of Florida. Celebrity trumped credentials, the fledgling frontier spirit beating out established New England gravitas. Jackson's victory over Adams signaled that the times were changing. Historians, from Arthur Schlessinger Jr. and his landmark study *The Age of Jackson* (1945) to Nathan Hatch and his *The Democratization of Christianity* (1989), have observed how none of this change was lost on religion. The age of Jackson, which signaled a new era for politics, also signaled a new era for religion in America, a religion not like their fathers' and their grandfathers' before them. Gone was the hegemony of New England and the East Coast establishment.

Jacksonian era religion would be a democratized one, as the individual usurped the reign of the clergy and the religious elites. Such individualism was set in motion as far back as the 1740s and the Great Awakening. But it would come to full flower in the Jacksonian era, represented well in the religious version of Jackson, Charles Grandison Finney. Finney's religion would favor Arminian tendencies over Calvinistic ones. Finney and his followers would have far more room for human action and human freedom than those old-time New England Puritans could ever imagine, yet alone countenance. Revivals were certainly prominent in early New England, but in the age of Jackson and in the hands of Finney the American church moved from having revivals to becoming a church of reviva*lism*. Revivals would indeed be the new norm of church life.

These early nineteenth-century tendencies of democratization, Arminianism and revivalism have long been discussed by historians. But something else lurks here that specifically fills in the portrait of the American Jesus. With all of this frontier mystique, the need for a new Jesus emerged. One who could look a lot like Jackson, one who had what it took to survive on the frontier, one with virility and strength and rigor, and one with a healthy dose of masculinity.

Yet there are two icons in the nineteenth century that we should notice. Besides Jackson and the trickle down effect his image had on the American

Jesus, there is the image of Jesus himself from Victorian culture in the middle of the 1800s. This is the gentle Jesus, "meek and mild." Like the image of Jackson, this image has a lot of hair. Beyond that, however, there aren't many other similarities. The most striking contrast between the two is that while Jackson strikes the pose of the alpha male, the Jesus of Victorian culture looks pretty nearly like a woman. In the well-worn words of Ann Douglas, the Victorians feminized Christianity. In doing so, they feminized Jesus himself. The frontier, the age of Jackson and the image of Jesus as true grit all serve as good foils for the predominant impulse that would overtake nineteenth-century American Christianity, Victorian culture. Beyond Jackson and the frontier and Victorian culture, one more factor weighs significantly in this nineteenth-century equation, namely America's Civil War.

During the nineteenth century, theologians began seeking the freer environs of life outside of the "theological canopy" that Mark Noll spoke of in his discussion of the Puritans. Once outside of the canopy, Jesus and his interpreters became much more susceptible to the vicissitudes of the cultural climate. Consequently, in this tale of his American making and remaking, Jesus becomes increasingly culturally conditioned, eventually becoming merely ideological. Jesus is no longer the God above, the God-man who breaks into this world. Instead, he becomes interpreted by this world, conformed to cultural mores and ideological pressures, be they of Jacksonian era politics, frontier sensibilities, genteel Victorian manners or even Union ideals or Confederate dreams. This chapter explores the travels of Jesus through nineteenth-century America, focusing on Jackson and the frontier era, Victorian culture, and the Civil War.

BIBLE IN ONE HAND, RIFLE IN THE OTHER

Charles A. Johnson astutely captures the intertwining of culture and religion on the frontier in his description of the pioneer: "The distinctively religious attitudes of the pioneer have been succinctly summed up as the product of a dual force: his independent and bold nature in revolt against society's restraints, and the leveling influence of poverty." Johnson proceeds to list the resultant religious traits stemming from this sociological context as including "emotional fervor, a personalized religious experience, rejection of abstract creeds and formal ritual, lay leadership, a religious message that placed major emphasis upon such simple virtues as personal honesty, equality, sympathy with one's feelings, and the corollary urge of mutual helpfulness." We could add to this mix the personal experience of Peter Cartwright, the famous "Kentucky boy" who rose to prominence as a frontier Methodist Episcopal preacher and who also lost to no less than Abraham Lincoln in a race for a seat in Congress. Cartwright recalls his adolescent years in Logan County, Kentucky, during the 1790s:

> There was not a newspaper printed south of Green River, no mill short of forty miles, and no schools worth the name. We killed our meat out of the woods, wild; and beat our meal, baked our bread.... We raised our own cotton and flax. ... Our mothers carded, spun, and wove it into cloth, and they cut and made our garments and bed clothes, etc.

For such a place, only a rugged and plain and unvarnished religion would do. Cartwright, fellow Methodist Lorenzo Dow and disgruntled Presbyterians Alexander Campbell and Barton W. Stone, would be the leading architects of a new religion to meet these demands of frontier life. This new religion would also serve to tame the rowdiness of frontier life. By stressing holiness in life, symbolized in teetotaling, some semblance of an orderly society could be hacked out of the chaos.[1]

Dee Andrews's recent history of the Methodists reveals the secrets to their success in meeting such demands. Andrews first relates how Cartwright's masculinity especially suited him to bring in the unharvested sheaves of males along the frontier, who typically were too hung over from whiskey binges on Saturday night to even think of attending church on Sunday morning. Writes Andrews,

> The Methodists, especially on the frontier, now produced more explicitly pugnacious, even worldly, preacher-heroes. Among these were homegrown geniuses like Peter Cartwright who spent their youths indulging in boyhood pleasures until their conversion turned them into manly advocates of the gospel.

But Andrews ultimately attributes Methodism's success to something different, chalking it up to the genius of Wesleyan discourse: "plain preaching for plain folk, by birth or aspiration." For the frontier, simple will suffice.[2]

---

[1]Charles A. Johnson, *The Frontier Camp Meeting: Religion's Harvest Time* (Dallas: Southern Methodist University Press, 1955), pp. 16-17; Peter Cartwright, *Autobiography of Peter Cartwright, the Backwoods Preacher* (New York: Carlton & Porter, 1857), pp. 8-9.
[2]Dee E. Andrews, *The Methodists and Revolutionary America, 1760-1800* (Princeton, N.J.: Princeton University Press, 2000), pp. 229, 244.

The question remains as to what all this frontier masculinity, rawness and simplicity have to do with Christ and the formation of American Christology. In short, the answer is *everything.* The necessity of retooling Christianity for the frontier ethos has the corollary of a necessarily retooled Christ at the center of it. The first step in retooling Christ means freeing Christ from the abstractions of creeds and instead looking to the simpler Jesus who graces the pages of the New Testament. The second step entails an emphasis on personally experiencing Jesus over merely learning of him. More often than not, this second step means looking beyond the pages of the New Testament. This two-step process can be seen in the work of Alexander Campbell and Barton W. Stone and the movement they founded, which has trickled down to today as the Christian Church (Disciples of Christ) and as the Christian Churches/Churches of Christ. Paul Conkin has called this movement a truly "American original." Moving ahead into the late twentieth century, the writings of Max Lucado illustrate this second step vividly. Lucado is likely the most famous and certainly the most widely read of Churches of Christ ministers, a group that came about in a major split in the Stone-Campbell movement at the turn of the nineteenth century. Lucado writes vividly of experiencing Jesus, allowing his imagination to provide those missing pieces in the biblical narrative. Consider this insight into the calling of Matthew, which Lucado uses to discuss the nature of friendship:

> Jesus starts to smile and shake his head. "Matthew, Matthew, you think I came to quarantine you? Following me doesn't mean forgetting your friends. Just the opposite. I want to meet them." "Are you serious?" [asks Matthew.] "Is the high priest a Jew?" [asks Jesus.] "But Jesus, these guys . . . half of them are on parole. Josh hasn't worn socks since his Bar Mitzvah."[3]

Lucado next has Jesus asking Matthew what he likes to do for fun, even prompting Matthew with suggestions, "Bowl? Play Monopoly? How's your golf game?" All this imagined dialogue leads Lucado right to the point he wishes to make: "Jesus wants to be your friend. He wants you to understand your relationship with him not as servant to Master, but as a friend to a Friend." Lucado doesn't say *both and,* as in both a servant-to-Master and friend-to-Friend relationship. For Lucado, it's *either-or.* Further, by stressing

---

[3]Paul Conkin, *American Originals: Homemade Varieties of Christianity* (Chapel Hill: University of North Carolina Press, 1997). See pp. 1-56 for his discussion of the Restoration Movement and the formation of the Christian Church (Disciples of Christ); Max Lucado, "Jesus, the Friend," in *Jesus* (Nashville: W Publishing, 2004), pp. 49, 62.

the friend-to-Friend relationship, the humanity of Christ rises to the surface, perhaps even bringing about a theological eclipse.

As the editors write in the introduction to this selection from Lucado—which happens to appear in a book hailed as "The essential book on the biblical Jesus," according to the back cover copy—"In an increasingly depersonalized culture, punctuated by dysfunctional nuclear families and neighborhoods constantly in flux with people moving in and out, it is refreshing to realize that Jesus wants to be your friend." The editors proceed to note how Lucado "*creatively* describes Jesus as just such a friend." Fortunately, for those beaten by the storms of depersonalized culture, Lucado didn't let the text, or better to say the lack of a text, get in his way. Lucado is no doubt sincere in his presentation of Jesus as our friend. There remains the question, however, as to how this particular way of experiencing Jesus reflects the biblical text vis-à-vis cultural proclivities. Again, the back cover copy of the book lets potential buyers know that the Jesus they'll meet in these pages is "the real Person," and "The best friend you'll ever have, dependable, committed, and great company." American evangelicals do indeed like Jesus; we just don't always like him straight.[4]

In his discourse on Jesus as our friend, Lucado is appropriating the biblical story in light of the depersonalized and fragmented culture in which he lives and ministers. For Campbell and Stone, the two who stand at the headwaters of the Restoration Movement and the eventual Churches of Christ and Christian Church (Disciples of Christ) groups, the driving cultural force is the frontier and all of the demands of frontier life. It's likely fair to assume that Lucado, as well as Stone and Campbell, take the Bible seriously, and that they are trying hard to be biblicists. That exact same biblicism, however, has opened them up to allowing these cultural pressures to govern what they see in the Bible and what they take away from the Bible. Culture too easily takes the upper hand once one is freed from creedal formulations. With specific regard to Stone and Campbell, perhaps no historian has uncovered this better than Nathan Hatch and his decisive work on this era, *The Democratization of American Christianity.*[5]

---

[4]Back cover copy of the paperback edition of Lucado's *Jesus.*

[5]Conkin has identified three wings in the Restoration Movement, that of southern state Methodists and Baptists, New England "Christians," and the frontier wing in Kentucky and southern Ohio started by Campbell and Stone. See his *American Originals,* pp. 3-8. Recently, E. Brooks Holifield has argued that the Restoration Movement in America actually finds its "philosophical and religious roots in Britain and Europe" (*Theology in America* [New Haven, Conn.: Yale University Press, 2003], p. 293).

Nathan Hatch's narrative centers on the aforementioned quartet of architects of the new religion: Cartwright, Dow, Campbell and Stone. As for Alexander Campbell, Hatch declares that when it comes to tradition and history,
Campbell's approach was "to wipe the slate clean," advocating a radical interpretation of the priesthood of the believer to mean that all Christians can and
should go directly to the biblical text itself, bypassing tradition, creeds and
the faith of their mothers and fathers. In the opening pages of *Christian System,* Campbell's definitive text, he wrote, "Our opposition to creeds arose
from a conviction that whether the opinions in them were true or false, they
were hostile to the union, peace, harmony, and joy of Christians, and adverse
to the conversion of the world to Jesus Christ." He further declared that
churches that adhere to any such creeds "are not churches of Jesus Christ, but
the legitimate daughters of the mother of harlots, the Church of Rome."
Campbell eventually broke from one of Rome's daughters, the Presbyterian
Church, due in part to the constant entanglement he was in for defending the
frontier revivals and to his distaste for the straitjacketing effect of creeds and
confessions. So Campbell opted for raw biblical simplicity. He formed a new
movement called Disciples, restoring the church to the simpler days before
the denominations, the days of the book of Acts. His fellow laborer in the
vineyard of the Restoration Movement, as it was called, was Barton W. Stone.
Stone traveled an independent, yet parallel path to that of Campbell. Stone
not only relinquished his Presbyterian credentials, he led in dissolving his entire presbytery, leaving behind its "Last Will and Testament" before establishing the "Christian Church." Stone and Campbell met for the first time in
1824. By 1831, the two groups merged, forming the Disciples of Christ,
which, by the eve of the Civil War, had grown to be, notes Hatch, "the fifth
largest protestant body in the United States." This movement also had a significant impact on Jesus. Stone allowed that two previously held nonnegotia-
ble doctrines, the Trinity and the death of Christ as a substitutionary atonement, were in fact up for grabs. Eventually, Stone became a subordinationist.[6]

Brooks Holifield pointedly explains Stone's christological departure:
"Stone rejected Trinitarian belief on the grounds that the language was not
biblical," adding that Stone "also thought it unreasonable that a substantial be-

[6]Alexander Campbell, *Christian System* (St. Louis: Christian Publishing, 1890), p. 9; Nathan O.
Hatch, *The Democratization of American Christianity* (New Haven, Conn.: Yale University Press,
1989), pp. 65, 71. See also Conkin, *American Originals,* pp. 12-13.

ing could beget itself or be begotten by itself." Curiously, both in terms of his conclusions and his arguments that got him there, Stone found himself in the company of the early church heretic Arius and of New England's William Ellery Channing. Douglas A. Foster observes that already by 1824, "Stone had long been charged with teaching an 'Arian' Christology and 'Socinian' views of the significance of Christ's death," adding that "many Presbyterians, Baptists, and Methodists viewed him as the 'Great Heresiarch of the West.'" Stone's views even gave Campbell pause. In fact, Campbell for a long time hesitated to join forces with Stone precisely because of Stone's trinitarian views. Foster, however, isn't convinced that the charge of heresy sticks. He'll concede heterodoxy, but not heresy. Foster and fellow Stone-Campbell scholar, D. Newell Williams, contend that Stone was caught off guard in his reading of the Dutch theologian Herman Witsius on the Trinity, which led to a misunderstanding of Witsius and the creedal view of the Trinity as teaching that there are three Gods. Williams notes that Witsius was the first theologian Stone ever read. Consequently, Stone "was not familiar with the method of doing theology that defined Christian truth by holding in tension seemingly contradictory propositions." Stone's inability to decipher theological formulations led him further in dismissing aspects of his Presbyterianism. Stone ended up then with a strange doctrine of the Trinity and Christology to be sure, but not, in the view of these Stone-Campbell scholars, a heretical one.[7]

As for Alexander Campbell, Holifield observes that he couldn't quite go along with Stone in his antitrinitarianism. Like Stone, he too rejected the extrabiblical terminology of *Trinity* and *substance*, but nevertheless saw a plurality and complexity in the society of the divine being. Campbell said pointedly, "In the first place I object to the Calvinistic doctrine of the Trinity." Calvin might have been flattered that Campbell attributed the doctrine of the Trinity to him. Of course, the doctrine preceded Calvin by only about fourteen centuries. What Campbell really had in mind was the classical formulation of the Trinity. Paul M. Blowers thinks that, on the whole, Campbell was more at home with the language of the Trinity as three persons than was Stone. But Campbell preferred the term *personal manifestations,* a bit differ-

---

[7]Brooks Holifield, *Theology in America* (New Haven, Conn.: Yale University Press, 2003), p. 305; Douglas A. Foster, "Stone, Barton Warren (1772-1844)," in *The Encyclopedia of the Stone-Campbell Movement,* ed. Douglas A. Foster et al. (Grand Rapids: Eerdmans, 2004); D. Newell Williams, *Barton Stone: A Spiritual Biography* (St. Louis: Chalice Press, 2000), p. 30.

ent from persons. Blowers himself notes how both Stone and Campbell
shared an "aversion to the traditional Niceno-Constantinopolitan language of
the one divine *essence (ousia)* in three co-eternal 'Persons' *(hypostases)*."
Whether it was heterodox, strange or unusual, or whether it was heretical may
be up for debate, but the Christology of Stone and Campbell did not resemble
the orthodox view of Christ. And the fact that it did not resemble orthodox
Christology had everything to do with the backdrop against which Stone and
Campbell set Christ in their place and time.[8]

Campbell once wrote that "a religion requiring much mental abstraction
or exquisite refinement of thought . . . is a religion not suited to mankind in
their present circumstances." One begins to get a sense of the particular circumstances that Campbell might be referring to by sifting through accounts
of frontier preachers. Most recall whole towns, such as they were, without a
single Bible among the residents and an absolute lack of things spiritual. In
his book on the pioneer ministers who brought religion to the frontier, *Bible
in Pocket, Gun in Hand,* Ross Phares chronicles humorous encounters of
outsider ministers and frontier people. What worked best on the frontier,
as Phare's account shows, was homegrown ministers who didn't receive formal training but "were educated between the handles of a plow," as a Nashville, Tennessee, resident duly noted. Phares then adds, "Another reporter
said that whenever [these] preachers arose to preach they 'usually threw
the reigns upon the neck of feeling, and let her run full speed.' " Phares further notes that a stentorian voice trumped seminary training as the greater
asset in these environs. Frontier life called for a suitable Savior, not one of
the theological exactitude of the creeds but one that reflects the simple stories of the Gospels. In the hands of Barton W. Stone, such simplicity led to,
at least in the eyes of many of his contemporaries, what the early church
called heresy. Later successors to the Stone-Campbell Movement, while
still appreciating and advocating the nondogmatic tendencies of its
founders, reigned in the heterodox formulations in favor of more explicitly
orthodox ones. Some, of course, went in the opposite direction, such as Edward Scribner Ames, whose *The New Orthodoxy* (1918) took classical trinitarianism, according to Paul Blowers, as "an unfortunate, irrelevant vestige

---

[8]Holifield, *Theology in America*, pp. 304-5; Alexander Campbell, *The Christian Baptist*, May 4,
1827. Paul M. Blowers, "God, Doctrine of," in *The Encyclopedia of the Stone-Campbell Movement*,
ed. Douglas A. Foster et al. (Grand Rapids: Eerdmans, 2004), p. 357.

of the patristic and medieval past." Those frontier impulses lived beyond the frontier.[9]

JESUS SUITABLE FOR FRAMING

While frontier life appealed to some, it did not appeal to all. As the frontier pressed westward, those towns left behind were looking for something more established and something a bit less rugged. The rough-hewn log homes might have had some charm at first, but eventually the desire for something a bit more refined won over. Victorian culture would fit the bill. Jesus would undergo a parallel transformation. If a masculine Jesus served the frontier well, then a feminized one would serve the needs of Victorians. And if what Victorians were spending their money on was any indicator, then they had an almost insatiable appetite for such a Jesus.

Victorians were buying and displaying the mass-produced art of a feminized Jesus by the carton. Jesus was showing up on fans, on note cards and prayer cards, as Christmas tree toppers, as the frontispiece in gift Bibles, on calendars, and in all sizes of lithoprints suitable for framing. American Catholics had their Madonnas and crucifixes, American Protestants had both in one. The Puritan predilection for word over image had given way to more of a place for the image, maybe even to image over word. As one example, consider a relatively little-known and understudied artifact of Victorian culture, *Sartain's Union Magazine of Literature and Art,* a monthly periodical based in Philadelphia that had a short run from 1849 through 1852. Heidi L. Nichols's groundbreaking work on this periodical—*The Fashioning of Middle-Class America:* Sartain's Union Magazine of Literature and Art *and Antebellum Culture*—argues convincingly that *Sartain's,* part of a "reading frenzy" of a booming market of periodical literature, served the needs of a blossoming American middle class and its religious appetite.

The burgeoning middle class was in search of a culture, a distinctly American culture, and *Sartain's,* Nichols observes, would give them one. It advised on the latest fashion, the latest artwork and the latest fads in interior decorating. It told its readers what music they should be listening to and what books they should be reading. In Nichols's words, "*Sartain's* sought to shape a distinctly American and middle-class culture through its literary offerings and engravings, and columns on art, music, flowers, architecture, and music." And not to be missed in the pages of *Sartain's* is the emphasis on religion. The first article of the very first issue was by New School Presbyterian minister and popular writer Albert Barnes, titled "The Announcement of the Angel to the Shepherds." John Sartain, the magazine's eponymous founder and famous artist, offered an accompanying engraving based on a painting by John Martin. Such sermons and essays were rare as the magazine churned out its monthly issues. Poetry came to be the preferred medium of transmitting religion to the middle class. But engravings and artwork were prominent all along the way. The zenith of such religious packaging for the new middle class was a series with both poetry and prose titled "Scenes in the Life of Christ." Alongside the words, John Sartain laid down his iconography of the Victorian Jesus, gentle, meek and mild, with flowing hair and high cheekbones, and a softness that only a womanly Savior can muster. Charles H. Lippy has argued that religious periodicals and religious novels likely had more of an impact on popular American religion than anything else. And he notes these works had primarily an audience of women. *Sartain's* knew its target audience well.[10]

The series on "Scenes in the Life of Christ" commenced in the first issue of the 1851 run with a prose piece on "The Offering of the Magi." Next followed a poem on John the Baptist, and then came "the Sermon on the Mount," by the Reverend John Todd, introduced with the words, "As the light of the bright morning broke over the hills of Judea." Todd describes Jesus as a having a "soft" voice, adding, "His countenance is meek and lowly." Todd later writes, "There was never a being who, in words so few, so simple, so childlike, bowed, subdued, and controlled so many hearts, as Jesus Christ." Nichols contends that the overriding picture of Jesus throughout the pages of the *Sartain's* is of Jesus "offering comfort as a good shepherd." Nichols adds, *"Sartain's* reveals what David Morgan describes as a nineteenth-century trend among North American evangelicals, whose 'descriptions of their relationship with Jesus were often infused with a longing for a sympathetic, gentle, and tender savior.'" Nichols also refers to the work of Barbara Welter in this regard. Welter con-

---

[10]Heidi L. Nichols, *The Fashioning of Middle-Class America:* Sartain's Union Magazine of Literature and Art *and Antebellum Culture* (New York: Peter Lang, 2004); Charles A. Lippy, *Being Religious, American Style: A History of Popular Religiosity in the United States* (Westport, Conn.: Praeger, 1994), pp. 73-74.

tributes to Anne Douglas's thesis on the feminization of American culture in the antebellum era, which has the corollary of the feminization of religion, by drawing attention to the hymnody of this era. Welter concludes that these hymns overwhelmingly depict Christ as "friend and helper."[11]

If *rugged* and *manly* might be the watchwords for Jesus on the frontier, *meek, gentle* and *mild* will suffice for Victorians. Not only is Jesus mild, but the kingdom that he brings is often described in Victorian literature as mild too. And, fortunately for Victorian poets, mild rhymes with child.

JESUS FOR THE CHILDREN

If Victorian culture feminized Jesus, then he must be up to the task of the Victorian woman, namely, motherhood. Consequently, two episodes in the life of Christ became prominent, if not omnipresent in Victorian culture. The first is Jesus' own childhood, and the second is Jesus blessing the little children. The problem with Jesus' own childhood, of course, is how sketchy it is. There just isn't much to go on. What's worse, what is there is somewhat problematic. As a twelve-year-old, he's rebuking his parents and teaching adults, flying in the face of the well-mannered Victorian child who "speaks only when spoken to." That being the case, the alternative is to add to the biblical account, to fill in the gaps. As Mason Weems invented the cherry tree episode for the apocryphal boyhood of George Washington, so Victorians took to some creative fiction for the boyhood years of Jesus.

In the nineteenth century a popular literary trend concerned lives of Jesus. This trend has a German trajectory, the so-called *Leben Jesu* movement, and an Anglo one. As Daniel Pals observes in his scholarly analysis of this movement:

> During the Nineteenth century, authors in Britain, as elsewhere in Europe, developed a keen interest in the historical life, or biography of Jesus. Especially after about 1860 Lives of Christ became in fact a sort of vogue among the Victorians, to which every type of writer—devotional, radical, clerical, or eccentric—was sooner or later attracted.

Pals goes on to add that such books promulgated a "wealth of interpreta-

---

[11]John Todd, "Scenes in the Life of the Savior," *Sartain's Union Magazine of Literature and Art* 8, no. 1 (1851): 7, 8, 10; Nichols, *Fashioning of Middle-Class America*, p. 95. Citation of David Morgan is from *Visual Piety: A History and Theory of Popular Religious Images* (Berkeley: University of California Press, 1988), p. 83. See also Barbara Welter, "The Feminization of American Religion: 1800-1860," in *Religion in American History: A Reader*, ed. Jon Butler and Harry S. Stout (New York: Oxford University Press, 1998), pp. 158-78.

tions" and "mirrored many facets of the Victorian mind," which is to say that Jesus became a Victorian to the Victorians. In America the lives-of-Jesus genre expanded to include lives of Jesus for children, a popular genre that ran from the 1860s through the 1950s, being replaced in the contemporary market by the explosion of children's religious books and Bibles.[12]

One salient example from the later decades of these lives for children comes from the pen of J. Paterson-Smyth, B.D., LL.D., Litt.D., D.C.L.—as the title page recounts his degrees. Paterson-Smyth previously authored *A People's Life of Christ,* before writing *A Boys and Girls Life of Christ* in 1929, long after the Victorian era had passed, but it is rather Victorian in its outlook nevertheless. Paterson-Smyth begins the chapter devoted to Jesus's boyhood by letting his imagination run a bit, "Now I am seeing pictures in my mind of that Nazareth childhood. If you shut your eyes and think hard you can make those pictures with me." Next, Jesus as a six-year-old boy goes off to the village school. After school Jesus is running through the marketplace and singing child rhymes and playing games. As he grows, Paterson-Smyth adds, "I can picture him in the older games of boyhood." Then Paterson-Smyth writes of an actual event in the boyhood of Jesus. Paterson-Smyth concedes, "It is not in the Bible," but then adds, "but it is a true picture of what Jesus is like." Jesus and the Nazareth boys, Paterson-Smith informs us, "One day saw a little dog by the roadside. 'What an ugly little brute,' they said. 'What a nasty smell!' Then young Jesus came up. 'Oh what lovely white teeth,' said He. 'They are whiter than ivory.' You see he just saw at once the only beautiful thing in that ugly little dog." It's not in the Bible, but it's certainly true.

Admittedly, this may be seen as rather innocuous. Clearly Jesus liked dogs and that's a good moral lesson. Nevertheless, the deeper issue is the need to fill in the missing text. If the life of Jesus is reduced to one grand moral example, then those missing childhood years are quite the embarrassment of the Gospels. Paterson-Smyth doesn't let his imagination stop at Jesus's childhood years, for much can be gained by thinking of Jesus as a young adult, employed as a carpenter. "I always think of that workshop," muses Paterson-Smyth, "as a friendly sort of place." Such musings on the "missing years" of the life of Jesus were commonplace among the Victorians.[13]

---

[12]Daniel L. Pals, *The Victorian "Lives" of Jesus* (San Antonio, Tex.: Trinity University Press, 1982), p. 3.
[13]J. Paterson-Smyth, *A Boys and Girls Life of Christ* (New York: Fleming H. Revell, 1929), pp. 46, 50, 62.

Also capturing the imaginations of Victorians is an episode from the Gospel accounts, the story of Jesus blessing the children. This not only became an oft-told story but the image of Jesus surrounded by children achieved iconic status, portraying dutiful and happy children surrounding a calm and gracious Jesus as he freely dispenses love and affirmation. In the series "Scenes in the Life of Christ," the event of Christ blessing the children takes the form of a poem. Miss Hannah P. Gould, muses, "His eye benign o'erlooks the crowd, / As bends the rainbow o'er the cloud." And, of course, that benign eye falls upon the children, "the *little* ones," which she describes as children, babes and infants. As for the babe, Gould adds, "The babe, upon whose sinless tongue / The fist caught accent hath not rung."[14] In an earlier issue, apart from the series on "Scenes in the Life of Christ," the popular poet Mrs. L. H. Sigourney also offered reflections on this event of blessing the children, referring to the "guileless" children of "innocence," whom Christ was drawn to. Sigourney then turns her poetic imagination to the mothers of these children:

> With what high rapture beat the matron heart,
> When those fair infants in His sheltering arms
> Were folded, and amid their lustrous curls
> His hand benignant laid.
> Oh Blissful Hour!
> None save a mother's thrilling love can know
> The tide of speechless ecstasy, when those,
> Whom she hath brought with pain into the world,
> Find refuge with the Unforsaking Friend.

Sigourney closes by having the matron "exulted," as "she saw the children's angels near the father's throne." If only the Gospel writers had thought of this.[15]

On the one hand, there's nothing necessarily wrong with drawing attention to this episode. Unlike the desire to add to narrative to the childhood of Jesus, the story of Jesus blessing the children is in the Gospels. On the other hand, what is truly occurring here should not go unnoticed. By so emphasizing this story of Jesus blessing the children, the Victorians proffered a narrow view of Jesus, one that ignored those episodes less compatible with Victorian

---

[14]Hannah P. Gould, "Christ Blessing Little Children," *Sartain's Union Magazine of Literature and Art* 8, no. 2 (1851): 87.

[15]L. H. Sigourney, "Christ Blessing the Children," *Sartain's Union Magazine of Literature and Art* 6, no. 3 (1850): 231.

sensibilities, one that could not contain the full complexities of the biblical narrative, the darker sides of wrath and judgment and the ravages of sin. The Bible of the Victorian world is too genteel for such things. Not to be missed, either, are the Victorian sensibilities of childhood innocence that overrun their interpretation of this Gospel episode.

In Melville's *Moby-Dick,* Queequeg the harpooner reels after his hand is almost caught in the jaws of a great white shark. This ferocious display of nature at its beastly worst leads him to declare, in pigeon English, "Queequeg no care what god made him shark . . . wedder Fejee god or Nantucket god; but de god wat made shark must be one dam Ingin." The Victorians had room for the God of the rainbow, the God of the butterfly and the sunset, but not much room for the God that made the shark. And what was true of their view of God also was true of their view of Christ.[16]

This tendency of the Victorians to have a selective understanding of Jesus based on a selective use of the Gospels will be repeated time and again as the story of the American Jesus unfolds. To counterculture disestablishment types of the 1960s, the episode of Jesus that achieved iconic status was the throwing of the moneychangers out of the temple. To those fundamentalists and evangelicals who singularly focus on giving invitations, the image of Jesus standing and knocking on the doors of hearts, drawn from Revelation and not from the Gospels, assumes iconic status. To evangelicals of a pacifist stripe, Jesus turning the other cheek reigns supreme. To the socially conscious, Jesus embodied in the poor becomes the rallying point. To just about all American evangelicals Jesus becomes the best friend, the Savior next door. All of these are biblically based images. The problem comes when such a focus on a particular episode in the Gospels or a particular characteristic or trait of Jesus leads one to downplay or even dismiss other episodes of the biblical narrative and other aspects of his character. Jesus comes to us as a complex figure, and reducing him does an injustice to the Gospel accounts. Reducing him does an injustice to Jesus himself.

WHEN WORDS FAIL

Sartain's subtly reveals the failure of the Word, the Bible, to speak to modernity, packaged in this case in Victorian trappings. It is a failure on two counts.

---

[16]Herman Melville, "The Shark Massacre," in *Moby-Dick* (New York: Penguin Books, 1992), chap. 66.

The first concerns that of the image. The second concerns that of the limitations of or problems with the biblical words themselves. And, what's more, this twofold failure of the Bible is of an unprecedented nature. Some could argue that the image (or icon) has held a perennial place in Christianity, which means that criticizing the Victorians on this point is a bit unfair. It certainly wasn't driven by illiteracy, which helps account for much of the iconography of the Middle Ages. The image triumphed then almost because it had to. One of the things the myriad Victorian periodicals and pulp novels attest to is the staggering rates of literacy. The pressing need to tell the story of the gospel in pictures due to the inability to read that story in words simply didn't exist in most of mid-nineteenth-century America, especially among the blossoming middle class. Rather than illiteracy as the cause, in the Victorian subtext of modernity, image trumps word due to the overwhelming urge for a human Jesus. Not the God-man of the historic creeds but the man from Nazareth who suffered and loved; not Jesus Christ, of whom one makes a confession and to whom one submits in reverence and worship, but the very human Jesus, on whom one can depend like a good and faithful friend, and to whom one can turn for solace and comfort. Looking at a picture of Jesus as he lovingly plays with the children takes on far more worth than sifting through a handful of parables and discourses.

The Bible not only fails due to the overwhelming power of the image but also because of the limitations or problems of the Bible itself. There are simply too many gaps in the Gospel narratives of the life of Jesus. What kind of child was he? How did he manage to live in a family and never get embroiled in an argument? How did he manage to attend school and never tear his shirt in a playground fight? These are questions for which eager disciples trying to live out their Christianity in the modern world want answers. And the Word fails them by offering no such answers. Consequently, they turn to filling in those gaps.

Though this will be mentioned later in chapter six, a sneak peak at Mel Gibson's *The Passion* might illustrate this matter concisely. Part of Gibson's story line is the grief of Mary. To set that up, he's at a bit of a loss if he has a dogged commitment to tell only the story of the Gospel narratives. In between the birth of Jesus and his trial and crucifixion, there simply isn't much to go on regarding Jesus and his parents. And what is there doesn't exactly play into Gibson's story line. The Word has Jesus rebuking his parents (who, by the way, leave him behind in the big city as a twelve-year-old) only to re-buke his mother again at a wedding. So Gibson adds words where the Word fails. He has a playful Jesus splash water in Mary's face when she offers him a washbowl to clean up from a day's work in the carpenter shop before sitting down for dinner. Cinematically it's brilliant. For the viewer who knows the end of the story, such playful scenes can only be tinged with bitterness, knowing that this doting mother will watch her son face a horrific death. It is not, how-ever, in the Word, in the text of the Gospels. Imagination, the image, fills in the gaps of the biblical narrative.

The need for Gibson, as well as the need for Victorians (such as the writers in *Sartain's* or the authors of the lives of Jesus for boys and girls), to fill in the gaps stems from modernity's perception of the limitations of the Word. There is one final problem with the Word in the modern world. Not only is it overwhelmed by the power of the image, and not only does it have limitations and gaps, but it is also a problem in and of itself. Now enters biblical scholar-ship of the modern era. To put it directly, the Word makes a modern person blush or snicker.

Before a rundown of the litany of usual suspects—mostly German schol-ars—who undermined the Bible, a few things need to be mentioned here, per-haps all of them deriving from the lost traction of theology and biblical studies in the academy. Reigning through the early days of the university and on through the Reformation and Renaissance eras, Augustine's dictum that "the-ology is the queen of the sciences" meant that theologians were perched safely atop the academy. Modernity dethroned the queen, and the other disciplines (science, history and later sociology and psychology) scrambled to ascend to the throne. History as a discipline lent little support for thinking of religious claims in absolutist terms. Lessing's infamous designation of history as the "ugly ditch" went even further, challenging what, if anything, from history can be carried forward as meaningful for today. Georg W. F. Hegel would tell us that looking back simply doesn't make sense. History is about the triumph of progress in the evolution of ideas. The Bible is a relic of a bygone era, a myth-ological age in which one's understanding of the world was merely elementary.

Speaking of evolution, one can't miss the rising star of science among the disciplines, hitched, as it was in the mid to late 1800s, to Darwin's view of the world. Even a person without training in science knows enough to know that virgins don't give birth and a supply of bread and fish doesn't multiply without

bakers and fishermen. But in a world where science is on the rise, voicing belief in these aged stories can prove rather embarrassing. Of course, this is not
to suggest that the Germans are responsible. America and the Anglos, as
seen in such figures as Locke, Hobbes, Jefferson and Paine, have their own
history of biblical criticism, which is to say that we have only ourselves to
blame. Nevertheless, the period 1850 to 1900 marked a significant shift in
what American popular religion and even more specifically American Christianity was willing to affirm when it came to the Bible and the Gospel accounts
of the life of Jesus. At the very least this period marks a significant shift in what
popular American Christianity was willing to emphasize when it came to the
Bible and Jesus. In the broader popular culture, Jesus had become all too human, overflowing with the milk of kindness. The popular Christian culture
lagged not too far behind.

Through all of these assaults, the triumph of the image, the perceived limitations and gaps of the word, and the perceived embarrassment of the word,
the Word lagged in the modern world. Yet, Jesus still managed to thrive.
Richard Wightman Fox uses Octavius Brooks Frothingham to punctuate this
point. Fox notes that after Frothingham left Unitarianism, following in the
footsteps of Ralph Waldo Emerson, "Jesus remained his guiding light." Frothingham himself put it this way in 1867, "The religion of Christ passes away;
the religion of Jesus enters on its career. Christendom declines; Jesusdom
awakes."[17]

CANON FODDER

Our discussion of nineteenth-century American religion has neglected,
some would argue, the most significant and defining moment, namely America's Civil War. Recent books by Mark Noll and Harry Stout have made compelling arguments that America's Civil War fundamentally changed America's religion; it was not just a political or constitutional crisis but a
theological crisis. Civil War reenactor, the Reverend Alan Farley, did not
need to wait for those historians to weigh in on interpretations of the Civil
War. Farley knew back in 1984, the year he started his Re-enactor's Mission
for Jesus Christ, that you can't quite understand America's Civil War without

---

[17]Octavius Brooks Frothingham, "The New Birth of Jesus," *The Radical* 2 (1867): 330, cited in Richard Wightman Fox, *Jesus in America: A History* (New York: HarperSanFrancisco, 2004), p. 283.

understanding both the war's influence on religion and the role religion played in the war. The chaplains, organized by the various regiments and by the United States Christian Commission (an organization given birth in 1861 by the YMCA) were very busy during the war between the states. Farley is one of their many reincarnations, not merely reliving the past but also "ministering to the Civil War re-enacting community" in the present. Christ was in the camp then, and during the days of reenacting, Christ may be found in the camps of Civil War battlefields again.[18]

The Christ of the Civil War is rather conflicted; he may be found in both camps. As Abraham Lincoln famously put it in his second inaugural address on March 4, 1865, those in the North and South "both read the same Bible, and pray to the same God; and each invokes his aid against the other." The United States Christian Commission saw to it that plenty of Union soldiers heard the gospel, enlisting the likes of D. L. Moody as director of the North West United States Christian Commission, with a job description that included preaching tours on the battlefield. But it seems that Christ fared better in the Confederate camps. The revival accounts and exploits recorded in diaries of Confederate chaplains lead one to wonder if Southern soldiers were too busy with religion to be paying attention to the war. Christ also dominated southern Civil War-time politics. So replete was it with Christ that, as Harry Stout tells the story, southern evangelicals, "who [already] had God in their constitution, wanted even more: a specific identification with Jesus Christ." All the while, Stout notes, northern evangelicals were prone to "fret constantly over the missing reference to God in their constitution."[19]

These fretting Northerners went so far as to advance a proposal for a Christian amendment to the Constitution, thinking it might win divine favor for their cause. A group of religious leaders delivered it to the White House on February 10, 1864. They sought to add the following lengthy interjection to the preamble:

> We, the people of the United States, humbly acknowledging Almighty God as the source of all authority and power in civil government, the Lord Jesus Christ,

[18]Mark A. Noll, *The Civil War as a Theological Crisis* (Chapel Hill: University of North Carolina Press, 2006); and Harry S. Stout, *Upon the Altar of the Nation: A Moral History of the Civil War* (New York: Viking, 2006).
[19]Stout, *Upon the Altar of the Nation*, p. 409.

as the ruler among the nations, and His revealed will as of supreme authority, in order to constitute a Christian government, and in order to form a more perfect union . . .

Lincoln received them "politely," but nothing ever came of their efforts.[20]

The Christ in the Confederate world was multiplex, taking on many images. To some it was his manliness that took center stage. Again, Stout retells the occasion of a sermon by the Richmond, Virginia, Baptist minister Jeremiah Bell Jeter. Preaching on Paul's exhortation to be good soldiers for Jesus Christ in 2 Timothy 2:3, Jeter took to a little saber rattling to get his congregation to fall in line behind, in his words, their "Captain Jesus Christ[, the] Captain of Salvation." Out on the battlefield with the terrors of war pressing in, however, things could look a bit more grim. Here sermons with such titles as "Christ and Our Loneliness" reflect more typical appropriations of Christ. What's true of both of these perspectives is that the exigencies of the situation were causing those looking to religion generally and Christianity more specifically to identify with Christ. Or, rather, they were hoping Christ would identify with them.[21]

Some went even further, identifying their beloved leader as a Christ figure. Akin to the attempts to lift Washington to messianic status, there were those who attempted the same for Abraham Lincoln. Of course, it didn't hurt that Lincoln died on April 14, 1865—Good Friday. Jon Meacham observes, "That the assassination took place on Good Friday, at the time of Passover, in the closing weeks of a war of liberation from the sins of the past was lost on no one." No less a figure than Herman Melville could not let go of the uncanny coincidence. The day after Lincoln's death, Melville mused messianic in his poem titled "Martyr":

> Good Friday was the day
> Of the Prodigy and the crime,
> When they killed him in his pity,
> When they killed him in his prime.

He continues:

> And, though conqueror, be kind:

---

[20]See Jon Meacham, *American Gospel: God, the Founding Fathers, and the Making of a Nation* (New York: Random House, 2006), p. 130.
[21]Stout, *Upon the Altar of the Nation*, p. 409.

But they killed him in his kindness,
In their madness and their blindness,
And they killed him from behind.

The sad result is a "sobbing of the strong / and a pall upon the land." Whitman's famous lament, "Oh Captain, my Captain," also reveals the place that Lincoln held.[22]

These appropriations of Christ for the cause, not to mention the messianic overtones attached to Lincoln, further entrenched American perceptions of America as the Promised Land, bequeathed by the Puritans, and the concomitant divinely favored nation status, first nurtured in the throes of the Revolutionary War. America's civil religion, which we began exploring in chapter two, was, in the immortal words of Julia Ward Howe's "Battle Hymn of the Republic," triumphantly marching on. Jon Butler offers a rather insightful analysis of this dance between the church and culture in his cleverly titled *Awash in a Sea of Faith*. For Butler, Lincoln embodies the climax of the plot of America's civil religion. Lincoln infused his politics with religious rhetoric, emphasizing providence and deliverance, but according to Butler, Lincoln's rhetoric was "only loosely Christian at best and perhaps not substantially Christian at all." Lincoln preferred to refer to God impersonally as "Maker" and to salvation as "of the nation and of the nation's soul, not individual salvation." Lincoln was "indeed religious, perhaps profoundly so," Butler concludes. So Lincoln embodies the nation he represented as he held its highest office. Indeed, a national religion by definition cannot be all that strong on the particulars.[23]

What may be true of the Victorians and of both sides of the Civil War is that religion ran deep, and as with Lincoln, it ran profoundly deep. This religion was certainly in debt to Christianity, the Bible and Christ. Yet this religion trended away, first, from the creeds, which had a narrowly and explicitly defined Christ as the God-man who died "for us and for our salvation," in the words of the Nicene Creed. America's civil religion next trended away from the Bible itself. Christ became liberated and consequently better suited for the variegated needs of the nineteenth century. American evangelicals were

---

[22]Jon Meacham, *American Gospel*, p. 131; Herman Melville, "The Martyr," in *The Columbia Book of Civil War Poetry*, ed. Richard Marius (New York: Columbia University Press, 1994), pp. 333-34.

[23]Jon Butler, *Awash in a Sea of Faith: Christianizing the American People* (Cambridge, Mass.: Harvard University Press, 1990), p. 294. Butler concedes that at one time Lincoln referred to Christ as "the saviour of the world," but, Butler adds, "the reference was singular and undeveloped" (ibid.).

not immune to these trends occurring in the broader circles of American culture. They weren't in the nineteenth century, and they aren't even today.

CONCLUSION

In the 1790s, the first full decade after America gained its independence,
church attendance reached an all-time low. By the 1820s the numbers had
climbed out of the slump and then some. Jesus and Christianity were reborn,
largely through the efforts of the new denominations, the Baptists and the
Methodists, and the new movements of Alexander Campbell and Barton
Stone. These leaders and their followers were fleet of foot literally, as they
crisscrossed the frontier on horseback, and fleet of foot theologically, as they
dumped burdensome theology. The old wineskins of the New England Puritans gave way to the new wineskins of Jacksonian and frontier Christianity,
complete with a masculinized Jesus and preachers toting a Bible in one hand,
a rifle in the other. Jesus, lean and mean. But by the middle of the 1800s such
imagery lost its cultural hold, giving way to the new models of a genteel and
feminized culture. The American Jesus followed suit. He became the moth-
erly figure, portrayed with feminine features and softness, and embodying the
new values of gentleness, meekness and mildness. Jesus, meek and mild. Both
cases, the frontier Jesus and the Victorian Jesus, hold something deeply in
common, however. In both, Jesus became much more human, and he became
known primarily through personal experience rather than by confession of a
creed.

The malleable American Jesus, which both the Puritan and Revolutionary
eras had incubated (see chaps. 1-2) was coming into its own. To those on the
frontier, he became one of them. To those Victorians of the new middle
class, he became a Victorian. This also rings true of the Civil War manifestations of Jesus. The wartime experiences of those both at home and on the
battlefields shaped their perspectives of Jesus. Jesus could be both stalwart
captain, victorious in battle, and the sympathizer of the lonely and desolate
and betrayed. The prevailing contribution of the nineteenth century to
American Christology is that Jesus, whether he was on the frontier or in a
Victorian sitting room and regardless of whichever side he was on in the
Civil War, became captive to ideology. Jesus was not the God-man breaking
in to this world. Instead, he was much more this-worldly. After his lengthy
and intricate discussion of theology in America from Jonathan Edwards to

Abraham Lincoln, Mark Noll acknowledges the great success of American evangelicalism in influencing culture as it "almost converted the nation." Then Noll offers his final assessment, "so too did the nation mold the Christian gospel in its own shape." Evangelicalism, Noll contends, fell victim to its own success.[24]

It seems that of all these cultural forms Jesus took in the nineteenth century, the feminized Jesus, gentle, meek and mild, won out. The transcendent One became domesticated, and in both senses of that term. First, Jesus became tamed, no longer the lion of the tribe of Judah but the lowly friend of sinners. Second, Jesus became feminized and consequently well-fitted for genteel home life, the model for harmonious domestic life. To achieve this, above all, the baby Jesus took prominence, right alongside of the Gospel story of Christ blessing the children.

There is likely nothing more incompatible with the Victorian culture of the nineteenth century than NASCAR culture in the twenty-first. Nevertheless, in the movie spoof on the latter, *Talladega Nights: The Ballad of Ricky Bobby,* an all-too-striking parallel resounds. In one scene, Will Ferrell's character, at that point a highly successful NASCAR driver, offers a prayer of thanksgiving before a meal, mostly of take-out food. He directs his prayer to Baby Jesus, which sets off an argument between him and his wife, Carley, played by Leslie Bibb. She counters that Jesus grew up and is Lord, to which Ricky Bobby returns that he prefers the little Lord Baby Jesus of Christmas, complete with little baby hands and little baby feet. This hapless theological go-round makes for a highly comedic scene, one of Will Ferrell's funnier moments, and this in a whole career of such moments. Despite the comedy, and desperately anemic theology, Carley Bobby got something profoundly right. Baby Jesus grew up. There is the Christ of Christmas, and there is the Christ of Easter too. And there is also the Christ of Good Friday. The Victorians preferred little baby Jesus and his innocent, little baby feet and hands.

Such rhapsodizing of the baby and child Jesus isn't restricted to the Victorian and NASCAR spoofs. Beth Moore also joins in. Her *Jesus, the One and Only,* in which she vividly and emotively describes her "romance with Jesus," sets out "under the sound guidance of Scripture, to picture what Jesus was

---

[24]Mark A. Noll, *America's God: From Jonathan Edwards to Abraham Lincoln* (Oxford: Oxford University Press, 2002), p. 443.

like" as an infant and child. Quite often, though, imagination fills in where the Scriptures fall silent. Imagination picks up where the Word leaves off. Her imagination helps readers palpably feel what it would be like to, along with Mary and Joseph, look at and hold the baby Jesus and to watch him playing with his siblings and his mother. Moore offers an exploration of the infancy and childhood of Jesus, territories largely left unexplored in the narratives of the Gospels.[25]

The Victorian image of Jesus continues to reach into our own times. As the nineteenth century was drawing to a close, however, it would meet its match. "Muscular Christianity," as historians have come to call it, would supplant this romanticized infant/child Jesus and feminized Jesus of the Victorians. Even Billy Sunday would fall in, hailing Jesus as "the greatest scrapper who ever lived." And, as in the nineteenth century, twentieth-century American Christianity would continue to emphasize both the humanity and the malleability of Jesus, known, of course, through personal experience—the golden thread that holds all of these disparate images together.

---

[25]Beth Moore, *Jesus, the One and Only* (Nashville: B & H Publishing, 2002), pp. xi, 37.

JESUS, HERO FOR THE MODERN WORLD

Harry Emerson Fosdick, J. Gresham Machen
and the Real Meaning of Christmas

*Are you willing to believe that love is the strongest thing in the world—
stronger than hate, stronger than evil, stronger than death—
and the blessed life which began in Bethlehem nearly
nineteen hundred years ago is the image and brightness of Eternal Love?
Then you can keep Christmas.*

HENRY VAN DYKE

*Liberalism regards Jesus as the fairest flower of humanity;
Christianity regards him as a supernatural person.*

J. GRESHAM MACHEN

It might be hard for contemporary audiences to imagine a time when a scandal between a parishioner and a pastor made the *New York Times,* a theological scandal, that is, and not a sexual one. But in 1923 it did. Henry Van Dyke, best-selling author, Princeton University professor and U.S. Ambassador to the Netherlands, gave up his pew at Princeton's First Presbyterian Church. The few Sundays that Van Dyke was not out speaking and was able to attend First Presbyterian's services, Van Dyke blasted, "are too precious to be wasted in listening to such a dismal, bilious travesty of the gospel." In an earlier generation Van Dyke's words would have set the stage for a duel. The preacher of such desolation was Princeton Seminary professor J. Gresham Machen. Machen was no stranger to readers of the *New York Times*. His editorials frequently appeared in its pages and the paper outed him as a "wet," an advocate of drinking alcohol in an era of prohibition, on the front page in 1926.

J. Gresham Machen managed to frustrate many more than Van Dyke. He faced off with Harry Emerson Fosdick, America's most beloved pastor in the 1920s. We could add to this list the faculty and board of Princeton Theological Seminary, the mission board of the Presbyterian Church in the U.S.A., along with its famous missionary novelist Pearl S. Buck, and eventually the entire denomination itself in a widely publicized church trial—again splashed on the pages of the *New York Times*, resulting in his ouster. All this for insisting that his denomination be true to its creed.

J. Gresham Machen's theological throes were just one chapter, though a highly significant one, of the fundamentalist-modernist controversy that dominated the American religious scene of the early twentieth century. Much has been made of this controversy, focusing on views of the Bible, Darwinism and evolution, modernity's notion of "progress," emerging eschatologies, and ecclesiastical power politics. Here we will revisit the familiar terrain of the controversy, focusing specifically on views of Christ. The controversy did much to shape, if not to define, twentieth century American religion, leaving an indelible mark on American understandings of Jesus. Whether contemporary evangelicals realize it or not, the fallout of this controversy has also significantly shaped the American evangelical Jesus.

PUTTING CHRIST BACK INTO XMAS

One of the bestsellers in 1895, just on the shelves in time for Christmas, was Henry Van Dyke's *The Story of the Other Wise Man*, published by Harper. At the time, Van Dyke (1852-1933) was pastoring Brick Presbyterian Church in New York City. His book, along with his other writings, landed him a spot on Princeton University's literature faculty, a post he held until his retirement with a slight interruption while he served as U.S. Ambassador to the Netherlands in the years leading up to World War I (1914-1918), appointed by his former Princeton colleague, Woodrow Wilson. Machen and Van Dyke had a history. While simultaneously working toward his divinity degree at Princeton Theological Seminary and an M.A. in philosophy at Princeton University, Machen, ever literary, enrolled in Van Dyke's literature seminar. Machen found the lectures wanting, more like the droll of a literary circle around a coffee table than what one should expect from a graduate seminar. Van Dyke and Machen were cut from very different cloth. Van Dyke was the consummate Victorian and Romantic, his portraits with his finely combed mustache attesting to his role as a Victorian icon, while Machen was not so in any way. Van Dyke found Machen "irritating" and "schismatic"—his own words. When one looks at Van Dyke's *The Story of the Other Wise Man*, it does not take long to understand why Van Dyke couldn't stomach Machen's penchant for orthodoxy.[1]

After Machen left the pulpit at First Presbyterian to be replaced by the more palatable Charles Erdman, Van Dyke returned to his pew as publicly as he left it. This time he told the *New York Times* that he looked forward to Erdman's reassuring and peaceful nature, adding that Erdman will "preach to us the unsearchable riches of Christ—good news and peaceful doctrine." Van Dyke liked the word *peace*. It occurs more than just about any other word in his Christmas book. In fact, in a later anniversary edition of it, he referred to his own book as a "peaceful sailing vessel" in the wide and stormy sea of literature. His story of Artaban, the "Other Wise Man," ranks with the best of Victorian literature, such as examined in the previous chapter. But Van Dyke also signals a significant and fundamental shift in thinking about the nature of the work of Christ on the cross within the conservative religious establishment. As Darryl Hart observes in *Deconstructing Evangelicals*, the term *evangelical* as we use it today largely came about through developments in the early and middle twentieth century. On the eve of the twentieth century the distinctions between the conservatives and the liberals within the major denominations and American Christianity were not as pronounced, especially for the majority of the laity. In other words, writing in 1895 from his study at the Brick Church, Van Dyke was not writing as a self-pronounced liberal, and he was not being read as one either. The tensions in the 1910s to 1930s would reveal that he fit much better with theological liberals than theological conservatives, but in 1895 his book would have been standard fare for all persuasions in the church. Consequently, what it reveals about the shaping of the American evangelical Jesus bears notice.[2]

---

[1]See Tertius Van Dyke, *Henry Van Dyke: A Biography* (New York: Harper, 1935). A curious description of Van Dyke may be found in Katherine M. H. Blackford and Arthur Newcomb, *Analyzing Character: The New Science of Judging Men* (New York: Blackford Publishers, 1922). Though relying on now debunked pseudo-techniques of phrenology, the authors might be on to something when, analyzing Van Dyke's head; they conclude that he is "refined, intellectual, sensitive, responsive, optimistic, but well-balanced, poised, and keenly discriminating" (p. 59). For a full discussion of the controversy in Presbyterian circles, see Bradley J. Longfield, *The Presbyterian Controversy: Fundamentalists, Modernists, and Moderates* (New York: Oxford University Press, 1991).

[2]See D. G. Hart, *Deconstructing Evangelicalism: Conservative Protestantism in the Age of Billy Graham* (Grand Rapids: Baker Academic, 2004), p. 21. Not all agree with Hart's argument. Hart's interpretation, however, accords with previously offered interpretations of Nathan Hatch and Jon Butler (pp. 36-37).

Van Dyke's book complements the Gospel narratives. In reality, the story only tangentially relates to the Gospel narratives. The prose flows. Consider: "The shiver that thrills through the earth ere she rouses from her night sleep had already begun, and the cool wind that heralds the daybreak was drawing downward from the lofty, snow-traced ravines of the mountains." Artaban travels separately from the three unnamed wise men of the biblical narrative. And, unlike them, he never meets up with Christ. In fact, he manages to be one step behind Jesus for the entire thirty-three years of his earthly life. And over the years Artaban's cache of treasures he has brought for his gift to the Christ child dwindles. He is left with one solitary jewel, a "soft and iridescent" pearl "full of tender, living lustre." In desperation, he makes one last trip to Jerusalem during Passover in the hopes of meeting up with Jesus. In yet another strange turn of events, he ends up using his pearl to ransom a slave girl, all the while struggling over "the expectation of faith and the impulse of love." He resolves the conflict by asking himself rhetorically, "Is not love the light of the soul?" At the very next moment, Christ is dying on the cross—we are led to assume since the action of Jesus is taking place offstage—and Artaban finds salvation "because he had done the best he could from day to day. He had been true to the light that had been given to him." Van Dyke then writes, "A calm radiance of wonder and joy lighted the pale face of Artaban like the first ray of dawn on a snowy mountain peak." Artaban has been warmed enough to melt the cold winter snows of his heart. Van Dyke followed *The Story of the Other Wise Man* with other Christmas stories, such as *The First Christmas Tree* and *Even Unto Bethlehem: The Story of Christmas*, all with the goal of inspiring audiences "to live Christmas." In the preface to *Even unto Bethlehem*, published as a gift book in 1928, Van Dyke reveals that he "was given this story" while "thinking and dreaming over the reality of the first Christmas," adding that "it is a picture drawn by imagination looking for truth."[3]

The questions the reader should be asking in all of this are, where is Christ

---

[3]First published in 1895, *The Story of the Other Wise Man* (New York: Harper) has been reprinted in numerous editions. It is currently available through Random House (1996). References here are from Harper's 1923 edition, pp. 21, 70, 71, 72, 74. Van Dyke wrote of his goal to inspire "to live Christmas" in the preface of his *The First Christmas Tree, and Other Stories* (1906; reprint, Orleans, Mass.: Paraclete Press, 2002). Henry Van Dyke, *Even unto Bethlehem: The Story of Christmas* (New York: Charles Scribner's Sons, 1928), p. ii. Van Dyke closes his story with the holy family's return from the flight to Egypt, noting specifically that Mary "came again to the little grey house that she loved and the carpenter-shop in Nazareth" (p. 103). Boldly for a Protestant, Van Dyke dedicated the book to Mary: "Ave Maria, Gratia Plenia, Mater Benedicta."

and what does he have to do with Artaban? He is, in fact, strangely absent in the narrative, ever present, yet only by hearsay and implication. His death on the cross relates to Artaban by the mere thread of example. Artaban's devotion to Christ empowers him to make that final act of selfless love, mirrored in Christ on the cross. Van Dyke once identified selfishness as *the* curse of sin. In articulating these views, he reflected the influence of such theological stalwarts of a liberal persuasion as Horace Bushnell and Friedrich Schleiermacher. Van Dyke was translating and popularizing these ideas for the masses. He was reducing Christ to a moral example because he had reduced Christianity to a set of moral platitudes. This also carries with it the necessary correlate of an elevated view of humanity and a diminished view of sin, all of which serve as the ingredients of classic theological and religious liberalism. Van Dyke was simply wrapping up that teaching in an attractive package, just like a Christmas present.[4]

Van Dyke did not limit his writing to Christmas stories for popular audiences, however. He was first a pastor, and a rather gifted and prominent one at that. Two of his books deserve further mention, both taking a place among the Macmillan Standard Library: *The Gospel for an Age of Doubt* and the sequel, *The Gospel for a World of Sin*. In the preface to the former, originally his Lyman Beecher lectures at Yale, Van Dyke bares his theological soul, informing readers that "the vital experience of faith is deeper than the theories of theology." He shares the sentiment in the preface to *The Gospel for a World of Sin*, there telling readers that his book "is not meant to present a theory of the Atonement," continuing, "On the contrary, it is meant to teach that there is no theory broad or deep enough to explain the fact."[5]

Van Dyke, however, may have been better off if even only occasionally he allowed his penchant for experiencing Christ and the cross to be reigned in by theology. In *The Gospel for an Age of Doubt* he offers his own thought on Christ's divinity, noting that "it differs" from that of others. For Van Dyke, presaging later developments in Christology, Christ is best understood from his vantage point of humanity first: "The Godhood that was in him was such as

---

[4]For a thorough study of the liberal influence in the nineteenth century, see Gary Dorrien, *The Making of American Liberal Theology: Idealism, Realism, and Modernity, 1805-1900* (Louisville, Ky.: Westminster John Knox Press, 2001).

[5]Henry Van Dyke, *The Gospel for an Age of Doubt* (New York: Macmillan, 1896), pp. xiii-xvii; *The Gospel for a World of Sin* (New York: Macmillan, 1899), p. vii. Both books enjoyed numerous reprints and editions in the early twentieth century, and both were reviewed widely.

manhood is capable of receiving." He finds this "makes [Christ's] Divinity at once easier to be believed, and more precious in its significance." Later in the book Van Dyke distills the concept of deity itself to its essence, or as he may prefer, its "loftiest summit," which is that "God is Love." The upshot is that while Christ is perfect in deity and humanity—Van Dyke even uses the term *homoousios*—he is perfect in deity to the extent that he manifests divine love. So too follows Van Dyke's theologizing on the atonement. He is not opposed to the substitutionary theory of the atonement. He just finds it wanting, as he does all theories of the atonement. In fact, he finds a "final definition" of the atonement unattainable. Humanity, instead, needs to keep on experiencing the atonement, continuing to fill our collective capacity till we reach the grand heights of "experienc[ing] the love of God in Christ."[6]

Both of the *Gospel* books were met with negative criticism, charging Van Dyke with wandering from orthodoxy, albeit subtly. And in prefaces to later editions Van Dyke responded. In short, theological bickering, he observed, serves only to obscure the preciousness of the gospel for an age and a people in need. Remember, Van Dyke liked peace. He also, however, shot off his rebuttals with a bit more than this typical salvo at hairsplitting theologians, for what mattered to Van Dyke was chiefly the experience of the human soul with the living God. Christ was the "brother of all men," and what he did was for all in a universal sense. Returning to Artaban makes the point more clear. Artaban was drawn to Christ by an inner sense, not by any direct revelation or body of teaching. Further, Artaban was empowered to his selfless act not by direct knowledge of what Christ was doing on the cross but instead only indirectly and remotely at best.

The combined result of Van Dyke's efforts is nothing short of a rendering of the moral influence theory of the atonement with Victorian trappings. He inched the religious establishment along in rethinking the person of Christ, redefining his deity and the orthodox two-nature Christology. Not to be missed either is Van Dyke's loose treatment of revelation. Artaban had been true, it may be recalled, "to the light given him," which, in the pages of the story, amounts to his visions and a still, small inner voice that egged him on. Both viewpoints would come to be foundational to the liberalism of the early twentieth century, picked up by no less than Harry Emerson Fosdick.

---

[6]Van Dyke, *Gospel for an Age of Doubt*, pp. xxi, 161; Van Dyke, *Gospel for a World of Sin*, p. 155.

FAIREST FLOWER OF HUMANITY

What Van Dyke may represent for the later Victorian religious novella, Harry Emerson Fosdick (1878-1969) represents for the genre of the liberal sermon. Preaching, Fosdick once said, "is personal counseling on a group basis." Some of the sermon titles that captivated his congregations—as well as his national audience tuned in every Sunday afternoon to the National Broadcasting Company's "National Vespers"—include "The High Uses of Serenity," "Handling Life's Second Bests," "Making the Best of a Bad Mess" and "Facing the Challenge of Change." He pre- and out-Pealed Norman Vincent Peale, and, were he alive and preaching today, he would likely rival Robert Schuller. Fosdick, like Van Dyke, loved the word *peace.* But for all of Fosdick's popular psychology and warmed over philosophy, he knew exactly what he was doing.[7]

Taught and mentored by Colgate's William Newton Clarke, whose *Outline of Christian Theology* (1898) takes pride as America's first liberal systematic theology, Fosdick went on to graduate study at Columbia University and its sister institution, Union Theological Seminary in New York City. An ordained Baptist, Fosdick nevertheless managed to hold on to the pulpit at First Presbyterian Church in New York City from 1918 to 1925. A church with a long history, First Presbyterian was founded in 1718 and originally located on Wall Street. Jonathan Edwards held his first pastorate with a splinter group from this church. In a few short months Edwards counseled the group, then meeting near the city's docks, to reunite. They retook the pews on Wall Street and an out-of-work Edwards returned to his New England home. In the early 1920s, controversy revisited First Presbyterian as a group from outside the church, led by the colorful William Jennings Bryan and others in the church's parent denomination (the Presbyterian Church of the U.S.A.), called for Fosdick's ouster. For one, Fosdick never relinquished his Baptist sensibilities or credentials; for another, he denied, among other things, inerrancy and the virgin birth of Christ. In response, Fosdick left, moving three miles uptown to New York's Central Park and settling into the pulpit at Park Avenue Baptist Church. This church had just completed construction of a new, Gothic structure in 1920, funded by John D. Rockefeller Jr. But even its large sanctuary could not contain the crowds thronging to hear Fosdick. So Rockefeller again

---

[7]For these sermons and more, see Harry Emerson Fosdick, *The Hope of the World: Twenty-Five Sermons on Christianity Today* (New York: Harper, 1933).

reached into his pockets and on October 5, 1930, he and Fosdick led in the dedication of the new Riverside Church—notice the absence of "Baptist"— nestled along the Hudson River and modeled after the thirteenth-century Gothic cathedral in Chartres, France. The carillon, at the time, was the second largest in the world, the tower reaching 392 feet. By all accounts an impressive church. From 1930 until his retirement in 1946, Fosdick preached to millions, both in person and over the radio from the church's pulpit.[8]

Around the sanctuary there is a series of stone carvings, depicting significant figures of history grouped by such categories as physicians, teachers and humanitarians. In the middle of each section is Christ, depicted accordingly as healer, teacher, humanitarian. Visitors and congregants were inspired by these heroes, who themselves had gained inspiration by the example of "some aspect of the life of Christ." In these stone carvings Jesus became the ultimate hero for life in the modern world. Christ was all-important for Fosdick. Riverside was, after all, a Christian church; the first of its three stipulations for membership being "affirmation of faith in Christ." The stipulation came, however, without any elaboration of either faith or Christ, begging the question of what Fosdick and the Riverside Church meant when they said *Christian* and *Christ*. At least as far as Fosdick was concerned, he did not leave us guessing.

Fosdick's most famous sermon came not from his time at Riverside but from earlier when he occupied the pulpit of First Presbyterian Church. On May 21, 1922, he preached "Shall the Fundamentalists Win?" Rockefeller, through his public relations man, Ivy Lee, arranged for the sermon's publication and distributed copies gratis to Protestant ministers across the country. Here Fosdick compares two approaches: the narrow and persnickety fundamentalism, which threatens the very heart of Christianity, and the open-armed and accepting liberalism. He contrasts how these different approaches affect specific doctrines, such as miracles and the virgin birth of Christ, the inspiration of Scripture, the substitutionary atonement, and the second coming of Christ. "This is a free country," Fosdick bellows, and "anybody has a right

---

[8]For the life of Fosdick, see Harry Emerson Fosdick, *The Living of These Days: An Autobiography* (New York: Harper, 1956); and Robert Moats Miller, *Harry Emerson Fosdick: Preacher, Pastor, Prophet* (New York: Oxford University Press, 1984). For Fosdick as theologian, see Gary Dorrien, *The Making of American Liberal Theology: Idealism, Realism, & Modernity, 1900-1950* (Louisville, Ky.: Westminster John Knox Press, 2003), pp. 356-434.

to hold these opinions or any others, if he is sincerely convinced of them." In one sentence, Fosdick sums up American civil religion: predicated on democracy, religion is privatized, with the only test being sincerity. The religion of my neighbor, as long as it's free and not forced, "neither picks my pocket," as Thomas Jefferson famously put it, "nor breaks my leg." Fosdick proceeds with even more patriotism, appealing to "the cause of magnanimity and liberality and tolerance of spirit."[9]

What matters for our study is the portrait of Christ drawn from Fosdick's sermon and his other writings. In reference to the person of Christ, Fosdick understood the virgin birth as the product of the first disciples' overzealous imaginations, simply recasting his special birth in the form of a biological miracle. Fosdick further paralleled Christ's birth with the other "founders of great religions," including Buddha, Zoroaster, Lao Tzu and Mahavira. As for the work of Christ, Fosdick failed to elaborate, in this sermon at least, on the issue of the atonement. He sketched out the fundamentalist view, claiming that the "special theory of the atonement" holds "that the blood of our Lord, shed in a substitutionary death, placates an alienated Deity and makes possible welcome for the returning sinner." Based on the pattern of how he treated other theological issues in the sermon, we can surmise that Fosdick held to the opposite. Against all this back and forth of the fundamentalists and liberals, Fosdick lamented that the one thing that mattered most, that people "in their personal lives and in their social relationships should know Jesus Christ," lay buried under the rubble of the theological battle. But what Fosdick had to say about Christ extends far beyond this famous sermon.[10]

A MAN'S MAN

Billy Sunday and Harry Emerson Fosdick had very little in common. Both

---

[9]Harry Emerson Fosdick, "Shall the Fundamentalists Win?" reprinted in *American Protestant Thought in the Liberal Era*, ed. William R. Hutchison (Lanham, Md.: University Press of America, 1968), p. 173. Thomas Jefferson, *Notes on the State of Virginia*, in *Thomas Jefferson, Writings*, ed. Merrill D. Peterson (New York: Library of America, 1984), p. 285.

[10]Fosdick, "Shall the Fundamentalists Win?" pp. 174, 173, 181. In his sermon reply, "Shall Unbelief Win? An Answer to Dr. Fosdick," Clarence Edward Macartney observed of Fosdick's treatment of the substitutionary atonement, "Dr. Fosdick does not dwell at length on this central doctrine of Christianity, but in the very sentence in which he caricatures the traditional evangelical belief in the atonement he reveals his complete and profound aversion to the New Testament teaching on the great and mysterious subject," reprinted in *Sermons That Shaped America: Reformed Preaching from 1630 to 2001*, ed. William S. Barker and Samuel T. Logan Jr. (Phillipsburg, N.J.: P & R, 2003), p. 341.

would likely gasp at the mention of each other in the same breath without the word *attack* lurking somewhere in between. But they did have one point in common: both liked to talk about manhood, and especially the manhood of Christ. Sunday once declared Christ to be "the greatest scrapper that ever lived." And, he intoned, "The manliest man is the man who will acknowledge Jesus Christ." Stephen Prothero locates all of this machismo in the cultural swing toward masculinity in the early twentieth century, a sort of Victorian culture meets Teddy Roosevelt, America's virile and "strenuous" president. Book titles bear out Prothero's contention of a masculine revolution sweeping American Christianity's portrait of Christ. These include Jason Pierce's *The Masculine Power of Christ* (1912), Carl Delos Case's *The Masculine in Religion* (1906) and R. W. Conant's *The Manly Christ: A New View* (1904). Chalk up all of this machismo to counterreactions to decades of Victorian cultural feminization. Conant's contribution merits some attention. Long before Ann Douglas wrote about the feminizing of American culture, Conant bewailed the "feminizing of Christianity." The church and Christianity simply can't appeal to the modern world by offering a feminized Christ, what Conant calls "that kind of a Christ." Instead, Conant declares, using italics for emphasis, *"Christ stands for the highest type of a strong, virile man, and there was nothing effeminate about him."* He held out hope for a revival if only Christ's manliness could be restored. So he dreamed:

> Let us consider what it would mean for Christian art and for preaching to present to the world a man's Christ. What sort of Christianity would command the admiration and reverence of the lawyer, the banker, and the reporter; of the teamster on the street, of the cowboy on the plains, of the engineer at the throttle?[11]

Also throw into the mix of the masculine revolution Sunday's sermonizing and Fosdick's 1913 devotional book, *The Manhood of the Master,* a book not intending to contribute "to the theology of the church about Jesus" but "an endeavor . . . to see the Man Christ Jesus himself." Fosdick's book is a character

---

[11]The citations by Sunday are found in Stephen Prothero, *American Jesus: How the Son of God Became a National Icon* (New York: Farrar, Strauss & Giroux, 2003), p. 94. For Prothero's discussion of Jesus as a "manly redeemer," see pp. 87-123. R. W. Conant, *The Manly Christ: A New View* (Chicago, 1904), pp. 9-11. Conant's popular book was reissued as *The Virility of Christ: A New View* (Chicago, 1915). Both editions privately published. See also Ann Douglas, *The Feminization of American Culture* (New York: Knopf, 1977); and Clifford Putney, *Muscular Christianity: Manhood and Sports in Protestant America, 1880-1920* (Cambridge, Mass.: Harvard University Press, 2001).

study, intended to be read over twelve weeks. The twelve chapters are struc-
tured around virtues of Christ's life. Each chapter consists of readings and
brief meditations for each day of the week, ending with a lengthy comment.
While titled *The Manhood of the Master*, there isn't a great deal of it that one
might say is specifically masculine, especially not in an "Iron John" vein. What
the book is about, however, is character, an important topic for Fosdick, who
also wrote *Twelve Tests of Character* (1923). And Jesus is the model character for all, both men and women. One influence becomes clear in the book:
Horace Bushnell's *Christian Nurture* (1847). Fosdick, with the help of Bushnell, celebrates Christ's malleability. He possesses character traits that often
go mismatched in the rest of us. He possesses all virtues, while other ages or
cultures manage to hold on to a mere handful of them. In fact, Christ's complexity is perhaps his greatest virtue, and Fosdick adds, "This study of the bal-
anced qualities in the Master's character could be extended almost without
limit." But, Fosdick reminds his readers, imitating him is not a matter of following him blindly. Obviously, his language and dress is of another era, but on a
deeper level Christ cannot be merely imitated because "his modes of thought
and speech were necessarily conformed to the customs of his country and
time." Consequently, when it comes to the letter of Christ's speech and actions, Fosdick tells us, "we cannot follow [Christ]." Instead, we are to follow his
character in its universal and ideal nature. We can follow Christ in his character, Fosdick assures us, because Christ represents in full what all humans possess in part: "The white light in him gathers up all the split and partial colors
of our little spectrums." We follow Christ not in the particulars but in his
personality.[12]

Fosdick took his thoughts on following Christ's character to a much larger
audience with his *The Man from Nazareth*. This book grew out of twin lifelong pursuits, his own fascination with the personality of Jesus and his desire
to bring Christ afresh into the twentieth century. Jesus, Fosdick observes, has
been interpreted since the beginning, since the time of the original disciples
and the penning of the Gospel narratives. Christ is not an "uninterpreted per-

---

[12]Harry Emerson Fosdick, *The Manhood of the Master* (New York: Association Press, 1913), pp. 5,
166-75. The book was published under the auspices of the International Committee of the Young
Men's Christian Association. The YMCA also produced a songbook titled *Manly Songs for Christian Men* (New York: Association Press, 1910). The reference to Bushnell is to his *Christian Nurture*
(New York: Scribner, 1847). For Fosdick's full discussion of personality, see his *On Being a Real Person* (New York: Harper, 1943), pp. 27-51.

son." On the contrary, Fosdick notes, "His very first disciples began interpreting him and, so far as the four gospels are concerned, this theological rendering of Jesus, which came to its climax in John, began in Mark." The disciples and biblical authors framed Jesus in the mental and philosophical and scientific, such as they were, models of their time and place in history, all the while concerned with the "deep and abiding" and timeless needs of man. In Fosdick's view, "The process which started in the experience of the first disciples has proved to be endless," a "perennial process" that "still goes on."[13]

As our study of the American Jesus attests, on one level Fosdick was quite right. On another level, however, his view bears scrutiny. Fosdick needed an interpreted Jesus by the disciples because he so wanted to reinterpret Jesus himself. The sticking point here is Christ's deity. The disciples framed Christ's personality in connection with divinity in a way that frightened Fosdick. So he adjusted the image to meet the needs of the twentieth century. Christ's divinity became redefined, if not defined away. Fosdick starts with a quote from John Ruskin. "As Ruskin said of the supreme artists," Fosdick observes, "they could not be proud because 'the greatness was not *in* them, but *through* them.'" Then he makes the application to Christ: "As Jesus saw the matter, it was not himself but God who was good, and who was using him in every good work he did." It was God *through* him. In Fosdick's view, he's in keeping with the Gospels in merely interpreting Jesus. There was the original Jesus, the Jesus of the disciple's making and the Jesus of the twentieth century's making, not to mention a host of reinterpretations intervening. As his interpretation unfolds in *The Man from Nazareth,* Fosdick concerns himself with the inner mental and relational dynamics of Christ, the Twelve and the other characters weaving in and out of the biblical narratives. "So to the twelve," Fosdick observes, "Jesus unbosomed himself, sharing with them alike his experience of, and his thoughts about, the divine resources that would sustain both him and them."[14]

Further, Fosdick's program of (re)interpreting Christ leads him to fill in the gaps of the Gospel narratives. While he makes good use of biblical citations, Fosdick will often writes "one suspects that . . ." or "I imagine . . ." before launching into some speculation of the inner mind of Christ or unrecorded

---

[13]Harry Emerson Fosdick, *The Man from Nazareth* (New York: Harper, 1949), pp. 247-48.
[14]Ibid., pp. 246, 176.

conversations he most certainly would have held with the Twelve. Here Fosdick reflects a deep and wide tendency to fill in the sketchy and episodic biblical story of Christ. Jesus, Fosdick informs us, "was a real man" who arrested crowds not so much through his teaching but through the sheer force of his personality. His speech was rigorous—and, Fosdick intones, "A Man's style of speech reveals him"—and he had the "extraordinary gift of being at ease with all sorts of persons." He was inclusive, openhearted, possessor of a unique power. The miracles didn't dissuade the crowds, either. Of course, Fosdick notes, "Indeed, our word 'miracle,' carrying the implication of broken law, completely misrepresents the thinking of Jesus' day." These were not scientific miracles, Fosdick assures us, but he never really gets around to telling us what they were. The specifics, however, matter little to Fosdick. Jesus's personality compelled crowds in the first century. Fosdick believed it had the same power to compel crowds in the twentieth century, a belief that was perhaps his raison d'être for all of his preaching and writing. His *The Man from Nazareth*, in the end, is most aptly titled.[15]

Fosdick's misunderstanding of Christ rippled through his theology, leading him to the conclusion late in life that "For me the essence of Christianity is incarnate in the personality of the Master, and it means basic faith in God, in the divinity revealed in Christ, in personality's sacredness and possibilities, and in the fundamental principles of life's conduct which Jesus of Nazareth exhibited." Fosdick had a faith to be sure, but one hanging by the tiniest possible theological thread, a thread that simply doesn't hold. The irony here is that with all of Fosdick's exaltation of Christ, he reduced Christ to nothing more than a superhero of human goodness. Machen once quipped that anything less than a view of Christ as infinite is infinitely less. So it is with Fosdick's Christ.[16]

Fosdick once preached a sermon at Riverside titled "What Does the Divinity of Jesus Mean?" Here he takes the divinity of Jesus as "the inner quality of his life" and as "God in" his life. But Jesus is not "an isolated phenomenon," instead revealing what all humanity possesses. Fosdick draws out the implication: "If Jesus is divine and if divinity is in each of us, like the vital forces which in winter wait in the frozen ground until the spring comes, that is a gospel!" In

---

[15]Ibid., pp. 42, 49-55.
[16]Fosdick, *Living of These Days*, p. 269.

another Riverside sermon titled "Taking Jesus Seriously," he lamented how theologians "grossly mistreated" Christ's divinity, adding, "Tell me, however, that Christ is the revelation of the Eternal Spirit, opening up a realm of Divine life and power into which I can enter, and that is the gospel." Elsewhere, he speaks of Christ's divinity as consisting of a highly attuned spiritual sense, noting that "To God through love for man was the road by which the Master reached his unique heights of spiritual vision." Fosdick loosed himself from the moorings of the biblical teachings of Jesus. And once loosed, he was bound to drift. It was not, of course, the spirit of Scripture or the spirit of Christology for that matter that he was drifting away from; it was the letter. Fosdick preferred the freedom of shaping Christ after his own experiences, the experiences of modernity. He was not ready to cast off Christ like the more progressive thinkers, neither would he suffer being bound to the old wineskins like the fundamentalists. Instead, he sought to recast Jesus, and in that he was far from alone.[17]

In Fosdick's day, not only was everyone reading him, they were also reading Bruce Barton's *The Man Nobody Knows: A Discovery of Jesus* (1924). In these pages, Jesus was portrayed as the "Outdoor Man"—again Teddy Roosevelt—"the Executive" and "The Founder of Modern Business." Further, Barton, himself an advertising executive, speaks of the arguments for Christ's existence as "advertisements." Fosdick painted Jesus as a hero for the modern person, leaving him open to private interpretations. Barton turned Jesus into a neon sign, making him into an entity open for business. Fosdick may not have liked Barton's overdrawn Jesus as businessman, but he had no grounds for objection since Barton was merely exercising his freedom to hold his own opinions.

A memorable section from Barton, reflecting on the King James Version's rendering of Luke 2:49, reveals just how far Barton was willing to go in bringing Jesus into the twentieth century. He writes:

> But what interests us most in this one recorded incident of his boyhood is the
> fact that for the first time he defined the purpose of his career. He did not say,
> "Wist ye not that I must practice preaching?" or "Wist ye not that I must get

---

[17]Harry Emerson Fosdick, *Riverside Sermons* (New York: Harper, 1958), pp. 269-73, 288; Harry Emerson Fosdick, *Adventurous Religion and Other Essays* (New York: Harper, 1926), p. 41. For Fosdick's freeing himself from the bounds of Scripture, see his *The Modern Use of the Bible* (New York: Macmillan, 1924).

ready to meet the arguments of men like these?" The language was quite different, and well worth remembering. "Wist ye not that I must be about my father's
business?" he said. He thought of his life as *business.*

Barton may have thought that he was following Scripture, even the letter of
Scripture. His misinterpretation of the word *business*, however, led him far
from the teachings of the Gospels. Unhindered by a proper interpretation of
the text, Barton proceeds to recall the life stories of America's captains of industry. He uses the life of Theodore N. Vail, founder of the American Tele-
phone and Telegraph Company, to illustrate Jesus's dictum that whoever
loses his life will find it. Barton notes that "to that great enterprise [AT&T]
[Vail] gave everything he had—'threw his life into it,' as we say—'lost his life in
it,' as Jesus said. And it gave him back larger and richer life, and a fortune and
immortality." In Fosdick, the letter of the Word had long since languished in
favor of its spirit. It appears that in Barton, even the spirit of the Word was
now to give way to the spirit of the age. The American Jesus entered the twentieth century, and he was ready to cash his check.[18]

WHAT (THE DIVINITY OF) JESUS MEANS TO ME

Reducing Jesus to a character that inspires—a hero or the consummate businessman—stretches beyond Fosdick and Van Dyke and Barton. In it we hear
echoes of Ralph Waldo Emerson and others from the past. But it also
stretches forward. Van Dyke and Fosdick reduced the value of Christ's work
to its example of self-sacrifice, an act of love conquering hate, evil and selfishness. Van Dyke arrived at this view on the tails of the Victorian virtue of gentlemanly altruism if not paternalism and patronage (not to be missed is Artaban's redemption of a *slave girl*). Fosdick exploited the war-hero genre
freshly minted after World War I. In the wake of the war, stories abounded of
the heroic and sacrificial deeds of soldiers in giving up their own lives for their
comrades. "No greater love," Fosdick liked to repeat, "has a man for his

---

[18]Bruce Barton, *The Man Nobody Knows: A Discovery of Jesus* (Indianapolis: Bobbs-Merrill, 1924),
pp. 162, 170. Among Barton's other writings are *A Young Man's Jesus* (Boston: Pilgrim Press,
1903), and a life of Paul, *He Upset the World* (Indianapolis: Bobbs-Merrill, 1932). Barton's interpretation of *business* encounters two obvious hermeneutical problems. Firstly, the Oxford English Dic-
tionary finds the word *business*, first used in Coverdale's translation prior to its appearance in the
KJV, meaning work to be done or matters to be attended to. Barton anachronistically fills it with the
modern notion of business as commercial enterprise. Second, *business* is a faulty translation of the
original text. The English Standard Version more accurately reads "my father's house."

friends than he who would lay down his life for them." The soldiers' deeds of self-sacrifice not only illustrated Christ's death, they replicated it in miniature. No doubt the railings of Van Dyke and Fosdick against selfishness in favor of self-sacrifice warrant applause. Fosdick once quipped that "a man wrapped up in himself is a very small package indeed," presaging the claims of sociologists of our current belly-button syndrome, so named for the tendency of infants to be so enamored with their own belly buttons that they can't seem to grasp that there is a world beyond their own self. But the key here is that Fosdick and Van Dyke reduced Christ's work to this. The selfless sacrifice is all it is, an example to empower us to the same. Perhaps the most significant reincarnation of this viewpoint among contemporary American evangelicals is in the form of videos and books for children.

In order to counter the negative media input, well-intentioned Christians have constructed an alternative world of entertainment for their young, what James Davison Hunter termed the phenomenon of "parallel institutionalism." High on morals and family values, though not always high on artistry—it's hard to compete with secular budgets—being nice to others in a selfish and self-centered world boomerangs through the genre. A Christmas book or video, aiming as it does at a season replete with greed, commercialism and opportunities to scream "I want" or "Give me," is the supreme place to preach selflessness and thinking of others. It's true that Christ died to conquer selfishness, but reducing "the meaning of Christmas" to that waltzes dangerously away from orthodoxy and differs not in the least from Van Dyke's books or Fosdick's sermons.[19]

Consider the Christmas episode *Electric Christmas* from the wildly popular and Focus on the Family-sponsored Adventures in Odyssey series of videos and DVDs. From the promotional literature, we learn that Dylan is mesmerized by the prospects of the "XR-7 limited edition speedster bicycle," just out of reach, his father informs him, of the family's budget. But then Dylan hatches a plan, learning that the very same bike is "the grand prize of the Christmas yard decorating contest." Dylan enters, originally intending to fol-

[19]James Davison Hunter, *American Evangelicalism: Conservative Religion and the Quandary of Modernity* (New Brunswick: Rutgers University Press, 1983), p. 56. See also, Eithne Johnson, "The Emergence of Christian Video and the Cultivation of Videoevangelism," in *Media, Culture, and the Religious Right*, ed. Linda Kintz and Julia Lesage (Minneapolis: University of Minnesota Press, 1998), pp. 191-210.

low the true meaning of Christmas, keeping it simple and focused on the manger scene. But, alas, extravagant lights and props appear on the next-door lawn and Dylan faces the fact that his entry just doesn't compete. Intense rivalry ensues as each boy attempts to outdo the other, leading Dylan down the road of erecting dinosaurs and a likeness of Elvis. In the process, Dylan "lets Whit down by forgetting his Angel Tree gift." But then comes the happy ending. While Dylan loses the contest and consequently the bike to Jessie, Jessie "unselfishly gives" the longed-for bike to Dylan. Dylan turns around and gives the bike to Matt, his almost forgotten Angel Tree designee. If viewers did not learn "the real meaning of Christmas" from *Electric Christmas,* then they can also try the Christmas episode by Focus on the Family-sponsored McGee and Me series titled, *'Twas the Fight Before Christmas.*[20]

Both, however, pale in success and sales to Big Idea Production's Veggie-Tales. Extending well into Christian and secular markets, VeggieTales' Christmas episode *The Toy That Saved Christmas* also depicts, rather cleverly, "the true meaning of Christmas." The antagonist, Mr. Nezzer, embodies the consumerism that has overrun every child's favorite holiday. As owner of Nezzer's Toy Factory, he sells the whole town on the "need" for his latest toy, the season's must-have "Buzz-Saw Louie." But, with a nod to Dr. Frankenstein's monster, a renegade Buzz-Saw Louie escapes the assembly line and subverts all of the evil factory owner's plotting, teaching the whole town the "true meaning of Christmas." This true meaning is encapsulated in a memorable line in one of the more entertaining moments of the video: "Christmas isn't about getting," the vegetables sing, "it's about giving." Altruism once again trumps selfishness, the real package that needs to be unwrapped at Christmas.[21]

To be fair, *Electric Christmas, 'Twas the Fight Before Christmas* and *The Toy That Saved Christmas* teach of Christ, the true gift and meaning of Christmas. For instance, in *Electric Christmas,* Dylan is given the bike by Jessie despite his not deserving it. This sets up the punch line: "God gave us the gift of his Son, even though we didn't deserve it." But the nature of that

---

[20] *Electric Christmas,* Adventures in Odyssey (Focus on the Family/Tyndale Christian Video, 1994), citations from the summary of the episode on <www.aiohq.com>, the official website of The Adventures in Odyssey series; *'Twas the Fight Before Christmas,* McGee and Me (Focus on the Family/ Tyndale Christian Video, 1990).

[21] *The Toy That Saved Christmas,* VeggieTales (Big Idea Production, 1996). Citations are from the episode and from promotional material on video sleeve.

gift, the nature of the person of Christ and the true significance of his atoning death are all left unpacked. The resounding message is that we best understand Christmas when we give to others as God has given to us, when we get beyond our consumer culture and our selfishness—all good, moral messages and all lacking something significant. Similar messages fill the pages of Christian children's books for Christmas as well.

Such fare is not limited to the children's section of Christian gift and bookstores. Adults could treat themselves to any number of individual or group studies that take their cue from the life of Christ. Often, Christ's character or some aspect of his personality is abstracted and then held up as a model to follow. Old standards include Christ's humility and gentleness, sincerity and love. Studying these character traits in Christ enables those same traits to be reproduced in us. Such soul-searching via Christ's character actually provides a basis for an entire series of studies for individuals and groups by Willow Creek Resources and Zondervan, "The Reality Check Series." In *When Tragedy Strikes: Jesus' Response to a World Gone Wrong,* with an American flag-draped cover, readers are informed that by doing this study, "You'll get a bonus. You'll meet a man of amazing kindness who has deep insights into the human experience and who invites you to a quality of life once thought unimaginable!" In *Hot Issues: Jesus Confronts Today's Controversies,* group participants are to "encounter Jesus afresh" and "watch his example carefully." Finally, in *Jesus' Greatest Moments: The Week That Changed Everything,* the reader walks along with Christ during his last week, all leading up to the resurrection, an event referred to as Christ's "compelling comeback."[22]

Such books and DVDs fill both children and adult sections of Christian bookstores. They likely are succeeding in their aim at helping people, both Christians and non-Christians, as the promotional literature observes, think about the meaning and relevancy of Christ in their lives today. The questions that are asked about the work of Van Dyke and Fosdick and others of a few generations ago must be asked of these works too. This is not to suggest a perfect parallel between the two; certainly there isn't. But there is much in common, in fact too much in common for the health of the church. Reducing Jesus

---

[22]Mark Ashton, *When Tragedy Strikes: Jesus' Response to a World Gone Wrong* (Grand Rapids: Zondervan, 2002), p. 10; *Hot Issues: Jesus Confronts Today's Controversies* (Grand Rapids: Zondervan, 2002), p. 11; and *Jesus' Greatest Moments: The Week That Changes Everything* (Grand Rapids: Zondervan, 2002).

to a mere exemplar of desirable character traits will only take one so far.

Of course, not everyone read Van Dyke and Fosdick appreciatively. Some saw right through their work and traced out its deleterious implications. One such critic was J. Gresham Machen. Reading Machen not only helps in seeing the shortfalls in Fosdick and early twentieth-century liberalism, it may also serve to tighten our vision as we look at contemporary American evangelical reflections on Christ.

MACHEN AS ANTIDOTE

Whenever Fosdick referred to his obscurantist antagonists, he was thinking chiefly of J. Gresham Machen (1881-1937). Raised in Baltimore, Machen studied at Johns Hopkins, briefly at the University of Chicago, Princeton Theological Seminary and Princeton University, and the universities of Marburg and Göttingen before settling in his teaching career in New Testament at Princeton Seminary, interrupted for service with the YMCA in France during World War I. Ironically, both Machen and Fosdick were kicked out of the Presbyterian Church of the U.S.A., but for opposite reasons—Fosdick for rejecting the Westminster Confession, the doctrinal standards of the denomination, and Machen for clinging to it. In 1929, following the reorganization of the board of Princeton Seminary, Machen felt forced to resign. He moved across the Delaware River to the brownstones of Philadelphia, where he established Westminster Theological Seminary. A few years later he felt compelled to start another institution, the Independent Board for Presbyterian Foreign Missions, due to the tolerance of liberalism by the denomination's official mission board. That action eventuated in his church trial, which led to his being defrocked in 1936. Machen responded by founding his third and last institution, the Orthodox Presbyterian Church that summer. Six months later, Machen died on January 1, 1937. His last words: "I am so thankful for the active obedience of Christ. No hope without it." For Machen, both in life and in death, theology mattered.[23]

As a New Testament scholar trained in Germany under the leading lights of higher criticism and theological liberalism, Machen was well suited to be the spokesperson for theological conservatives, a role he grudgingly, though ex-

---

[23]See D. G. Hart, *Defending the Faith: J. Gresham Machen and the Crisis of Conservative Protestantism in Modern America* (Baltimore: Johns Hopkins University Press, 1994); and Stephen J. Nichols, *J. Gresham Machen: A Guided Tour of His Life and Thought* (Phillipsburg, N.J.: P & R, 2004).

pertly, took on. His *The Origin of Paul's Religion* (1921) and *The Virgin Birth of Christ* (1930) were hallmarks of conservative scholarship, debunking the brightest and best of liberalism. The book that gained him his national reputation, however, was a piece of theology, *Christianity and Liberalism* (1923), a book-length reply to Fosdick's "Shall the Fundamentalists Win?" Machen followed his classic text with a sequel, *What Is Faith?* (1925). In these last two books, Machen surprisingly agreed with Fosdick that there were, at that given time in the church, two different views on significant theological issues. He vehemently disagreed with Fosdick, however, on whether or not those differences mattered. To Fosdick, they were simply two different perspectives on Christianity; to Machen, one was Christianity and the other was something altogether different. Crucial to the discussion was Christology.[24]

"There is a profound difference, then," Machen observes in *Christianity and Liberalism,* "in the attitude by modern liberalism and by Christianity toward Jesus the Lord. Liberalism regards him as an Example and Guide; Christianity as a Saviour: liberalism makes Him an example for faith; Christianity, the object of faith." Then he puts it with a bit of rhetorical flourish, "Liberalism regards Jesus as the fairest flower of humanity; Christianity regards Him as a supernatural Person." Machen is not denying the role of Christ as example. In fact, he states, "The imitation of Jesus has a fundamental place in Christian life; it is perfectly correct to represent Him as our supreme and only perfect example." Machen further observes that Christ did not come to offer mere guidance; he came to offer salvation. Here Machen finds himself to be in good company, as he notes, "Not the example of Jesus, but the redeeming work of Jesus, was the primary thing for Paul." Building on this, Machen proceeds to argue that it was not the faith of Christ, but faith in Christ. Christ is not, in Machen's words, the example of faith but faith's object.[25]

Machen drives this latter point home in *What Is Faith?* in a chapter he titled "Faith in Christ." He states the problem this way, "The truth is that in

---

[24]J. Gresham Machen, *The Origin of Paul's Religion* (1921; reprint, Eugene, Ore.: Wipf & Stock, 2002); *The Virgin Birth of Christ* (1930; reprint, London: James Clarke, 2000); *Christianity & Liberalism* (1923; reprint, Grand Rapids: Eerdmans, 1997); *What Is Faith?* (1925; reprint, Edinburgh: Banner of Truth Trust, 1991). All of these books are discussed in Nichols, *J. Gresham Machen,* pp. 81-134.

[25]Machen, *Christianity & Liberalism,* pp. 80-96. It should be noted that even in this book, which was intended for a popular audience, there is a depth to Machen's thought and crispness to his logic. It garnered praise from such secularists as Walter Lippmann and H. L. Mencken, the latter seldom dishing out words of praise to anyone.

great sections of the modern Church Jesus is no longer the object of faith, but has become merely an example for faith; religion is based no longer upon faith in Jesus but upon a faith in God that is, or is conceived to be, like the faith that Jesus had in God." Machen further takes on the theological complacency of Fosdick and others. He writes, " 'Let us alone,' some devout pastors say, 'we are preaching the gospel; we are bringing men and women into the Church; we have no time for doctrinal controversy; let us above all have peace' . . . 'Let us sink our doctrinal differences.' " Machen responds by noting sympathy with such concerns and even that he understands some speak such words sincerely. He concludes, however, "But for us, and for all who are aware of what is really going on, the policy of 'peace and work,' the policy of concealment and palliation, would be the deadliest of sins." Not because Machen relished a good fight but because maintaining "the redemptive religion known as Christianity" was at stake.[26]

Machen was actually promoting a both-and approach against Fosdick and liberalism's either-or approach. Fosdick set the impasse: theology or devotion, obscurantist bickering or proclaiming the gospel. Machen knew, as the history of the church had taught him, that the church's devotion runs shallow without theological depth, and that preaching the gospel apart from all of its biblical trappings is not preaching the gospel at all. It was Fosdick who stressed Christ's example only; it was Machen who stressed both Christ's example and Christ's necessary and substitutionary work of redemption. Fosdick said that Christianity is a lifestyle and not a doctrine, but Machen countered that Christianity was a doctrine first and lifestyle second. Fosdick may have won the rhetorical battle by his word choice and his crisper image, but Machen was far closer to the truth. All too often Machen got painted as the one who took his marbles and went home because he couldn't get along with anyone—an unfortunate caricature that persists to the present day despite the fact that his former students and colleagues lined up to attest to his sense of humor, his charitable spirit and good nature. All too often, as well, Machen and those seeking theological exactitude find themselves depicted as opposed to the church's true task of evangelism, all of that theologizing merely diverting attention from weightier matters. The reality of Machen's life and his activity in the church point in the opposite direction of the caricature.

---

[26] *What Is Faith?* pp. 98-101.

There are crucial lessons here that have perennially dogged the church. Fosdick was able to make the inroads that he did because of his rhetoric and because of the caricatures he drew of the theological conservatives and fundamentalists. Fosdick knew the words to say—Riverside was, after all, a Christian church that promoted Christ. Further, he held to the "divinity" of Christ, and he proclaimed the gospel. Machen and others just drew attention to the fact that Fosdick denuded Christology of its biblical and orthodox meaning, dressing it up instead in the fashions of modernity.[27]

In both of their studies of the American Jesus, Stephen Prothero and Richard Wightman Fox highly estimate Machen's criticism of liberalism's Jesus, commending the rigors of his scholarship. While Fox spends more time on Machen, recalling the main points of Machen's arguments, he then intones, "Machen wholly missed the depth of liberal Christians' attachment to Jesus." Fox, however, is the one missing the mark. First, Machen well understood the depth of liberalism's piety, so much so that while he was in Germany the depth of the pietism he encountered by the liberals there threw him into a crisis of faith. But Fox misses Machen on a much deeper level. Piety was not the measure of religious devotion for Machen. Machen had difficulty understanding how someone could claim to be Christian when not taking seriously what the Bible teaches about Christ. Machen did not begrudge Fosdick his view of Christ. He simply didn't want Fosdick to call it Christian. In Machen's view, all the devotion in the world matters little if it is pointed in the wrong direction. Contrary to Fox's judgment, Machen indeed understood the depth of the liberals' attachment. Machen just wasn't sure to whom or to what they were attached.[28]

CONCLUSION

Fosdick liked to speak of the religion *of* Jesus versus the religion *about* Jesus. Creeds, theologizing and the like all were a lost cause in his view, displacing

---

[27]As one example of Fosdick's either-or thinking, consider this passage from *The Meaning of Faith* (New York: Association Press, 1917): "Nothing but *experience* can give us a living estimate of anything; without that any theory is in vain. . . . After that, theology may help or hinder him, whether it is wise and vital or cold and formal; but with theology or not, he knows the heart of the New Testament's attitude toward Christ" (pp. 287-88). It may indeed be the case that scores of contemporary evangelicals would applaud Fosdick's sentiment without realizing the conclusions about the Bible, the gospel and Christ that such a sentiment led to for Fosdick.

[28]Prothero, *American Jesus*, pp. 26-27, 114; Fox, *Jesus in America* (New York: Harper San Francisco, 2004), pp. 333-36.

the virtues of a devoted life for "obscurantisms and perversions." Even in "Shall the Fundamentalists Win?" he played the devotion card, hailing those "devoted lovers of the Lord and servants of the gospel," regardless of whether or not they held to the virgin birth of Christ. Van Dyke too passed on the petulant quarrels caused by those who cared for theological precision. Not to be missed either is Van Dyke's and Fosdick's motivation. Both thought they were doing the gospel a favor. But getting Christology right or insisting that one have it right is not petulant, quarrelsome or obscurantist. The residue of the controversy for contemporary American evangelicals is that the tug of war between devotion to Christ, on the one hand, over precise thinking about Christ, on the other, often goes in the direction of devotion. Fosdick's methodology and approach wins out over Machen's. The sampling of the Christian market for Christmas DVDs and Bible study guides sadly bears this out.[29]

It's too much to dream of a world of small group studies on the Nicene and Chalcedonian creeds, much less a world in which such books would be competitive in the Christian marketplace, let alone imagine a world with a children's video on the Nicene Creed. Such a thing belongs in its original medium, in fact. The point is that in Fosdick and Machen's day, it was clear that there was a difference between the two and between their renderings of Christ and Christianity. That difference was not just a matter of emphasis. It wasn't that Fosdick wrote for a popular audience while Machen wrote for a scholarly one, an argument that one might make to defend "Electric Christmas" as innocuous. The difference between the teaching of Machen and Fosdick was fundamental, essential. These were two different Christs.

The American evangelical church of today needs to consider whether or not it can still identify the difference between the two and, having done so, see the dangers in the one. It is not enough for us to assume that a foundation of orthodox Christology is in place when we look to the Christmas story for a lesson on selfishness or to the life of Christ for the marks of godly manhood or for deep insight into human experience. Before such criticisms of Christian children's fare are dismissed as the nitpicking of theologians, we should be reminded of what is at stake. Jesus is not merely or supremely the man from Nazareth of ideal character and virtue. He is not the mere exemplar of selflessness for a self-absorbed world. He is that and so much more, infinitely

---

[29]Fosdick, *Adventurous Religion and Other Essays*, pp. 322-24.

more. He is Lord and Savior, the God-man who died for us. That is the real meaning of Christmas. Even the classic *A Charlie Brown Christmas* (1965) reveals that we at least have to quote Luke 2 if we're attempting to tell the true meaning of Christmas. Above all (again the *Peanuts* gang helps out here), we have to show that Christmas is ultimately about the miracle of Christ's birth. That, Charlie Brown, is the real meaning of Christmas.

The crucial foundation of two-nature Christology must be explicit, must be elaborated on and, in some cases, must be taught in the first place. Such an understanding of Christ is all the more important when we consider the seeming inability of contemporary evangelicals to recognize the problem with the way Jesus is appropriated in our own subculture. It should not escape notice that what got checked at the door as liberalism in previous generations of evangelicals now finds a home in the current generation. In the next chapters, we'll continue exploring the shaping of the American evangelical Jesus throughout the twentieth century in the contemporary marketplace of music, film, trinkets and politics. Listener, viewer, buyer and voter beware.

JESUS ON VINYL

From the Jesus People to
Contemporary Christian Music

*Singing overt praises to Jesus through rock 'n' roll
music makes about as much sense as
shouting Sex Pistols lyrics during a church hymn.*

NATE LEVIN

Why should the Devil have all the good music?

MARTIN LUTHER
(WITH A LITTLE HELP FROM LARRY NORMAN)

One of Elvis's bestselling albums of a pretty long string of bestselling albums was one of his many forays into gospel and hymns, *Christmas,* originally recorded in 1957 and re-released in 1970. The album that Johnny Cash longed to make from the very beginning was one of the first releases on the Columbia label. Once the man in black was freed from his original Sun Records contract, he cut *Hymns by Johnny Cash* (1959). Music has significantly shaped American culture from its roots. This is especially true of the twentieth century, especially true when it comes to America's youth, and especially true of the musical genre of gospel. All three, music, youth and gospel came together in perfect confluence in the 1960s as burned-out hippies turned on to Jesus. Like the little drummer boy, the only things they had in their hands were drum sticks and maybe a few guitars. So they played for Jesus. They began playing for him in Haight-Ashbury in San Francisco, in Hollywood and in Seattle's North End. Then the movement spread. Over the next decades this Jesus-music industry grew into the powerful, multibillion dollar market force known as CCM, Contemporary Christian Music. Gospel music sales in 2004 alone topped 700 million dollars. In the old days, they just called themselves Jesus People. *Time* magazine called it "The Jesus Revolution."[1]

Not all onlookers gave the Jesus People and their revolution a thumbs up. The press had watched America's youth experiment with any number of things throughout the 1960s. Now spirituality had captured the attention of the youth, and like any fad, many commentators mused, this one would quickly pass. Folks espousing a high view of the church weren't sure what to make of Pat Boone baptizing hundreds in his swimming pool. Fundamentalists were sure that the movement focused on the wrong things. Many lined up to castigate the movement for its criticism of the institutional church and setting up "house churches" instead. The Jesus People also looked like hippies. Of course they did, for they were, retaining almost everything from the hippie culture except drugs and sex. Admittedly, that doesn't leave much to being a hippie, but it was still enough to rile the fundamentalists. Jack Hyles, the irascible fundamentalist, delivered what he believed to be the death knell to the Jesus People movement in the form of a sermon he titled "Jesus Had Short Hair."[2]

The Jesus People, however, failed to accept Hyles and the other fundamentalists' rebukes. For them Jesus had long hair, and he was also the consummate countercultural rebel. The famous "Wanted: Jesus Christ" poster appeared almost ubiquitously, being published in the *Hollywood Free Paper*, Berkeley's *Right On!* and even in *Time*. It declares Jesus to be a "Notorious Leader of an underground liberation movement," with the appearance of a "Typical hippie type—long hair, beard, robe, sandals, etc." In fact, you could argue that the Jesus People happened to be the hippies that found what all of the hippies were looking for: the answer to the hypocrisy and inauthenticity of the establishment. In Jesus they found the real thing. And in Jesus they found real love.[3]

TRY JESUS

"Experience Jesus." "Try Jesus." "Turned on to Jesus." Such slogans punctu-

---

[1]The *Time* cover story ran as "The Jesus Revolution." Inside, the article was titled "The New Rebel Cry: Jesus Is Coming!" June 21, 1971, pp. 56-63. "Today's Gospel Sound: Moving Millions, Industry Overview 2005" (Nashville: Gospel Music Association), p. 1.

[2]Jack Hyles, "Jesus Had Short Hair," first preached in 1971.

[3]See *The Street People: Selections from "Right On!" Berkeley's Christian Underground Student Newspaper* (Valley Forge, Penn.: Judson Press, 1971), pp. 10-11; and *The Hollywood Free Paper* 1 no. 1 (October 7, 1969).

ated the message of the Jesus People, stressing the difference of their approach from both the hippie culture they crawled out of and from the institutional church or formal religious culture they weren't about to become
connected with. And they captured everyone's attention from Billy Graham
to the editors of the national news magazines. In the *Time* cover story, the authors use the words *startling* and *surprising,* as well as a host of superlatives
to depict this phenomenon, all the while telling the story with, even considering journalistic standards, an unusually fast pace. Something large and significant had arrived on the cultural scene, leaving many shaking their heads in
bewilderment and not a few quite curious. Consider this telling of one of
Chuck Smith's Pacific Ocean baptisms:

> Most of the baptized were young, tanned, and casual in cut-off blue jeans, pull-
> overs, and even an occasional bikini. A freshly dunked teen-ager, water stream-
> ing from her tie-dyed shirt, threw her arms around a woman and cried, "Mother,
> I love you!" A teen-age drug user who had been suffering from recurring un-
> scheduled trips suddenly screamed, "My flashbacks are gone!"

"Drug cures," the article goes on to recount, "are not the only attraction for
conversion." People also turned to the Jesus movement for "the direct approach to Christ" it freely offered. This accounted for a large number of Roman Catholics and those from the mainline denominations. Those who left
these faith traditions found the immediate experience offered by the Jesus
People to be real. The Jesus movement also found a home among Pentecos-
tals and charismatics, led by such figures as David Wilkerson, whose story of
Nicky Cruz, *The Cross and the Switchblade,* racked up over six million in
sales. The Jesus People comprised a diverse group, offered plenty of curiosi-
ties to look at and had a contagious enthusiasm. People from across the spectrum of American culture, in other words, had plenty of reasons to take notice of the Jesus movement.[4]

The critical year that started all this is more than likely 1967, as Ted and
Liz Wise set up a commune of four couples, formerly drug addicts and hippies who got turned on to Jesus, in the Haight-Ashbury district of San Francisco. Ted recalls that his conversion, in 1966, occurred while he was on LSD,
giving him the title of the first hippie convert. They eventually rented a store-
front, turning it into a coffeehouse and christening it The Living Room. They

---

[4]Julian Wagner, "The New Rebel Cry," *Time,* June 21, 1971, pp. 61-62.

offered hippies a place to crash, free soup (hippies indeed found it hard to live off of just love) and plenty of talk about Jesus. An early convert was Lonnie Frisbee. After joining the four couples in the commune, he later moved to Costa Mesa, where he opened a commune dubbed the House of Miracles. Frisbee eventually became the youth pastor at Chuck Smith's Calvary Chapel in Costa Mesa. Christian communes sprung up in cities across America. A sampling of these include His Place in Hollywood; Hosanna House in Eugene, Oregon; House of Joy in Portland, Oregon; House of Prayer in Detroit, Michigan; House of Judah in Buffalo, New York; and the House of Smyrna in Toronto, Ontario.[5]

Besides Ted Wise and Lonnie Frisbee, early leaders in the movement also included Arthur Blessitt, Hal Lindsey, Duane Pederson and Moses David Berg. Blessitt, originally from Mississippi, opened His Place in Hollywood in 1968, famous for its "toilet service." Invariably, those milling about His Place would find themselves in the bathroom watching as the newest convert would flush away his or her stash of drugs, giving new meaning to Paul's command to "put off" the old ways. Neighboring businesses pressured authorities to shut down Blessitt's coffeehouse. He responded by chaining himself to a large, twelve-foot cross. Blessitt then traveled across the country with his cross, which by then had a wheel affixed to it. He next took his cross around the world, having set the goal, which came to him by divine fiat, of carrying his cross in every country by the year 2000.

Hal Lindsey wrote his runaway bestseller *The Late Great Planet Earth* while working at his own Jesus Christ Light and Power Company, a ministry aimed at UCLA students that also ran the JC Light and Power House, a coed commune that could house up to forty people.

Then there is the aberration led by Moses David Berg. He established the Children of God, considered himself a prophet, and preached a radical, doomsday message, going to even more eschatological extremes than Lindsey. Berg brought a great deal of aspersion on the movement through his technique of "flirty fishing," which meant that the female members of the

---

[5]For an overview of the movement, see David D. Sabatino, "Jesus People Movement," in *Encyclopedia of Religious Revivals in America,* ed. Michael McClymond (Westport, Conn.: Greenwood Press, 2006), 1:227-30. For a discussion of the communes, see Hiley H. Ward, *The Far-Out Saints of the Jesus Communes: A Firsthand Report and Interpretation of the Jesus People Movement* (New York: Associated Press, 1972).

Children of God used sex to attract new members and converts. Berg called them "Hookers for Jesus."

That the Jesus People movement encompassed the likes of Blessitt, Lindsey and Berg, though of course those within the movement readily denounced Berg, shows its diversity.[6]

The movement also diversified enough to give a prominent role to women in its leadership. Chief among them is Linda Meissner, who moved out from David Wilkerson's ministry to start her own, The Jesus People Army. Meissner would join with Berg and the Children of God, but not before her group established a commune in Milwaukee. A splinter of that group migrated to Chicago, establishing Jesus People USA. This is one of the few communes from the Jesus movement that remains to the present, numbering about 500.[7]

No wonder this diverse movement captured the attention of so many, both friend and foe alike. One person who decided to take a closer look was none other than Billy Graham. Larry Eskridge—in a retrospective article on Graham's relationship to the "Jesus Generation," the title of Graham's 1971 book—argues that Graham gave cover, "gave his blessing," to the Jesus People, allowing them to gain acceptance in the evangelical world. Further, Graham's "irenic inclination" and "tolerant inclusivism" of the youth of that era—whether they had long hair or crewcuts—also signaled that the church would make a home for youth, while the culture at large had cast a skeptical eye on them. This leads Eskridge to conclude that Graham's affirmation "looms surprisingly large in the resurgence and future direction of American evangelicalism." In other words, had Graham not stepped in as an ally, the Jesus People and their direct and indirect impact would have amounted to nothing more than a passing fad. Since he stepped in, however, this movement indelibly impacted the shape of current American evangelicalism.[8]

The Jesus People would eventually exchange their hippie ways for more settled lifestyles, but as they came into evangelical churches and even formed new

---

[6]See footnote 5 for sources, as well as the various articles on Blessitt, Lindsey and Berg in Randall Balmer, *Encyclopedia of Evangelicalism* (Louisville, Ky.: Westminster John Knox Press, 2002).

[7]See footnotes 5 and 6, as well as <www.jpusa.org>.

[8]Larry Eskridge, "'One way': Billy Graham, the Jesus Generation and the Idea of Evangelical Youth Culture," *Church History* 67:1 (March 1998), p. 106; see Billy Graham, *The Jesus Generation* (Grand Rapids: Zondervan, 1971). The cover of Graham's book, which came out late in the year 1971, looks remarkably akin to the *Time* magazine cover published earlier in June.

denominations or affiliations, such as Calvary Chapel and the Vineyard movement, they brought something with them, namely, their music and their very
warm, personal, experience-based relationship to Jesus. The Jesus People also
inched American evangelicalism along in its suspicious ecclesiology. Even as
they settled into pews and enjoyed the patronage and moral support of such
churches as Hollywood's First Presbyterian Church, the Hollywood Baptist
Church and Peninsula Bible Church, the Jesus People remembered their richest
experiences came not while sitting in pews but while attending concerts, or while
simply living out their love for Jesus on the streets. One thing they certainly did
for American evangelical Christology was to focus on the love of Jesus.

ALL YOU NEED IS LOVE

In their scholarly study of the Jesus People, Ronald Enroth, Edward Erickson
and C. Breckenridge Peters discuss what they see as a shallow and fundamen-
talist-inspired approach to the social issues of the day in the pages of Duane
Pederson's *Hollywood Free Paper*, one of the Jesus People papers. Pederson
coined the term *Jesus People* and led the movement in Los Angeles. In sub-
sequent years he would convert to the Eastern Orthodox tradition. But in
those days he was all for the movement. Headlines in his paper used social
issues as teasers to talk, almost incessantly, about one's inner, personal relationship with Jesus. A headline running "How Moral Is War?" introduced an
article that dealt with inner spiritual warfare and not the Vietnam War, which
was raging at the time. Another headline on pollution dealt with "spiritual
ecology" and sin's pollution of the soul, and so on. Enroth, Erickson and Peters conclude that Pederson's paper, disjointed and shallow, constantly
turned to a simplistic "Jesus is the answer" approach without probing the
depths of the questions people were asking. According to their study, even
the folks at Hollywood's First Presbyterian Church, who first desired to support Pederson and his paper, backed off, sensing that the anti-intellectualism
rife in the *Hollywood Free Paper* proved to be of little help. The church established its own paper, *The Alternative*, with a lot more Francis Schaeffer
and a lot less sloganeering.[9]

---

[9]Ronald M. Enroth, Edward E. Erickson Jr., and C. Breckenridge Peters, *The Jesus People: Old-Time
Religion in the Age of Aquarius* (Grand Rapids: Eerdmans, 1972), pp. 73-79. See "Ecology," *Holly-
wood Free Paper*, January 6, 1970; "Is War the Problem?" *Hollywood Free Paper*, June 16, 1970; and
"Pollution Conspiracy," *Hollywood Free Paper*, July 21, 1970.

Duane Pederson was nonplussed by such criticisms. In his 1971 book *Jesus People*, which is largely a compilation of articles from his paper, Pederson exclaims, "The Jesus People Movement is a movement of love. It isn't a new denomination. It isn't even a church. It's a movement, made up of people who express love when they come face to face with lonely, frightened, completely lost people." He continues to explain how the Jesus People connect, noting, "The street people—for one reason or another—are castoffs from society. But the love that Jesus gives me for them causes them to respond. And as a result, many of them come to Jesus Christ. The Jesus People exemplify Jesus' love. Simply. Beautifully, without undue display."

The 1990s produced a cottage industry of critiques of evangelicals by evangelicals for evangelicals. David Wells, Mark Noll and Os Guinness all lined up to decry the shallowness of evangelicalism. Who can forget Noll's opening salvo: "The scandal of the evangelical mind is that there is not much of an evangelical mind"? Though these books neglect to mention the Jesus People movement, it significantly contributed to the lackluster intellectualism rife in American evangelicalism.[10]

But the Jesus People, if numbers count, were effective at winning souls. It was, after all, a movement of love aimed at a generation looking for it. Not only were they effective due to their message of love, they were also effective on account of their medium of music. Among those early converts stands Larry Norman, the founder of Christian rock (Jesus music back then). His 1969 album *Upon This Rock* is hailed as the first album of the genre. By 1975 he established his own label, Solid Rock Records. Soon, record store clerks across America were stumped, not knowing what bin to put these new albums in. It would take some time for this new genre of Christian rock to reach the place it holds in the music industry today. But that didn't stop the production of albums. Randy Stonehill, an early signer to Norman's label also takes his place among the pioneers of the genre. His first album, *Born Twice* (1971), was financed by the legendary Pat Boone. Boone not only opened his pool, he also opened his checkbook, not to mention the doors he opened in the music industry for these young musicians. Pat Boone ex-

---

[10]Duane Pederson with Bob Owen, *Jesus People* (Pasadena: Compass, 1971), pp. 37-38. See David Wells, *No Place for Truth?* (Grand Rapids: Eerdmans, 1993); Mark Noll, *The Scandal of the Evangelical Mind* (Grand Rapids: Eerdmans, 1995); and Os Guinness, *Fit Bodies, Fat Minds* (Grand Rapids: Baker, 1994).

plained what motivated him, Norman, Stonehill and a host of others to pioneer this new route:

> It hit me like a brick, or one of those beach hot dogs. Of course—it's possible!
> Why not talk to young people about Jesus in their own language, and with the
> sound of their own music? Why not be completely honest about a human being's search for something real in a world that so often accepts substitutes and
> dehydrated religion?[11]

This new sound came of age rather quickly, helped along by an eight-hour Christian rock concert concluding Explo '72, a six-day evangelism conference in Dallas sponsored by Campus Crusade for Christ. It didn't hurt Jesus music either to have some celebrity conversions, like Noel Paul Stookey of Peter, Paul, and Mary, and Phil Keaggy of Glass Harp. This was also the era of the rock operas *Jesus Christ Superstar* and *Godspell*. Coming to rapid maturation, the 1970s witnessed the birth of bands like Petra, which is the Greek word for *rock*, Resurrection Band, and Sweet Comfort Band, as well as more folk-sounding bands and artists like Agape, The Second Chapter of Acts, Keith Green and John Fischer. The 1970s also witnessed the rise of Christian rock shows on already-established Christian radio stations, as well as the establishment of new radio stations specifically to play these new records. Jesus music also hit at a time when the Christian Booksellers Association, a trade organization of Christian retailers, enjoyed rapid growth in both sales and stores. If secular record stores hadn't quite caught on to the trend by the end of the 1970s, Christian youth could purchase plenty of vinyl from their local Christian bookstore.[12]

But the fact that Christian rock quickly became, as sociologists like to say, ghettoized—meaning it became parochial and insular within the Christian world—bothered people like Larry Norman and John Fischer. They wanted the movement to remain as it started, an evangelistic outreach. The problem was that by becoming Christian rock stars, they no longer enjoyed the secular audiences they once had. In fact, some Christian rockers, like Larry Norman, soon had a hard time finding a home anywhere. Jay Howard and John Streck argue that Norman would be "marginalized in both the realm of rock music, where he was considered too religious, and in the burgeoning Christian music

---

[11]Pat Boone, "prelude" to Paul Baker, *Why Should the Devil Have All the Good Music? Jesus Music—Where It Began, Where It Is, and Where It Is Going* (Waco, Tex.: Word, 1979), p. vii.
[12]See chap. 7 for a discussion of the rise of the Christian Booksellers Association and its relationship to the Jesus People.

industry, where his music was believed to be too aggressive." Initially, however, they enjoyed wide audiences of fellow hippies. And when they got to play for these audiences, their songs had plenty of Jesus. On their album *I Love You,* Larry Norman and the group People! recorded a song titled "We Need a Whole Lot More Jesus and a Lot Less Rock and Roll." Interviewed in an article on Jesus rock in the June 1971 issue of *Rolling Stone,* Chuck Girard of Love Song declares, "When you ask somebody what our songs are about there's no ambiguity. It's right there in plain simple language with no deep intellectual vibes. What we're saying is Jesus, one way. If you want the answer follow it." In one sense there is a profound countercultural impulse here. The exclusivity of Christ, that he is the *only* way, tends not to be a palatable doctrine in any age and place, but especially in the free-thought world of California in the 1960s and 1970s. But on the other hand, the advocacy of an experiential Christianity was rather in tune with that culture at that time.[13]

That very same *Rolling Stone* article notes how grassroots the Jesus rock movement really was. These were, for the most part, not polished studio musicians with the backing of large record labels and concert promoters. These were bands whose members were out on the streets handing out handbills to get people to come to their free concerts. These were largely "amateur musicians." "The music isn't always a great quality," confesses one such musician also interviewed for the *Rolling Stone* piece, "but it's funky because it's about Jesus." Before long this loose movement of mostly amateur musicians, with a few standouts among them, comprising the Jesus music of the 1970s would morph into the well-oiled machine of Contemporary Christian Music of the 1980s and on. The crucial question is what would become of the Jesus funk?[14]

THE TIMES THEY ARE A-CHANGIN'

A cartoon appearing in *Right On!* and the *Hollywood Free Paper* traces the evolution of an almost military-looking, youthful, bearded figure spouting off on the revolution: "The only way to purify the system is to destroy it and start all over again." The man ages and morphs, with each passing frame, into an old,

---

[13]Jay R. Howard and John M. Streck, *Apostles of Rock: The Splintered World of Contemporary Christian Music* (Lexington: University Press of Kentucky, 1999), p. 31; Patrick Corman, "Freaking Out on Jesus: True Testimonials from the Street," *Rolling Stone,* June 1971, pp. 24-25.
[14]Corman, "Freaking Out on Jesus," pp. 24-25.

bald man in a suit, playing the part of "The chairman of the central committee," whose duty it is "to enforce party discipline on the masses." The cartoon offers a parable to these youth of Berkeley and elsewhere to beware lest they subtly lose their idealism, blend in and conform. It is a call to avoid becoming a part of the very thing that they have directed their energies against, the establishment. It is actually a perennial parable, warning of the loss of youthful idealism as the realities of life set in. Perhaps they included this cartoon in their papers to remind themselves of the dangers of caving on those idealistic principles. They should have listened to the parable. Despite a few holdouts, like the Jesus People USA commune in Chicago, the tens of thousands of Jesus People eventually cut their hair—Jack Hyles would be so proud—settled into family life, took corporate jobs and waxed anxious over their pension plans. The industry they started, Christian rock, also transformed itself into big business. While catching occasional snippets of criticism from its founding musicians and from the pockets of remaining fundamentalism, CCM and the Gospel Music Association (GMA) by and large rolls on, accumulating fans and amassing record sales with each passing year. CCM and the GMA have a glossy monthly magazine, corporate representation, annual trade shows and a well-watched annual award show. While the Dove Award doesn't quite rank next to the Grammy, it comes pretty close. The times have changed since 1969 and the strumming of guitars at Haight-Ashbury.[15]

Adelaida Reyes notes that "after World War II, popular music gained momentum and transformed itself from a mere purveyor of music that sought a common denominator into an active promoter of the new, spurred on by commodification and a market that is continually in search of novelty." Both factors may go a long way in explaining the evolution of the songs of the Jesus People to the business of CCM. Terry Mattingly puts the matter directly when it comes to the transition of the earlier Jesus music to CCM, wryly observing, "And, lo, the counterculture became the corporate culture, one that was increasingly competitive and relentlessly contemporary." Bill Romanowski concurs. In fact, he sees what happened to Christian music as it increasingly became commodified as an archetype of the way "religious subcultures are co-opted, perhaps even converted, by the dominant American consumer culture." He adds, "As the Christian music industry was increasingly incorporated by mainstream in-

---

[15]*Street People*, pp. 22-23.

dustrial practices, however, evangelistic ideals were eclipsed by business imperatives." Competition for "slim markets" led to cooperation between Christian labels and secular ones, leading to the crossover controversy, as artists like Amy Grant and Michael W. Smith began writing and performing songs that could be generic enough in their lyrics to make it onto secular radio stations. Romanowski contends that while such crossing over resulted in expanded markets or "ministry," it also "threaten[ed] the loss of specific religious identity to the homogenizing effects of mass culture."[16]

Some artists within the world of CCM also agree. In a famous debate between John Styll and Keith Green over the role of corporate structures in CCM, Styll argued that "the reason that there *are* such things as [Christian] record companies is primarily to take the burden of business, distribution, and manufacturing headaches and hassles off an artist so that artist can concentrate on what they do best." Keith Green returned, "The central reason that there are record companies is for corporations to make money." Recording artist Steve Camp launched a similar salvo at the industry in some of his 107 Theses that comprise his "Call for Reformation in the Contemporary Christian Music Industry." Camp, along with other recording artists, established Audience One, a movement geared to reforming CCM. But still, profits rule. The Gospel Music Association's industry report for 2005 has a cover tag line that reads "Moving Millions," attaching a double meaning to the word *moving* (in retail lingo the word means selling products; in spiritual lingo it means, presumably, the work of God). Once you get past the cover page, you see that the retail meaning of the word, however, trumps the spiritual, as page after page of the report ticks off millions of albums sold, millions of concert tickets sold, millions of viewers of movies who are listening to Christian artists on the soundtracks and the "millions of consumers . . . who comprise a major buying force in today's economy." CCM has come a long way from the days of the Jesus People.[17]

Romanowski, however, laments something worse when he writes, "The

---

[16]Adelaida Reyes, *Music in America: Experiencing Music, Expressing Culture* (New York: Oxford University Press, 2005), p. 38; Terry Mattingly, *Pop Goes Religion: Faith in Popular Culture* (Nashville: W Publishing, 2005), p. 21; and William R. Romanowski, "Evangelicals and Popular Music: The Contemporary Christian Music Industry," *Religion and Popular Culture in America*, ed. Bruce David Forbes and Jeffrey H. Mahan (Berkeley: University of California Press, 2000), pp. 107-8.

[17]These citations may be found in Howard and Streck, *Apostles of Rock*, p. 169. The exchange between John Styll and Keith Green was originally published in *Contemporary Christian Music*, March 1980.

Christian music industry promoted an evangelical popular culture based on the rules of commercialism and not those of churches, elevating consumer values and taste at the expense of doctrine and tradition." This new evangelical popular culture furthers the experientialism and individualism of evangelicalism spawned by the Jesus movement; the music stresses personal faith and personal experience. The charge of individualism against the Jesus movement may appear to be strained given that a heavy dose of communalism characterized its early days. It nevertheless spawned individualism by so stressing the personal experience of Christ. It would take a band outside of the genre of Christian rock, Depeche Mode, to alert evangelicalism to what it had done in their song "Personal Jesus." Jesus becomes your own, your personal Savior, to "hear your prayers," who becomes "someone who cares." Which brings us to answer the question posed earlier: What would become of Jesus as Jesus music passed from the hands of the Jesus People to the tentacles of CCM? He became even more personal and even a bit blurred. Returning to Steve Camp's 107 Theses, thesis 41 declares, "Christian music, originally called Jesus Music, once fearlessly sang clearly about the gospel. Now it yodels of a Christ-less, watered down, pabulum-based, positive alternative, aura-fluff, cream of wheat, mush-kind-of-syrupy, God-as-my-girlfriend kind of thing." Jesus especially becomes blurred when he is dropped for a message of implicit faith, the types of messages found in the so-called crossover songs.[18]

CROSSOVER CONTROVERSIES

From the beginnings of Christian rock, artists had a choice to be either Christians who played music or to play Christian music. As the gospel music industry grew, a third way emerged; artists could be Christians who play wholesome, faith-implicit music that would garner secular airplay. Amy Grant was the first of the contemporary generation to officially break the secular sound barrier with "Baby, Baby." Christian artists would follow, with even bigger chart-toppers, like Jars of Clay's "Flood" and Sixpence None the Richer's "Kiss Me." Of the latter, Randall Balmer has quipped, " 'Kiss Me' has roughly

---

[18]Howard and Streck, *Apostles of Rock*, p. 109. Admittedly, for me at least, when Johnny Cash covered "Personal Jesus," he took what was intended to be mockery and filled it with sincerity. In Cash's gnarly old voice, he truly revered the personal Jesus that Depeche Mode used as a foil for all they disliked about Southern Christianity. Steve Camp, "A Call for Reformation in the Contemporary Christian Music Industry," posted at Audience One's website <www.a1m.org>.

as much spiritual content as a steel-belted radial tire."[19]

A great deal of controversy surrounds the crossing over to secular markets by Christian musicians, primarily because these Christian musicians want to keep their feet in two market shares, the worlds of pop music and Christian music. They would like to stay in the running for Dove awards, keep their CDs in Christian stores and have youth pastors bring busloads to their concerts. Balmer notes how this has caused not a little consternation within the world of the Gospel Music Association, leading them to "com[e] up with an unwieldy set of definitions that make the tax code read like a nursery rhyme." In their study of CCM, Howard and Streck present a sympathetic case for the artists who crossover. They note how DeGarmo & Key's original video for "Six, Six, Six" was rejected by MTV. The band tweaked the video and it enjoyed "light rotation." "Hard feelings remained," however. The band enjoyed a measure of revenge in their song titled "I Use the J-Word." So they were "banned from MTV," the song's lyrics muse, because they take their religion "a bit too seriously." Howard and Streck also chronicle the reports of Christian bands who were offered touring and record contracts if they "were less 'gospel' and more 'inspirational,' " a line that Bob Hartman of Petra takes to mean that they are to "take the Jesus out."[20]

Those who do take out Jesus stand a better chance of success, though of course there are no guarantees. Many bands have left their Christian labels to sign with secular ones only to be dumped after less-than-stellar sales. Successful bands, however, tend to capture the attention. "Butterfly Kisses" stands out; what it lacks in theology, it certainly makes up for in sentimentality. MercyMe's "I Can Only Imagine" catapulted that band all the way to appearances on NBC's *Tonight Show with Jay Leno* and other national media outlets. The latter has a rich sound and explicitly religious, even Christian, lyrics, but in the end it presents a rather vacuous theology. These crossover artists remind me somewhat of the Osmonds. They are wholesome, safe and clean-cut, especially compared to their purely secular counterparts, but you can listen for a long time and not hear anything overtly Mormon. Perhaps the same could be said of Christian crossover artists. They too are wholesome,

---

[19]Randall Balmer, *Mine Eyes Have Seen the Glory: A Journey into the Evangelical Subculture in America*, 4th ed. (New York: Oxford University Press, 2006), p. 306.

[20]Ibid.; Howard and Streck, *Apostles of Rock*, pp. 90, 180-81 (originally from James Long, "Petra's Bob Hartman: No Doubt About It," *Contemporary Christian Music* 18, no. 11 [1996]: 38-39).

safe and clean-cut, but not much Christianity crosses over with them.

In some ways this problem confronts more than the crossover artists. The whole sweep of CCM may come under its purview. CCM itself attempts to crossover, combining tastes and styles of the popular culture with the sensibilities and (a modicum of) the lyrics of church music. How well it straddles that fence becomes a point of debate. One problem that arises, however, is what CCM communicates in general about evangelicalism's ambivalence to culture. While the early days of Jesus music had an edge, arising as it did from the streets, CCM today has dulled the edge, producing music that is safe, not all that complex and artistically ranking a little below the songs on pop albums that don't make it into radio circulation. CCM has become ghettoized, the Christian suburban youth's counter to what their unchurched friends listen to. James Davidson Hunter refers to this dynamic as parallel institutionalism, which means that you can listen to Christian music on Christian radio stations or at Christian concerts or on CDs bought at Christian stores. You can even download Christian ringtones for your phone bought, hopefully, from a Christian-owned-and-operated kiosk at the mall. You can even download the ringtones straight from a Christian website. Hank Hill, the character from the animated series *King of the Hill,* sagaciously quipped in relation to Christian rock, "You aren't making Christianity better, you're just making rock and roll worse."[21]

Perhaps as an alternative we could argue that there is church music (avoiding murky waters here, let's not even mention worship style), and then there is the music that entertains you or even enriches you, in other words secular music, ranging all the way from opera to grunge. The problem with this proposal is that it requires discrimination, which requires thought, and at times can even be dangerous. To recourse to CCM because it's safe, however, comes with its own package of problems. A more robust view of culture accepts that in the process of engagement there might be some missteps. It recognizes that sometimes you might come away with a little dust on your feet.[22]

The other problem with this view is that it smacks of compartmentaliza-

[21]"Reborn to Be Wild," *King of the Hill,* November 9, 2003.
[22]Jon Fischer, a figure from the early days of the Jesus People, laments the transformation of the CCM industry from boldly engaging the world in evangelism to simply providing a safe environment for an insular Christianity. See his *Fearless Faith: Living Beyond the Walls of "Safe" Christianity* (Eugene, Ore.: Harvest House, 2002).

tion. If the Jesus People wanted anything, they wanted Jesus and their Christianity 24/7 (though this horrid phrase hadn't been invented yet). They wanted Jesus to be everywhere in what they did. Their motivation, however, tended to be evangelism. Chuck Smith speaks of how the young Jesus freaks would just walk around neighborhoods looking for people sitting on their porches or hanging out their laundry. As soon as they saw someone, they would walk right up to them and within minutes would be talking about Jesus. "If you'd sit still," Chuck Smith recalled, "they'd tell you about the Lord." Evangelism in music, however, has become eclipsed as CCM has morphed into what it is today. Many of the early pioneers actually chastise the industry on this very point. Today, too, evangelicals are fond of speaking of their holistic devotion to Christ, if not for reasons of evangelism, then simply because they want to "surrender all." The problem is that most evangelicals today have a too narrow view of what spirituality and devotion to Christ means. They have delimited their enjoyment of God through the good gifts of his creation. A broader view opens the horizons, avoiding ghettoization and the parallel institutionalism. Curiously enough, such an approach to culture, of being a worldly disciple, as Dietrich Bonhoeffer put it, may just return that evangelistic edge that has grown dull.[23]

CHRISTAPALOOZA

Perhaps the ghettoization and parallel institutionalism of CCM manifests itself nowhere more apparently than at the numerous Christian rock festivals. These festivals offer something for just about every taste, excepting maybe opera, and even something for every member of the family. Those into the punk or grunge scene can mosh for Jesus in the pits while their younger siblings sit in tents watching VeggieTales. The first of these festivals was the aforementioned Explo '72, the brainchild of Campus Crusade's Bill Bright. In June of 1972, "teenagers, college-aged youths, and older adults began the pilgrimage to Dallas," with the result that "Dallas had never seen such an onslaught of people." Remember, this was an era when the youth made society nervous. Crowds at the evening meetings topped 80,000. A daytime concert scheduled for downtown pulled in an audience of over 180,000 to hear the new Jesus music artists and the likes of Johnny Cash. Bright's overriding goal

---

[23]Randall Balmer, *Mine Eyes Have Seen the Glory*, p. 23.

for Explo '72 was evangelism, and that has remained a professed goal of the festivals since. Andrés Tapia states, "Evangelicals stage their own Lollapaloozas to save teen souls." How many unchurched actually attend most of the festivals is another thing altogether. Like the rest of CCM, the festivals have evolved into a safe place for Christian teens to hang out with other Christian teens and listen to some music while they are at it. Howard and Streck note, "While some fifty thousand people will be drawn to the Christian music festivals in any one summer, only the smallest percentage of these will be something other than evangelical Christians." Christian music, they add, "can hardly be expected to offer salvation to an audience that already possesses it." Their numbers are actually low, but otherwise, they make a point worth considering.[24]

In chapter three, we briefly looked at the Methodist camp meeting revivals occurring in the frontier in Kentucky in the early years of the 1800s. Now, two hundred years later, their descendants can gather for a week-long music festival (attracting mainly Methodist youth from Kentucky and the surrounding regions) called Ichthus, from the Greek word for fish and a common Christian symbol. In addition to Ichthus, there is also Spirit West Coast in Monterey, California; Creation Festival in Mt. Union, Pennsylvania; and one of the oldest and an original from the Jesus People, Cornerstone in Bushnell, Illinois. There are many smaller festivals around the country with names like Acquire the Fire, Jesusfest and Lambjam. Woodstock lives, though manifested in much tamer versions. These festivals are not limited to the United States. Since the early 1970s, from those early days of the Jesus People, British Christian-rock fans have made the pilgrimage to Greenbelt Festival, which still pulls crowds, thirty-odd years later, of twenty thousand. Larger crowds, reaching nearly thirty thousand, attend the Parachute Music Festival in New Zealand, which has as its goal "to raise the standard of Christian music in New Zealand"—with apologies to my New Zealand friends, I hadn't realized that the threat of substandard Christian music ranked as such a significant problem for the Christian community there.[25]

One of the earliest of these festivals got its start straight from the source of

[24]Baker, *Why Should the Devil Have All the Good Music?* pp. 107-8; Andrés Tapia, "Evangelicals Stage Their Own Lollapaloozas to Save Teen Souls," *Icon,* July 25, 1996, p. 10; Howard and Streck, *Apostles of Rock*, pp. 59-60.
[25]See Parachute Music's website at <www.parachutemusic.com>.

CCM. The Jesus People USA started the Cornerstone Festival and continue to run it to this day. The festival has expanded over the decades, now stretching over five days. Cornerstone has also expanded beyond Illinois to include Cornerstone Florida and, at least for one year, Cornerstone North Carolina. At the original Cornerstone in Bushnell, the headliner bands got the prime-time spot, at midnight, for the "Evening Encores." But, reflective of the changes in the Jesus music world, the festival now features a "New Band Showcase," touting bands in a variety of genres: postpunk, alternative, experimental, indie, metal, hardcore, metalcore and even posthardcore. Many of these bands, at least according to their MySpace websites, reject the label Christian, or at least take it ambivalently, preferring to frame their music as presenting "hopeful lyrics" that focus on "overcoming problems" in life. They come to Cornerstone, which offers one of the most sought-after venues for such aspiring bands, in search of an audience and maybe even a better record deal. They live in a world not unlike that detailed in the documentary DVD on the life of Jay Bakker (the son of the infamous televangelist), *One Punk Under God.*[26]

While Cornerstone pushes the creative envelope, Creation tends to cater to more mainstream tastes. Organizers promoting the 2007 Creation Festival, which tends to draws from fifty to eighty thousand people, focused the attention on worship, noting, "Worship, in all its forms, has always been the most important part of Creation Fest." Additionally, outfitting Christian teens in the latest T-shirts, hats and accessories also ranks near the top of the list. John Leland, reporting for the *New York Times,* titled his piece on Creation Fest "At Festivals, Faith, Rock, and T-Shirts Take Center Stage." The article mentions that shirts bearing "I mosh for Jesus" sold pretty well, as did shirts and hats bearing "I Love Christian Boys." These festivals are a place where Christians can meet other Christians of the opposite sex, after all some of their church youth groups have slim numbers. Leland labels the goods hawked as "irreverent and trend driven." Some respond, as one interviewee in the piece did, "You've got to buy clothes, why not have a message?"[27]

Creation Festival has gone bicoastal, with Creation Northwest, held at the Gorge in George, Washington. Of this conference, a writer for *The Stranger,* Seattle's weekly magazine, took this away from his visit to one of the merchan-

---

[26] *One Punk Under God,* dir. Jeremy Simmons, New Video Group, 2007.

[27] "Creation Fest Announces Line-Up for 2007 Events," *ChristianMusic.com;* John Leland, "At Festivals, Faith, Rock, and T-Shirts Take Center Stage," *New York Times,* July 5, 2004.

dise tents of T-shirts, many bearing the image of Christ,

> This iconic appeal to such gross capitalist sensibilities is one of the most tragic
> aspects of modern Christianity's loss of substance. Christ, as a spiritual prod-
> uct, has undergone a stunning military-industrial make-over, emptied of con-
> tent and shrink-wrapped for the television generation.

The writer goes on to note, "Even the somber event of Jesus' crucifixion
was given a glib and self-congratulatory updating by such t-shirt slogans as
'Hang Out With Jesus, He Hung Out For You.'" Tim Stafford, offering a state-
of-the-industry report on CCM for *Christianity Today*, also visited one of the
many Christian music festivals. The festival's organizer, Stafford relays,
"spoke of the three-day event as a kind of retreat center, providing relief, restoration, and feeding." Stafford then adds, "At the same time, it is a commercial venture."[28]

Beyond merchandise tents, there are also prayer tents and various work-
shops on everything from dating to songwriting. When it comes to music,
again, there's something for all tastes. Most festivals have center stages with
headliner bands performing nightly. Side stages present venues for local and
regional bands, as well as coffeehouse-type venues for different styles. The
music of all of these styles is, in the words of Monique El-Faizy, herself at one
time an evangelical, "just good enough to do what it needs to do . . . to give
Christian teens a place to go that isn't filling their heads with secular, sexual
messages." "To fulfill this purpose," she adds, "this music only needs to seem
hip enough to make these kids feel like they're not missing out on something
better." But, as El-Faizy recognizes, the quality is actually pretty good. And
when one considers that a number of those headliner bands are crossover artists, the Christian teens can in fact listen to the same hip music that other
teens listen to. Having crossover bands perform at these festivals, however,
comes with controversy, the controversy that dogs these crossover artists.[29]

JESUS IS MY BOYFRIEND

Even those who stay on the evangelical side of the divide and do not cross
over face controversy from time to time, some of it seemingly warranted.

---

[28]Rick Levin, "Christapalooza," *The Stranger*, August 19-25, 1999; Tim Stafford, "Has Christian Rock
Lost Its Soul?" *Christianity Today*, November 22, 1993, p. 16.

[29]Monique El-Faizy, *God and Country: How Evangelicals Became America's New Mainstream* (New
York: Bloomsbury, 2006), p. 145.

Bud Bultman, writing an editorial on "Christian Muzak" in the now-defunct monthly magazine for InterVarsity Christian Fellowship, *His,* declared a moratorium on Jesus love songs: "I refuse to listen to one more Jesus-is-my-girlfriend song. You know the kind. You can substitute *Mandy* or *Barbara Ann* for *Jesus* and the rest of the lyrics still make perfect sense." He cited two lyric examples, "Lest Jesus do it to ya," and "He makes me giggle." Bud Bultman enlisted the aid of Jon Fischer, one of Christian music's pioneers, who railed against Jesus love songs when he said, "One of my biggest gripes is love songs to God. God is never identified, neither is anything he's done in history. The lyrics mean nothing." Bultman and Fischer are joined by no less than the creators of the Simpsons, who have a character explain, "Christian rock is basically rock, but you replace baby with Jesus." It seems like Christian artists listened to at least Bud Bultman, for instead of singing Jesus-is-my-girlfriend songs, the current market of CCM appears flooded with Jesus-is-my-boyfriend songs.[30]

Consider some of these lyrics from different songs of Rebecca St. James. In "Take All of Me," written by Marty Sampson, the first stanza ends with "Take all of me, yeah / all of me." She also croons, "Take me I am yours" and "All I want is you," in "Pray." In her cover of Rich Mullins's "Hold Me Jesus," she asks Jesus to, well, "hold her" because her life doesn't make sense, and she's "shaking like a leaf." She adds in another song that she has fallen for Jesus "harder than the first time." All of these songs focus not on any act of God in history, not on the concrete events of Christ's life and death and resurrection. These songs all lack exactly what Jon Fischer lamented as a great loss, linking Jesus' love not to anything done in history but to the personal experiences of feeling Jesus near, of feeling him close during those hard times. Like a good boyfriend, Jesus shows up at the right moment, says the right thing and knows how to hug. Take out the name *Jesus* that occurs from time to time and these songs could be sung to a boyfriend.

Casting Crowns also adds to the mix. In "Your Love Is Extravagant," they speak of the intimate friendship with Christ before revealing, "Your fragrance is intoxicating in our secret place." In non-Christian songs these lyrics would be taken directly as a double-entendre. Skillet in "Will You Be There," asks if

---

[30]B[ud] B[ultman], "Christian Muzak," *His,* February 1982, p. 32; "I'm Going to Praiseland," *The Simpsons,* May 6, 2001.

Jesus and his love will be there "as I fall to sleep" and "as I grow cold." FFH (Far From Home) sings of their need for Jesus' touch and for Jesus' love, wanting to rest on his shoulder and hear him whisper in "Jesus Speak to Me." "I need to hold You oh so close," they say. Then there's Kutless and "Arms of Love," extolling Christ for "holding me still / holding me near," wrapped up in his arms of love. One line expresses gratitude for the things Jesus has done, but then doesn't mention any. Perfect opportunity lost. Instead of informing listeners of some of these acts that Jesus has done, listeners are just supposed to envision those welcoming, warm arms of love wrapped around them in a cold and cruel world. Carman also reminds audiences, who have been "spurned and burned" and "used and abused," to "jam with the Lamb" in his song "Come into this House."

There are still some "Jesus is my girlfriend" songs afoot. Timothy Larsen, a church historian, shared with me an instance of hearing these lyrics while visiting a church, "When I look in your eyes I go weak in the knees," and "Your scent drives me crazy." Steven Curtis Chapman speaks of Jesus as his "magnificent obsession," asking him to "Take me to depths I've never been." He also wants to be "completely lost." Blinded by love? Jesus is, after all, everything we want and everything we need. In another song on the *Dedication* album, Chapman calls everyone's attention, "Ladies and Gentlemen, children of all ages," as he gives an answer to the confusion and debate over Jesus' identity. He speaks from the stance of "who Jesus is to me," as he declares that Jesus is "life." Another perfect opportunity lost. This answer isn't even close to Peter's answer in John; it even falls short of the answers given by the crowds in that text. But for American evangelicals in the 2000s, it works just fine. The group from Canada, downhere, raises a significant question of who is the real Jesus in the song "The Real Jesus," on their album *Wide-Eyed and Mystified.* "Can anybody show me the real Jesus?" they ask. Maybe they are asking the question of their fellow Christian artists.

Toby Mac of dc Talk once claimed that he is "never trite when I write." Of course, earlier in the same song he tells us that he's kicking it "Jesus style." It becomes hard to not see triteness in much of the lyrics in CCM when so many artists speak so glibly and vaguely of the love of Christ, reducing it to romantic notions and mere personal experience. It also becomes hard not to see how this love sung by Christian artists is on par with the way love is handled in the non-Christian songs adolescents also listen to. When adolescents hear Christian songs treat love the same way as the secular songs do, they will more than likely transfer the romantic notions they have of love, derived from the conditioning of those secular songs, to their love of Christ. The love of God and the love of Christ, however, are on a much different level than the "love" that comes across in these Christian songs. Of course, one could argue that Christian artists, like Rebecca St. James, are precisely countering such other songs and pointing their audiences away from love as romantic or even erotic. But when the songs are framed in personal experiences of rhapsodic moments punctuated by hugs, we are hard-pressed to see much difference.

Triteness in these lyrics also becomes hard to avoid when the overwhelming word in these songs is *feel*. "What will my heart feel" is something that can only be imagined in MercyMe's wildly popular crossover hit "I Can Only Imagine." From its beginnings in the late 1960s, Christian contemporary music has emphasized the experiential. Offering an early commentary on the movement, the astute observer of American church history Martin E. Marty declared, "It is in the realm of personal experience, however, that the Jesus revolution is making its strongest impact." While the genre has shifted to reflect shifts in musical taste, while the industry has transmogrified from some hippie bands turned on to Jesus to a multibillion dollar empire with radio networks and conglomerate record labels, it might be true that some things have stayed the same. "Try Jesus," since he's the real thing, worked then and works now. Then it sounded like hippie slogans. Now it sounds like the words of a lovesick teenager's diary. Again we return to the question lurking about in this chapter: What's happened to Jesus in CCM? He's become a faithful and true boyfriend or girlfriend. Steve Camp actually goes one step further, indicting the CCM industry for being Christless.[31]

At least some of these songs that have been critiqued can be taken as intending to express the same longing for God expressed by the psalmist. Some of the songs may even reflect the way different biblical interpreters, such as the Puritans and the Medieval mystics, have taken the Song of Songs. The longing to express a deep devotion to God is laudable. But caution enters in when that longing comes in a theological vacuum.

---

[31]Martin E. Marty, "Jesus: The Media and the Message," *Theology Today* 28, no. 4 (1972): 474; Camp, "A Call for Reformation."

CONCLUSION

"Contemporary Christian Music," writes Howard and Streck, "represents a microcosm of the contemporary American evangelical religious experience and, as such, offers important inroads to an understanding of the American cultural landscape." These could be just the words of scholars trying to argue that their particular work makes some larger and significant contribution to understanding culture. Or, more likely the case, Howard and Streck may very well be on to something. CCM is a microcosm of American evangelicalism. CCM is also a microcosm of the American cultural landscape, at least when it comes to the religious and spiritual horizons of that landscape. By telling the story of CCM, you likely will get most of the story of American evangelicalism from 1970 to the present. I was struck by this in reading through Randall Balmer's *Encyclopedia of Evangelicalism*. When I first realized that the article on the Christian rock band Stryper had more column inches than John Stott and even more than Harriet Beecher Stowe, I was ready to write Balmer a letter in protest. When I saw Sandi Patty beat out John Perkins, the letter was almost in the mail. But as I reflected on the column inch inequity, it struck me that the problem lay not with Balmer. In the immortal words of Pogo, "We have met the enemy and he is us."[32]

Andrew Greeley has written of popular culture as the *"locus theologicus."* We encounter God in popular culture. Whether or not Greeley is truly right I'll leave to others. As far as where one may find the evangelical God and Christ, however, Greeley's words couldn't be more true. Evangelicals tend to get their theology from popular novels, learning about spiritual warfare from Frank Peretti and learning about all things "rapture" from the dynamic duo of LaHaye and Jenkins. They also get their theology from popular music. If numbers can be trusted, then the amount of albums bought, songs downloaded and hours logged listening to Christian radio cannot tell a lie. This raises concerns about the type of theology CCM teaches. More specifically, what type of Christology does CCM teach? It appears to be circumscribed by the experiential. And that experience tends to focus on the romantic and heroic love of Jesus for the individual in the trials and storms of life, which leaves the person shaking like a leaf and needing to be held. Jesus, or the " 'J' word," cer-

---

[32]Howard and Streck, *Apostles of Rock*, p. 6; Balmer, *Encyclopedia of Evangelicalism;* Walt Kelly, author of the cartoon strip *Pogo*, on a poster for Earth Day in 1970, see Marilyn White, "We Have Met the Enemy . . . and He Is Us," *I Go Pogo* <www.igopogo.com/we_have_met.htm>.

tainly appears throughout these songs. Again, when all that Steven Curtis
Chapman has to say about Jesus is that he is "life," the theologian in me wants
to hear a little more. In fact, evangelicalism *needs* to hear more if it is to retain
its theological core. Jesus appears a lot in CCM. He also appears a lot in the
Jesus People movement of the late 1960s that started it all. He just needs
more said about him.[33]

The broader horizons of church history offer a most intriguing perspective
on this trajectory from the Jesus movement to CCM. The Reformation in particular stands out. The immediate few centuries leading up to Luther's famous posting of the Ninety-Five Theses witnessed a church that had lost its
way. The moral compass had gone awry, resulting in a time of deviant behavior, even within the church. Fiscal irresponsibility and social injustice ruled
both in the halls of the state and the church. To mask it all, religious formalism
trucked on. Not all felt comfortable with the status quo. One group, the Conciliar movement, championed a change in the administration or hierarchy of
the church to counter these downward trends. The Conciliar movement proposed a return to the first few centuries of the church, when councils ruled
and the plurality of the bishops forged theology, which was not in the hands
of a few or even one. Another group proposed a change regarding the spirituality of the church. The *Devotio Moderna*, the new or modern devotion,
called for a reform on the level of spirituality. Thomas à Kempis with his *Imitation of Christ* well represents this movement. The *Devotio Moderna*
charged the church as being lackluster in its spirituality at best. At worst, and
likely closer to reality, the institutional church fostered hypocrisy and inau-
thentic worship and spirituality.[34]

The parallels to the Jesus movement should be obvious. The Jesus People
too saw themselves in a moment that called for reformation, though they
would prefer the counterculture language of revolution. They too wanted to
counter the hierarchy and administration of the church. They eschewed
church buildings and church structures, preferring the more loosely struc-
tured house churches. They had, in other words, some things in common with
the Conciliar movement. They had much more in common, however, with the
Devotio Moderna. The Jesus People yearned for authentic spirituality. They

---

[33]Andrew Greeley, *God in Popular Culture* (Chicago: Thomas Moore, 1989), p. 9.
[34]See Stephen J. Nichols, *The Reformation: How a Monk and a Mallet Changed the World* (Wheaton,
    Ill.: Crossway, 2007).

didn't want a Jesus of hypocrisy and formalism. They may have wanted a far-out Jesus (I couldn't resist) but they certainly didn't want a far-off one. They didn't want the Jesus Christ of the creeds. They wanted Jesus near, very near. They wanted a Jesus who had the appearance of a typical hippie and, had he been alive in the late 1960s, a Jesus who shared the hippie ideals. Again church history is instructive. The Conciliar movement and the *Devotio Moderna* certainly made an impression, inching the church back to where it needed to be. Neither movement, however, waged a successful war in bringing about the deep reforms that were needed. That would not come until the Reformers and the Reformation itself. The Reformation was many things, indeed taking some unfortunate missteps along the way, but at its root the Reformation was about theology. The Reformers realized that for true change, merely reorganizing the organizational chart or promoting a more authentic spirituality simply wouldn't do.

This is not to minimize either the Conciliar movement or the *Devotio Moderna*. Neither do I intend to absolutize the Reformers and simply call for the transplant of the Reformation as the solution to all of evangelicalism's woes. Contemporary evangelicalism finds itself in a new, historically situated environment, different from that of the Reformers. In fact, it was the Reformers who said, "The church reformed, always reforming," presciently realizing that times change. In contemporary evangelicalism's situation, however, what the Reformers focused on still applies. When the Jesus People reacted to the religious formalism and hypocrisy of their day, they did not go deep enough in looking for a theological revolution, a revolution that should have had a little more to say than "Try Jesus." Even lovesick teenagers tossed on the shores of life or shaking like leaves need more than a hug from Jesus. Even they need to know that he is the God-man. If they don't hear it in the songs, the *locus theologicus* of today, then where will they hear it?

JESUS ON THE BIG SCREEN

The Passion for Hollywood

Before they can be anything else,
American movies are a product.

SIDNEY POLLACK

Every Jesus film has been about the current moment.

STEPHENSON HUMPHRIES-BROOKS

This film is not based upon the Gospels but upon
this fictional exploration of the eternal spiritual conflict.

MARTIN SCORSESE, OPENING TO *THE LAST TEMPTATION OF CHRIST*

Based on a survey of Hollywood insiders, *Entertainment Weekly* declared Mel Gibson's *The Passion of the Christ* the most controversial film of all time. But, surprisingly, for a Hollywood flick, the ruckus was not being raised by the Religious Right or the stalwarts of evangelicalism. Instead, the religious conservatives were buying tickets by the gross and renting out whole theaters for evangelistic outreaches. Gibson, a committed Roman Catholic, had found some good friends in unlikely places. He also stirred up quite a controversy.[1]

---

[1] *Entertainment Weekly,* June 9, 2006. The cover story runs "The Most Controversial Movies Ever," with *The Passion of the Christ* taking the no. 1 spot. The November 23, 2005, edition of the movie magazine named *The Passion* among "the top fourteen most notorious hot-button movies ever," along with *The Da Vinci Code* and Martin Scorsese's *The Last Temptation of Christ.*

CONTROVERSIAL SAVIORS

The controversy over *The Passion* movie seemed to come in two veins. First, was the violence—the "R" rating gave many of those aforementioned evangelicals pause and sent their leaders scrambling for damage-control spin. Second, and this far outshadowed matters of violence, was the charge of anti-Semitism. Some of the truly challenging questions that the film and the phenomenon it spurred raise, however, have been eclipsed by these issues that have garnered the headlines of the protest. American evangelicals on the whole tended to applaud the movie and to quickly seize the opportunity the movie presented for evangelism, all the while giving little critical thought to what they were doing and what they were watching. Roman Catholics defended the movie—and Gibson for that matter. The clearest defense came straight from the Vatican by Archbishop John Foley, president of the Pontifical Council for Social Communications, "If they're critical of the film," Foley reasoned, "they would be critical of the Gospel."[2]

The ironies abound when considering *The Passion* phenomenon. Evangelical organizations like Dobson's Focus on the Family often bemoaned Hollywood's offerings, especially chastising the industry for its depictions of violence. Yet from the moment these same leaders were privy to a personal screening they became the film's biggest cheerleaders. Neal King expresses this irony similarly:

> Evangelicals teach each other *how to be evangelicals* by recounting the ills of current cinema, the movies of craven Hollywood, and the poisonous effects of moviegoing on their children. . . . However, the prerelease marketing of *The Passion of the Christ* inspired the same groups to book whole theaters and to share its religious ritual.

Christian leaders also seemed to enjoy cozying up to Gibson, perhaps relishing being a part of that world even for a moment, despite the fact that in the past such associations of evangelicals with movie stars and moguls were to be shunned.

Moving away from film to the broader cultural landscape can be instruc-

---

[2]For a summary of the controversy surrounding the film, see Mark Silk, "Almost a Culture War: The Making of *The Passion* Controversy," *After the Passion Is Gone: American Religious Consequences*, ed. J. Shawn Landres and Michael Berenbaum (Lanham, Md.: Rowman & Littlefield, 2004), pp. 23-34; Archbishop Foley is cited in Steven D. Greydanus, "The Vatican Film List—Ten Years Later," <www.decentfilms.com/sections/articles/vaticanfilmlist.html>.

tive. Evangelicals and their fundamentalist forebears had been in a cultural semiretreat from the 1920s on. In the 1950s Billy Graham gained a seat at the table for evangelicals in American culture. In the 1970s evangelicals and some fundamentalists began battling for a seat at the table in American politics. In 2000 they had one, with a professing evangelical seated at the head of the table in the White House. Evangelicals began relishing these new roles, no longer the cultural outcasts they once were. Sitting next to Gibson for private screenings only furthered their sense of having arrived.[3]

Evangelicals and fundamentalists alike supported the movie for evangelistic reasons. Some congregations and other institutions of a more fundamentalist stripe who impose movie restrictions on their constituents lifted the ban, granting a special dispensation for *The Passion,* citing evangelistic purposes as the reason. This too, however, is a surprising irony given Gibson's explicit and the movie's implicit Roman Catholicism. Again, many of the more conservative evangelicals seemed to have no problem embracing Gibson during the film's run of success, while otherwise eschewing such evangelical and Roman Catholic bipartisanship. David Neff, a participant in a private screening cohosted by Gibson and Willow Creek's Bill Hybels, also points to this "surprising" evangelical enthusiasm given "that the movie was shaped from start to finish by a devout Roman Catholic and by an almost medieval Catholic vision." Neff then explains in part how "Evangelicals have not found that a problem," by explaining that "overall, the theology of the film articulates very powerful themes that have been important to all classical Christians."[4]

Leslie Smith suspects there are other factors at work, as well, in explaining the embrace of the movie by evangelicals. She too takes notice of the movie's violence and Gibson's history of making violent films, and of the movie's Roman Catholic tendencies as well as Gibson's explicit Catholicism. All of which leaves her with the question, "Why did evangelical Protestants so eagerly embrace [this] film?" Her answer is a complex one: "It exemplifies many of the qualities of modern American evangelical culture: it privileges emotional experience, it appeals to traditional American consumerism, and it asserts su-

---

[3]Neal King, "Truth at Last: Evangelical Communities Embrace *The Passion of the Christ*," in *Re-Viewing the Passion: Mel Gibson's Film and Its Critics,* ed. S. Brent Plate (New York: Palgrave Macmillan, 2004), p. 151.
[4]David Neff, "The Passion of Mel Gibson: Why Evangelicals Are Cheering a Movie with Profoundly Catholic Sensibilities," *Christianity Today,* March 2004.

pernaturalism and moral absolutism in a rationalistic, postmodern society." Her first point concerning emotional experience is worth unpacking. Smith later notes, while attending a Bible study built around Lee Strobel's accompanying workbook for the movie *Experiencing the Passion:*

> The people with whom I spoke gauged *The Passion's* [biblical] accuracy not by measures of specific historicity but rather by the emotions the film evoked in the viewer and the extent to which it could lead to a conversion experience. To put it simply, this group of evangelicals assessed the realism of the film by its emotional impact.

She then quotes from Strobel's workbook: "For the first time in my life I felt as if I were really *experiencing* what Jesus had endured." Smith adds to her list of experientialism, consumerism—based on the marketing campaign and related product lines the film spurred, not to mention its $370 million gross— and the tension with the larger culture: "The attention paid to *The Passion* was alluring to evangelicals because of the legitimacy that it granted both their group and their message."[5]

Evangelical leaders and their constituents applauded the film for its raw authenticity and verity in retelling the biblical narratives. So true was it to Scripture that the movie even ran the dialogue in Aramaic and Latin. Yet from the opening scene, Gibson nevertheless succumbed to the temptation facing all would-be cinematographers of Jesus: going beyond the biblical account. As David Neff pointed out, when the biblical narrative let him down, Gibson turned to Anne Catherine Emmerich's *Dolorous Passion of Our Lord Jesus Christ* to help the drama along. Gibson could also rely on his own creativity, so he has a playful Jesus flicking water in his mother's face as she offers him a washbasin to clean up before lunch. This touching scene is nothing less than gut-wrenching, for we know the trial that Mary will face in watching helplessly as her son is taken and suffers and dies a too-cruel death. And it is in the end that the violence of the film takes over. To be sure, the historical Jesus' trial was unjust, his precrucifixion torture brutal and the crucifixion itself despicable beyond comprehension. But in reading the Gospel narratives, we are hard-pressed to find the graphic depiction of violence that the movie relentlessly heaps upon its viewers. Gibson not only forces his viewers to watch, he

---

[5]Leslie E. Smith, "Living *in* the World, But Not *of* the World: Understanding Evangelical Support for *The Passion of the Christ,*" in *After the Passion Is Gone,* ed. J. Shawn Landres and Michael Berenbaum (Lanham, Md.: Rowman & Littlefield, 2004), pp. 48, 51, 56.

forces them to linger through his relentless recourse to slow motion, a technique film critics tend to see as not only amateurish but also deeply manipulative.

Gibson indeed succeeds in producing a visceral reaction, confirmed by Lee Strobel's aforementioned confession that he never *experienced* the true passion of Christ until he watched the movie. Donald Hodel, president and CEO of Focus on the Family, similarly chimed:

> *The Passion* was profoundly compelling and affecting. The quality and realism of the acting, the setting, adherence to the historical record, its intensity and pacing all amount to an outstanding and moving film. . . . For both Christian believers and for non-believers *The Passion* will penetrate the mind, heart and soul in ways that can only be memorable and positive.

Paul Crouch Jr. of Trinity Broadcasting Network offers his endorsement, "It is without a doubt the best portrayal of Christ and the Crucifixion I've ever seen. In fact, it makes you want to take all Biblical epics and most 'Christian' films and throw them right in the trash." Greg Laurie of Harvest Crusades stresses the evangelistic appeal of the movie, calling it the greatest moment of the century: "I believe *The Passion of the Christ* may well be one of the most powerful evangelistic tools of the last 100 years, because you have never seen the story of Jesus portrayed this vividly before."[6]

But what is the movie's impact now, even just a few years later? Or what was the average moviegoer's reaction even by the time they made it back to their car in the parking lot? *People* magazine dubbed James Caviezel, who starred as Jesus, "the Sexiest Savior" in its 2004 annual issue devoted to the sexiest men alive. It's unlikely that this was the cultural impact that evangelical leaders hoped for.

For all of its pungent reaction at the time, the ongoing effects of *The Passion* seem flaccid. The media and broader cultural circles have long since moved on. Posters may be found rolled up here and there in the corner of youth pastors' offices, but even the church has lost its passion for the movie. The movie, it appears, has gone the way of all fads, a bright meteor that became a bit of a spent force. *The Passion,* however, wasn't the only controversial Jesus film. In fact, it might come as a surprise that two of the most contro-

---

[6]These endorsements, as well as others by evangelical and Roman Catholic leaders alike may be found at "'The Passion of the Christ': Assessment by Conservative Christians," <www.religioustoler ance.org/chrgibson3.htm>.

versial films of the twentieth century both took as their subject the age-old story of Christ. And that's about the only thing these two films—Gibson's *The Passion* and Martin Scorsese's *The Last Temptation of Christ* (1988)—have in common. The controversy over Scorsese's film came from the side of the aisle that lined up behind Gibson. The American Council of Catholic Bishops organized protests, as did evangelical leaders. Bill Bright went so far as to offer ten million dollars to Universal Studios to destroy the movie. Hollywood insiders seemed to think that all of that protest only served to spur on box office tickets and draw attention to a movie that otherwise would have had a mediocre showing. The boycotts, however, came from the deeply rooted belief that the movie fell nowhere shy of blasphemy. Even the consultant hired by Universal Pictures to counter all of the negative publicity resigned three months before the movie's release, citing the film's blasphemous content as one of the reasons.[7]

Not only do Jesus films have a controversial history, they also have a long one. The first attempt to put Jesus on film came from the French Director Alice Guy, whose short, silent film *Jesus Before Pilate (Jesus Devant Pilate)* came out in 1898. Americans would produce their own short film in 1912, the Kalem Company's *From the Manger to the Cross*. But the honor of producing the first full-length film goes to American movie legend Cecil B. DeMille, who released the big-budget (for the time) silent film *The King of Kings* in 1927. Jesus films took a hiatus until the 1960s. Since then, however, Jesus films have been made with an impressive regularity. As Stephen Humphries-Brooks, an astute scholar of Jesus films, observes of all of these silver screen portrayals of Christ, they tend to have more to say about the cultural moment that produced them than the moment they wish to depict, the moment captured on the page in the Gospels. In fact, it seems that all films depicting historical events and all biopics suffer from anachronisms; they tend to reflect the times in which the film was made as much as the times in which the film is set. It might not be too much of a stretch that, for the most part, these Jesus films also have more to say about the directors, producers and screenwriters than they have to say about the central figure of the script. These problems seem to plague the effort of putting Jesus up on the big

---

[7]W. Barnes Tatum, *Jesus at the Movies: A Guide to the First Hundred Years* (Santa Rosa, Calif.: Polebridge Press, 1997), p. 163.

screen. To borrow an oft-repeated mantra since Marshall McLuhan first coined it, the medium does matter. He actually put it more strongly, "The medium is the message." Jesus, as this chapter argues, doesn't shoot well. He's not a very good celluloid savior.[8]

This is not to suggest that nothing can be gained from the enterprise of converting the Gospel accounts into film, evangelistically or otherwise. Some of these film projects have been quite successful, which is to say they work. This is especially true of the 1979 *Jesus* film and the Jesus Film Project, which occurs mostly out of the arena of commercial venues. But putting Christ on the silver screen involves tradeoffs—many things can be lost in translation. This chapter looks at this roughly one hundred year history of Jesus in American film, from the silent 1912 *From the Manger to the Cross: Jesus of Nazareth* to the most controversial film of all time, the 2004 *The Passion,* and even some 2006 additions to the genre.

THE GREATEST STORY EVER TOLD

The first attempt to put Jesus on the screen goes all the way back to 1898 with the silent film *Jesus Devant Pilate (Jesus Before Pilate).* A full decade later an American silent film was shot on location in Egypt and the Middle East, *From the Manger to the Cross: Jesus of Nazareth* (1912). These films' short scripts were taken directly from the Gospel accounts. Jesus himself tended to be "off camera," more present by allusion than by direct visual contact. Like other silent films, a few episodes would tick by before the words appeared on the screen to let the audience know what was happening. Most of the "dialogue" comes directly from the biblical text. Both films were placidly received as "solemn and overly reverential." Even audiences of silent black-and-white films wanted something more than church on a silver screen. These audiences found their wishes coming true when no less than the veritable Cecil B. DeMille released *The King of Kings* in 1927. This movie, like DeMille's others, came with all the grandeur of old Hollywood.

Gibson may very well have taken a few pages from DeMille's playbook. DeMille's colleague on the film, Jeremiah Millbank, saw the film as having evangelistic appeal. In his autobiography, DeMille reveals, "To this day Jeremiah Millbank has not taken a penny of profit from *The King of Kings:* All

---

[8]Marshall McLuhan, *Understanding Media: The Extensions of Man* (Boston: MIT Press, 1964).

his share in its continuing earnings goes to make and distribute new prints of it, principally for use by churches and missionaries." DeMille estimates that such efforts resulted in 800,000,000 people seeing the movie. In part those numbers are due to the religious leaders that DeMille courted and then mobilized on behalf of the film. Curiously, as with the lightning strikes during the filming of *The Passion,* events occurred around the shooting that made people think the heavens themselves were endorsing the film. In the case of *The King of Kings,* when doves were released to fly into the sunset, they instead "went straight by themselves to fly around the Cross of the Savior." DeMille also credits the film's success to H. B. Warner's "supernatural" performance. "All my life," recalls DeMille, "I have wondered how many people have been turned away from Christianity by the effeminate, sanctimonious, machine-made Christs of second rate so-called art, which used to be thought good enough for Sunday schools." DeMille gave the twentieth-century world a savior of "virility," the same as the original "Man of Nazareth had." Bruce Barton, who turned Jesus into a businessman fit for the early twentieth century, served as DeMille's theological consultant on the project. DeMille's *The King of Kings* would set the gold standard. Some have even argued that this film "proved so popular and enduring that it was some time, literally decades, before anyone had the courage or the reason to attempt another cinematic version of the life of Jesus."[9]

By the 1950s, however, filmmakers were ready to give it a try. Three movies in particular hover around Jesus and the Gospels, Mervyn LeRoy's *Quo Vadis?* (1951), Henry Koster's *The Robe* (1953) and William Wyler's *Ben-Hur* (1959), all three of which were originally novels. These movies have Jesus off-stage, though central to the storyline and the main characters. *Quo Vadis?* picks up the story after Christ's death, following Peter through the difficult persecutions of Nero's reign. *The Robe* too deals with the conflict between Rome and early Christianity by telling the story of Marcellus, the centurion who won Christ's robe at the foot of the cross. The story also moves along not only by political intrigue but also by romance between Marcellus and Diana. Both he and Diana met their fate together, at the hands of Caligula. Wyler's *Ben-Hur* is subtitled *A Tale of the Christ.* In it, Jesus appears at a dis-

---

[9]Cecil B. DeMille, *The Autobiography of Cecil B. DeMille,* ed. Donald Hayne (Englewood Cliffs, N.J.: Prentice-Hall, 1959), pp. 274-84; Richard C. Stern, Clayton N. Jefford and Guerric Debona, *Savior on the Silver Screen* (New York: Paulist Press, 1999), p. 62.

tance, and the only two times he speaks, his face is off camera. Jesus neverthe-less functions as the overwhelming figure in the life of Judah Ben-Hur, played by none other than Charlton Heston.

Having been emboldened by these attempts, in the 1960s not a few films returned Jesus to center stage. Two in particular are Nicholas Ray's *King of Kings* (1961) and George Stevens's *The Greatest Story Ever Told* (1965). The title of the first is a nod to DeMille. Otherwise, the film is pure 1960s. It offers a more human Jesus than that of DeMille's film. This Jesus, the authors of *Savior on the Silver Screen* argue, "is primarily a speaker of sayings, not a worker of miracles . . . a 'rebel with a cause,' who tries to bring about the revolution through a message of peace." Max von Sydow, lending his gravitas, takes Jesus in the opposite direction in *The Greatest Story Ever Told*. This cinematic tell-ing of the greatest story also racked up one of the greatest cast of characters, including Charlton Heston, Sidney Poitier, John Wayne, Martin Landau and Angela Lansbury. This film and its stars seem bent on portraying the ideas of Jesus over his action and over his sayings, and even over the events of the Gos-pels. According to the authors of *Savior on the Silver Screen,* "Jesus seems to be the most Gnostic in this film." One scene alone proves this point. As Max von Sydow's Jesus presides over the table of the Last Supper, arms out-stretched and angelically backlit, he nearly appears to levitate. This is Jesus hovering on the Earth, his white robes always pristine, not walking in the dust.[10]

Peter Hasenberg has noted that this moment of film history, like the broader culture of the 1960s, emphasized "(1) a dominance of the subjective point of view, (2) a critical view of society, sometimes even with a strong po-litical motive, and (3) a conscious and critical use of conventional narrative and genre structures." All of these tenets directly affect Jesus and the screen's portrayal of him. The dominating subjective viewpoint allows the filmmaker's or the scriptwriter's sensibilities to take over the Gospel portrayal. Hasen-berg's second point, a counterculture animus, also means that Jesus of the 1960s and 1970s takes on a hippie persona, with the overthrowing of the moneychangers from the temple—the rebel against the establishment—receiving significant attention. The third point, in effect, tells us that these new Jesus films aren't like the films of our fathers and grandfathers. These three tenets also have the cumulative effect of allowing for more artistic li-

---

[10]Stern, Jefford and Debona, *Savior on the Silver Screen,* pp. 69, 145.

cense. Filmmakers were free to roam beyond the Gospel accounts, and freely roam they did.[11]

Jesus films of the 1970s took the hippie Jesus to new heights and introduced the types of controversies that would later encircle *The Last Temptation* and *The Passion*. The two in particular are the musicals *Jesus Christ Superstar* and *Godspell,* both from 1973. Two other 1970s Jesus films represent the ridiculous and the sublime. The latter is Franco Zeffirelli's *Jesus of Nazareth* (1977), while the former is Terry Jones's *Monty Python's Life of Brian* (1979). Indeed, it was a strange decade. Zeffirelli's film has been hailed as the greatest cinematic achievement of portraying the life of Christ. That may very well be the case. One thing for certain, at over six hours running time, it easily ranks as the longest. Zeffirelli's directorial skill can be seen in just how riveting those six hours are. He seems to move almost seamlessly between the locally situated story of the first-century Jesus and the universal and perennial story that historically situated life tells. Then there's Monty Python's Jesus. The British comedy troupe's cinematic portrayal met with all of the criticism directed toward *Jesus Christ Superstar* and *Godspell.* Despite its maker's contentions that the film's acerbic wit was aimed at religious formalism and institutional Christianity, and not at Christ himself and the Gospels, Catholics and evangelical Protestants took the film as nothing less than blasphemous. The film actually isn't about Jesus; instead it tells the story of Brian, a hapless comic figure whose life eerily intersects with that of Jesus.[12]

At least one biblical scholar, however, takes Terry Jones to be nobody's fool. Philip R. Davies confessed, "I have long been of the conviction that Monty Python's *Life of Brian* is an indispensable foundation to any student's career in New Testament studies." (Welcome words for me since I tend to tell my students that *Monty Python and the Holy Grail* is indispensable for church history studies.) He tells them this because, in his view, the film "engages with a number of basic scholarly historical and theological issues." Davies may be right, watching the film likely hones one's hermeneutical skills.[13]

[11]Peter Hasenberg, "The 'Religious' in Film: From *The King of Kings* to *The Fisher King*," in *New Image of Religious Film,* ed. John R. May (Kansas City: Sheed & Ward, 1997), p. 43.

[12]For a discussion of *The Life of Brian,* see Stern, Jefford and Debona, *Savior on the Silver Screen,* pp. 233-63.

[13]Philip R. Davies, "Life of Brian Research," *Biblical Studies/Cultural Studies: The Third Sheffield Colloquium,* ed. J. Cheryl Exum and Stephen Moore (Sheffield, U.K.: Sheffield Academic Press, 1998), p. 400.

In the 1980s came the not-very-popular but critically well-received *Jesus of Montreal* (1989) by Denys Arcand. This is the classic story within a story; as the main character, Daniel (Lothaire Bluteau), plays Jesus in a passion play in modern Montreal. He soon, however, takes on a messiah complex, complete with an interesting twist on the well-worn cinematic episode of throwing the moneychangers out of the temple. In this case exploitive directors and movie financers are chased out of a theater as cameras and equipment are destroyed in a fit of righteous indignation. Daniel eventually dies, from a bizarre accident, getting knocked over while hanging on the cross playing Jesus in the passion play. *Jesus of Montreal* unfolds a cleverly embedded story within a story that works on a number of levels. The film to dominate the 1980s, however, was Martin Scorsese's *The Last Temptation of Christ*. Here too Scorsese unfolds a story within a story, as he tells the inner psychological struggle of Jesus, played by William Defoe, alongside of episodes vaguely reminiscent of the biblical story line.

Perhaps studios refrained from Jesus films in the 1990s in order to recover from *The Last Temptation*. But some made-for-television movies stepped in. Kevin Connor's *Mary, Mother of Jesus* aired on NBC in 1999, the same year that Roger Young's *Jesus* aired on CBS. Both movies seemed to have the net effect of creating some controversial headlines, such as "Dueling Saviors: CBS, NBC Face Off This Season with Jesus Movies," in the *Chicago Sun-Times*. Otherwise, they had little impact, reaching few viewers and garnering few other headlines.

Not so with the Jesus films so far in the 2000s. In fact, American Jesus films reach a crescendo in Mel Gibson's *The Passion of the Christ* (2004). His is not the only movie of the first decade of the 2000s, however. In 2006 Jean-Claude La Marre's *Color of the Cross* (2006) opened with a modicum of controversy and ended with a mere sliver of the attention and the profits of *The Passion*. La Marre was busy in this film, serving as its writer and director, and taking on the lead role of Jesus, the first black Jesus, that is, in a major motion picture. La Marre's film set another precedent in making race the issue that put Jesus on the cross. And then there's the much-hoped-for film by Catherine Hardwick, *The Nativity Story* (2006). The film had significant commercial backing and courted the same evangelical leaders that Gibson had. This film, however, had none of the controversy, offering a safe, tame retelling of the biblical tale. It couldn't live up to Gibson's success, not only falling way short of *The Passion's* gross but also getting eclipsed by Gibson's *Apocalypto* (2006) that hit theaters the same week as *The Nativity Story* opened.

This survey of the translations of the greatest story ever told to the silver screen raises a number of significant points worth developing. First, American movies work best when there's romance, a slight problem given the story line of Jesus. What American filmmakers, scriptwriters and novelists lack in material, however, they more than compensate for through creativity, inched along as they are by some developments in New Testament scholarship. The likely suspect for adding the romantic intrigue to the story is Mary Magdalene. From the days of Cecil B. DeMille, she has been well used for the part. She takes a rather strange route to the role of leading lady. Mary Magdalene, however, isn't the only element of the story that gets elaboration. The Gospel accounts in general disappoint if we're looking for good, cinematic material. Consequently, filmmakers and scriptwriters rush in where the canonical Gospel writers feared to tread. The medium almost demands departure from the biblical text.

Jesus films also reveal a tendency to transplant Jesus from his age to ours. Of course, more than films do this. Sermons, theological works, even Bible translations do the same things as these movies. The difference is the medium, which allows for a more intense contextualization. While some films like *Jesus of Montreal* (1989) explicitly and blatantly move Christ forward, other films, even ones sporting Aramaic dialogue, do it subtly. This moving of Christ forward has a curious effect on our reading of the Gospels. Film is a significantly powerful and influential medium, and has a tendency to overshadow our perceptions and interpretations of the people and the events that films depict. Do people think even a little bit differently about Nixon after watching Scorsese's interpretation of him (*Nixon*, 1995)? It might be the case that Jesus films, at least for the season they dominate the discussion, tend to have a significant impact on popular-level hermeneutics, the way people read the Gospel texts. Finally, Jesus films have difficulty, almost by definition, depicting the hypostatic union, Christ as the God-man. Stern, Jefford and Debona make the point directly when they charge that Jeffery Hunter, who plays Jesus in the 1961 film *King of Kings* "surely plays up Jesus' humanity." And since then Jesus films have tended to emphasize the humanity of Jesus. These four points emerge from the American Jesus films: the trumping of

Mary Magdalene's role, the virtual necessity of adding to the biblical story, the transplanting of Jesus from his context to the context of the filmmaker and audience, and the (again seemingly necessitated) emphasis on the humanity of Jesus. Each deserves some attention.[14]

THERE'S SOMETHING ABOUT MARY

Of all the supporting characters in the Jesus movies, one that has taken a rather interesting road is Mary Magdalene. The biblical narrative actually tells us very little of Mary Magdalene, but in the sixth century, Pope Gregory the Great taught that she was a prostitute. This requires some reading between the lines of the Gospel narratives and then some additional filling-in to boot. First, we have to identify Mary Magdalene as the same person who is the unnamed woman "sinner" who anointed Jesus' feet with a precious ointment kept in an alabaster box (Lk 7:37-39). Gregory was helped along by looking past Luke 7 to Luke 8:2, which speaks of Mary Magdalene, "from whom seven demons had gone out." Of course, there's nothing in the text that demands the unnamed woman of Luke 7:37 is the Mary Magdalene mentioned in Luke 8:2. But while there's nothing in the text to make the connection, the need for a good story does. In fact, Gregory's (over)interpretation of Mary Magdalene is rather tame compared to what happens to her at the hands of other interpreters. There's a rich French tradition that has Mary capturing Jesus' blood in the Holy Grail and escaping to somewhere in France. Over time, the Holy Grail became understood as code: Mary herself was the grail and the blood was in fact their love child, the bloodline of Christ. All we need now is a blockbuster novel, turned into yet another movie—*The Da Vinci Code*—and it's off to the races. This attention and interpretation runs counter to the sparse references to Mary Magdalene in the Gospels. As one writer has intoned, Mary Magdalene "wasn't bad, just interpreted that way."[15]

Mary Magdalene's history on the silver screen is also quite a ride. She actually opens Cecil B. DeMille's *The King of Kings,* which he did on purpose to "jolt" audiences "out of their preconceptions with an opening scene that

---

[14]Stern, Jefford and Debona, *Savior on the Silver Screen,* p. 63.
[15]Before Dan Brown's novel *The Da Vinci Code,* Michael Baigent, Richard Leigh and Henry Lincoln wrote *Holy Blood, Holy Grail* (London: Jonathan Cape, 1982), offering a self-proclaimed scholarly account of this fanciful story of Mary Magdalene as the mother of Jesus' child. In 1969, the Roman Catholic Church reversed the interpretation of Gregory the Great, arguing against identifying Mary Magdalene with the unnamed woman in Luke 7:37.

none of them would be expecting." Indeed, surely none of them did expect it, and likely none of them were prepared for what they were to see: Mary Magdalene looking rather seductive in her lavishly appointed courtyard villa being admired by courtesans while she pets a tiger. She also, especially for 1920s film standards, is dressed rather scantily and wearing an awful lot of makeup. It's easy to figure out, in other words, her profession. She's all abuzz at the news that Judas, one of her "admirers," has been "bewitched" by a carpenter from Nazareth. As the film progresses, she finally encounters Jesus, who heals her and rescues her from her life of sin. DeMille transforms the seven demons of Luke 8:2 into the seven deadly sins, each one leaving her as rather phantom-like creatures. DeMille also uses her conversion as the tipping point for Judas Iscariot. Apparently, Judas, found on Mary Magdalene's calling card, that he would no longer be able to visit her now that she was converted. First it was Mary Magdalene who was upset because Jesus took Judas away. Now Judas would be upset, and apparently, contrary to Shakespeare, hell's fury is stronger in a scorned man. Consequently, as Jesus heals Mary Magdalene and she converts, the camera pans left to catch an angry gleam forming in Judas's eye. That angry gleam eventually matures into his betrayal of his Master. Cecil B. DeMille, while drawing from tradition, added his own unique cinematic stamp to Mary Magdalene. And the American psyche was forever changed, thinking that, indeed, there is something about Mary.[16]

DeMille's cinematic license with Mary Magdalene, however, was only the beginning. Even the inimitable Johnny Cash would make his own contribution to the story. After his conversion in 1968, Cash set about a project that was for him a labor of love, entailing both an album and a full-length feature film retelling the story of Jesus. On October 23, 1972, most of Nashville gathered for the premier showing of *The Gospel Road*. Cash mostly self-financed the picture. He also shot it in Israel, hoping to bring as much authenticity to the story as he could. The disciples would be played by, fortunately for Cash, a group of European backpackers who just happened to be milling around the deserted town where the film was shot—this was the 1970s. The director, Robert Elfstrom, sporting long, blond hair and looking like a hippie, played Jesus. The part of Mary Magdalene went to June Carter Cash. Cash introduces the conversion of Mary with the narration, "I wonder what Mary

---

[16]Cecil B. DeMille, *Autobiography of Cecil B. DeMille*, p. 275.

Magdalene really looked like. The Scriptures don't tell a lot about her. But what little is told has made her the subject of more speculation and controversy than any woman I ever heard of." Cash also adds, "Jesus was to suffer much for his association with people of," at this point he stops looking down and drills his eyes directly into the camera, "questionable character." But Jesus, Cash reminds us, didn't come for the well but for the sick. In other words, Mary Magdalene "needed him." Cash next moves to add to the speculation and controversy in his encounter of Mary Magdalene and Jesus. As his biographer Michael Streissguth puts it, June as Mary Magdalene and the scene itself was "altogether sensuous."[17]

In the wordless interaction, until June's solo dubs over the scene, Jesus caresses June's face and removes her head scarf as it gently falls to the ground. Viewers actually view the scene no fewer than four times and from as many camera angles. At the end of the scene, June, looking mesmerized, speaks to the camera, "Seven times he touched me," apparently one time for each of the seven demons mentioned in Luke 8:2, "and each time he touched me I felt something go out of me and I'm clean. I am clean." Then Johnny Cash offers the final word, "Mary was the kind of woman that Jesus was to have a lot of love and compassion for," before adding with frankly an uncomfortable emphasis, "A lot of love and compassion for Mary Magdalene." No doubt both Johnny Cash and June Carter Cash were sincere in their movie and especially in this scene. Though true of Johnny more than June, prior to 1972 both of them had rather public contentions with their own "demons." When June, in character, said, having met Jesus, "I am so happy," she more than likely meant it from her heart. Their sincerity aside, the scene stresses a nearly romantic attachment between Jesus and Mary Magdalene, punctuated by the numerous references to the words *touch*, *feel* and *love*.

It would take Martin Scorsese, however, to bring the romance of Jesus and Mary Magdalene to its zenith. Scorsese's Jesus gives in to the temptation, a lapse that Scorsese celebrates. When we first meet up with Jesus in this film, we find him to be a rather tortured and conflicted individual, psychologically that is. He's plagued by pain, inner voices and sin. "I'm struggling," are the very first words that Jesus utters. Mary Magdalene becomes in many ways his

---

[17]Michael Streissguth, *Johnny Cash: The Biography* (Cambridge, Mass.: De Capo Press, 2006), p. 181.

special project; he will, in a stereotypical fashion, rescue the prostitute even though she doesn't want to be rescued. He doesn't make an ideal Savior, however. One evening he sits among the many men who came calling. When he finally does go in to see her after the last one leaves in the early dawn hours, his question of her is would she forgive him of his sins. Eventually and reluctantly Jesus goes to the cross. In what feels like a dream, a young, blond angel, complete with a British accent, comes to Christ, tells him that God doesn't want him to die and takes him down off the cross. In the next scene Jesus and Mary Magdalene consummate their marriage. Jesus raises a family and lives out his life.

Jean-Claude La Marre also picks up on the Mary Magdalene prostitute in *The Color of the Cross*. Following DeMille, La Marre has Judas as one of her clients. In fact, in his movie Judas uses the thirty pieces of silver to successfully tempt Mary Magdalene back to the life Jesus rescued her from on the night of the betrayal.

Scorsese's radical introduction of a sexual dalliance with Mary Magdalene has now, in a post-*Da Vinci Code* culture, become commonplace. Helped along by biblical and patristics scholars infatuated with Gnostic texts, the thesis that Mary Magdalene and Christ had sexual relations, produced an offspring, and triggered the greatest cover-up of all time has gained much traction. This is the conspiracy theory of all conspiracy theories. Quite recently a novel writer, whose qualifications include her quite confident self-claim to be in that long line of offspring from Jesus and Mary Magdalene, offers a treatment of the alleged romance between her first-century ancestors. Kathleen McGowan calls her novel "partly autobiographical." While (hopefully) not believing her, her publisher, Simon and Schuster, invested quite a bit in both a marketing campaign and a large first print run. What is it about Mary that has brought all this on?[18]

The better question might be what is it about contemporary culture that has brought all this on? Perhaps the answer is as simple as the notion that in order for it to be a truly good story it has to have romance. Every leading man needs a leading lady. The audiences of the silver screen thrive on this, as do the readers of novels. If you can't find the romantic plot line in the Gospels

---

[18]Kathleen McGowan, *The Expected One: A Novel* (New York: Touchstone/Simon & Schuster, 2006); Andrew Buncombe, "Kathleen McGowan: The Da Vinci Descendant," *The Independent*, July 23, 2006.

themselves, a little literary and cinematic license can help. It's quite likely that most evangelicals remain nonplussed by all of this ado about Mary Magdalene, which is to say that these movies have had little or no impact on American evangelical thinking about Christ. There still is, however, something about Mary that we should pay attention to, even if only as a cautionary tale. From Cecil B. DeMille to La Marre what happens to Mary Magdalene reflects the need to go beyond the text, to see more of the human dimension of Christ than comes off from the flat, two-dimensional text of the Gospels. In earlier chapters, especially in chapter three on the Victorians, we saw how the Word was perceived to have failed, not answering our unanswered questions about Christ, not filling in those scenes our imaginations call for. The perceived failure of the Word becomes by definition all the more acute when it comes to putting Christ on the silver screen.

JESUS LAUGHING

This extracanonical Mary Magdalene of American Jesus films represents a larger tendency to freely fill in the Gospels, to go where the text does not take us. After all, Jesus surely had times when he laughed with his family and with disciples. Surely he shared many tender moments with them. It's not too much of a leap to conclude that having a fuller picture of Jesus, having these gaps filled in, would most certainly be a good thing. Evangelicals applauded Mel Gibson's verity to the biblical narrative in *The Passion,* ironic because in many ways Gibson drifted from the biblical narrative, sometimes far and wide. First, the opening scene in the garden of Gethsemane, the moment of Christ's struggle in prayer over this final step in his messianic mission, Gibson has Satan appear to him off-camera, furthering his struggle and toil. Gibson then has Satan send a snake Christ's way, which Jesus forcefully—rather manly?—crushes. The scene becomes a stroke of cinematic and theological brilliance. It harkens the viewer back to Genesis 3:15 and the promise that while the serpent strikes the heel of the seed of the woman, the seed of the woman, whom later biblical texts identify as Christ, will crush the serpent's head. It's not, however, in the Gospel texts. I'm not being overly nitpicky: Gibson takes cinematic license quite often, maybe more often than the film's rather vocal proponents wish to admit.

Gibson's focus on Mary, the mother of Jesus, also requires him to fill in the gaps. In a flashback scene, Mary recalls a playful Jesus splashing water in her face before sitting down to eat dinner. Again it becomes a tender moment that helps his story line, but one absent from the Gospels. So too with Gibson having Pilate's wife offer Mary a fine linen cloth as Jesus' precrucifixion torture finally moves to an end. This scene comes from Emmerich's *Dolorous Passion of Our Lord*, not from the Gospels. Darren J. N. Middleton summarizes the film's sources, "Gibson blends late-medieval catholic visual art, the fourteen stations of the cross, Isaiah 53, and the visions of Anne Catherine Emmerich."[19]

Perhaps most troubling, however, is the movie's relentless focus on the gruesome violence. The Gospels themselves do not linger over the precrucifixion torture anywhere near the extent that Gibson does. Lorenzo Albacete contrasts Gibson's account with that of the Gospels, observing, "It is surprising to see how concise and devoid of detail the passion accounts in the Gospels are. One could read all four of them during the time it takes to watch the flagellation scene in Gibson's film." Albacete then explores the dangers of Gibson's obsession, noting that it has the effect of reducing the Gospel story to a gut-wrenching, emotional drain. Gibson's telling also fails to connect the story of the passion to the rest of the story of the incarnation, except by some relatively slim attempts through flashbacks. But even there Gibson exercises license. And, while we are on the subject of Jesus' mother, Albacete, himself a Roman Catholic, notes, "Gibson's depiction of Mary, the mother of Jesus, is entirely a result of his Catholicism."[20]

This criticism of Gibson is not to minimize the truly physically grueling and torturous nature of the passion event, nor does it dismiss the experiential in the lives of Christians today. But Gibson's movie wrests the passion account from its theological and historical context—despite all of the Aramaic and Latin—making it an existential moment. Albacete insightfully refers to this as a "disincarnation."

There are far more extreme examples than Gibson when it comes to adding to the Gospels to put Jesus on the screen. *The Passion* is the kind of film that most Christians, both evangelicals and Catholics alike on this one, hail as biblically accurate and faithful and true. As Pope John Paul II said after view-

---

[19]Darren J. N. Middleton, "Celluloid Synoptics: Viewing the Gospels of Marty and Mel Together," in *Re-Viewing the Passion*, ed. S. Brent Plate (New York: Palgrave Macmillan, 2004), p. 71.
[20]Lorenzo Albacete, "The Gibson Code," in *After the Passion Is Gone*, ed. J. Shawn Landres and Michael Berenbaum (Lanham, Md.: Rowman & Littlefield, 2004), p. 109.

ing the film, "It is as it was." If such a film, despite papal pronouncements, adds
to the script, then how much more do other films add to the script?

JESUS IN MONTREAL

Another phenomenon of Jesus movies worth considering concerns the desire to
recast him into our own cultural context. Denys Arcand's 1989 *Jesus of Montreal*
presents a salient example. In this rather existential film, an aging priest enlists the
services of a young actor to rewrite a thirty-year-old script for the passion play
staged by Montreal's diocese. Daniel, played by Lothaire Bluteau, begins re-
searching the scholarship of the quest of the historical Jesus. In the process he
learns that Jesus's death was an accident of history, as Jesus assumed a messiah
complex that got out of hand, ending in Jesus' death as an insurrectionist at the
hands of the Romans. Now enlightened, Daniel wishes to recast the play along
these lines, putting a much fresher face on it than the bishop bargained for. Daniel,
much like Jesus gathering the disciples, calls other actors to join him, some accepting, some choosing other work. The play, set outdoors, mystifies some and attracts
others. Church officials, however, decide to bring down the curtain, so to speak,
on the operation, thus playing quite well the role of the Pharisees.

The movie actually has much to commend it, having won the jury prize at
Cannes in 1989. It is probably by far the most engaging of Jesus films. Arcand's genius in the film, according to Brian Stone, is "the dynamic confronta-
tion of Daniel as Christ-figure and the Jesus-portraits among which he moves,"
the portraits including the Jesus of form criticism that Daniel researches, the
"lofty" Jesus of the church officials, the entertainer Jesus that the crowds went
out to see, as well as the many iconic images of Jesus that pepper the film.
Theologian Richard Walsh also applauds Arcand for depicting not a nostalgic
Jesus but one who is unnerving and disturbing, like the prophets of old. Critics
too praise the movie, but for far different reasons. One declared the film "valuable precisely because of [its] lack of dogma." In the words of one, "Arcand
penetrates Christianity with agnostic wit," giving moviegoers a "secular savior"
and suggesting that "where religion has failed, art may yet offer salvation." The
problem with removing Jesus from the boundaries of the Gospels, as the film
intentionally does, is that one indeed is left with a secular savior.[21]

---

[21]Bryan P. Stone, *Faith and Film: Theological Themes at the Cinema* (St. Louis: Chalice Press, 2000),
    p. 56; Richard Walsh, *Reading the Gospels in the Dark* (Harrisburg, Penn.: Trinity Press International,
    2003), pp. 45-68; the movie critics' citations are found in Tatum, *Jesus at the Movies*, pp. 187-88.

Most movies, however, tend to be more subtle in bringing Jesus forward. Again, Johnny Cash's *Gospel Road* is an example. Like just about every Jesus film, Cash includes the infamous expunging of moneychangers from the temple. In *Jesus in Montreal,* Daniel chases greedy directors out of a theater with electrical cords in his hand instead of a leather whip. Cash has Jesus walking through what is supposed to be the temple courtyard, overturning tables, chasing off livestock, smashing produce and hurling money boxes. He then has Christ rebuking the leaders and the merchants for their greed, hypocrisy and their sin of defiling God's, his father's, holy house. Cash then offers narration, commenting on Jesus' "public exposé" of the "religious establishment." Cash's word choice is instructive, as these expressions reflect more of 1970s counterculture than they do the biblical idiom. So ensconced are we in our own age that we hear Cash's word rather seamlessly alongside of the biblical words, not even taking notice of the difference. When we remember that the character playing Jesus looks exactly like a California hippie we see how much this scene reflects the 1970s.

The fast-forwarding of Jesus into contemporary settings may also be seen in the 1970s movie musicals *Jesus Christ Superstar* and *Godspell.* Both of these started life as Broadway musicals in 1971, the exact same year the Jesus People were garnering the covers of national news magazines. From the moment the brightly painted bus pulls up to the Roman pillars in the middle of the desert and unloads its enthusiastic troupe of actors, musicians and dancers, anyone sitting in the audience of *Jesus Christ Superstar* knows they are in for a 1970s rock opera and not a historical depiction of historical texts. The brightly colored spandex-clad dancers drive the point home in song after song. Some of the more telling anachronisms of this movie include Judas being chased across the desert by three tanks and King Herod asking Jesus to walk across his swimming pool. Lloyd Baugh speaks of the film's "almost total lack of correspondence between the film and the gospel." Baugh continues by noting that the film's lack of coherency and consistency as it moves from at least a biblical frame of reference to utterly foreign reinterpretations and retellings, creating what he wants to call "the first postmodern gospel."[22]

Godspell is even more blatant in contemporizing the message, having John

---

[22]Lloyd Baugh, *Imaging the Divine: Jesus and Christ-Figures in Film* (Kansas City: Sheed & Ward, 1997), p. 36.

the Baptist call followers to join him splashing around in a fountain in New
York City's Central Park—the equivalent to the baptisms by him in the Jordan
River. The followers look more like mesmerized zombies, hearing the call to
discipleship as if it were some dog whistle on some special frequency. The
Pharisees and Sadducees that rebuff Jesus in the Gospels become the police,
and Jesus, whose face is painted as a clown with a teardrop, hangs out with the
disenfranchised in a junkyard, when they're not twirling around the streets to
Barry Manilow-esque songs. At the end, Christ dies on a pedestal, fashioned
after the kind circus animals stand on, against a chainlink fence. His disciples
arise in the morning to take down the dead body and carry it through the
streets, singing "Day by Day," which initially sounds somber and chantlike before becoming more upbeat and hopeful. Both of these movies have been labeled "important cultural artifact[s]," which has a side effect of allowing aca-
demics to justify showing them in courses. To call them cultural artifacts also
means that they both represent and contribute to culture and to cultural attitudes about Christ. In both the cases of *Jesus Christ Superstar* and *Godspell*,
Jesus looks like he would be right at home in 1970s counterculture. Of
course, that's not the Jesus of the Gospels. Both films suffer irreversibly from
downplaying Jesus' divinity. As Richard Wightman Fox quipped, "*Jesus
Christ Superstar* displayed plenty of divinity. It was simply located in the Father, not in Jesus."[25]

Most evangelicals would give little, if any, time to either of these 1970s
movies or their soundtracks, or their continual on-and-off Broadway reincarnations. But evangelicals have, from time to time, sanctioned the rechristen-
ing of the Gospel story in contemporary fashion. Most such contemporizing
of the Gospels and of Jesus occurs off the screen and off the stage. The wildly
popular *Cotton Patch Gospel* transports the Gospels from the distant geo-
graphical region of the Mediterranean to the American South. There are also
more subtle ways, such as the ways most contemporary Christian writers
speak of Jesus in colloquial terms and current idioms, or the way they recast
and retell the Gospels in contemporary settings and circumstances. The desire to do so reflects the healthy impulse of bringing Christ and the Bible to
bear on the context of our lives. But it can also cause us to distort Jesus and

---

[25]Stern, Jefford and Debona, *Savior on the Silver Screen*, p. 193; Richard Wightman Fox, *Jesus in
America: A History* (New York: HarperSanFrancisco, 2004), p. 380.

the Gospels or to miss out on how Jesus and the Gospels could correct what we assume to be true, what we take for granted culturally. Putting Jesus on the silver screen invites the overtaking of current cultural forms in the telling of Jesus' story. In the process, Jesus himself gets swept away, as the case with the disciples in *Godspell* carrying him off through the streets of New York (or Quebec).

HOW DO YOU SHOOT THE HYPOSTATIC UNION?

It might be unfair to expect of film that which it cannot deliver. It appears to be too difficult to offer an entire biblically informed movie on Jesus. It appears to be even more difficult to portray Christ as the God-man on the screen. These limitations may not be so much the fault of the screenwriters, producers and directors, as much as they reflect the limitations of the genre. One exception to this contention, if not an exception to these Jesus films, is *Jesus* (1979) by John Krish and Peter Sykes, with the backing of Bill Bright and Campus Crusade. In the 1990s, the Jesus Film Project became a veritable institution, offering whole kits for screenings and postscreening classes. The film has been translated into hundreds of languages, with more translations added annually and more in the works. If you want to read the script, as the website for the project informs you, simply open your Bible to Luke. The film was shot on location to further its authenticity. As Bill Bright and five hundred others began to put the project together, they followed five principles. The first two are "The film, must be as archaeologically, historically, and theologically accurate as humanly possible. The presentation must be unbiased, acceptable to all as the depiction of Christ's life."[24]

The *Jesus Film,* as it has come to be called, is the exception, however, that proves the rule. But even here, too, as its creators realize, the film still needs to be interpreted. Depicting Christ's birth, life and death, and even his resurrection is one thing; understanding the full weight of all of those events is another. *The Passion of the Christ,* too, has been hailed for its evangelistic value. Given the intensity of the film, how anyone can escape without even a modicum of reaction defies imagination. Yet many moviegoers did. Having seen *Braveheart*, they expect violence from Gibson. Having seen many, many violent movies, American audiences may have been impressed by the sheer du-

---

[24]"History of the Project," *The Jesus Film Project* <www.jesusfilm.org/aboutus/history.html>.

ration of the violence Gibson put before them, but many likely could watch without wincing. Even if they did wince at the violence, something significant remains missing. *The Passion* can portray the violence of the crucifixion, but it can't portray the break in the eternal fellowship of the Trinity, the break in the divine union between the Father and the Son as the Son bore the wrath of God for the sin of humanity. It's not Gibson's fault. No director can pull it off.

Putting Jesus on the silver screen focuses almost necessarily on his humanity. Even the crowds who lived during the first century and encountered Jesus grasped his humanity much more readily than his deity. And when he confronted them with his true identity, they responded with incredulity and suspicion. Following the Puritan era in American theology, the humanity of Christ has been on the rise. In the nineteenth and early twentieth century the religious establishment belonging to denominations and movements—which in previous eras held strongly to the Nicene and Chalcedonian formulas of the two natures of Christ, that Christ is the God-Man—began to drift from and then eventually jettison such statements in favor of seeing Christ as a divinized or enlightened human. At times, American Christianity tilts the other way, allowing his deity to eclipse his humanity, as in the Christmas carol that goes, "The little Lord Jesus, no crying he makes." But by and large in our culture it's the humanity of Jesus that wins out. In the broader circles of popular culture, Jesus too shed his trappings of divinity and became mortal, one quite close to God but entirely and only just like the rest of us. This trajectory follows the cinematic portrayal of Christ almost to a T. As the century churned out films, Jesus became one of us.

IT'S A BIRD, IT'S A PLANE, IT'S A . . . CHRIST FIGURE?

Theologians who work with film and culture have distinguished between "Jesus figures" and "Christ figures." The Jesus figure is Jesus himself, played across a spectrum from the painstakingly authentic and realistic to the entirely stylized. Think Jesus of the Jesus Film Project versus the Jesus of *Godspell*. Christ figures, on the other hand, are messianic figures, playing the role of redeemer or savior. For this category, think of Rocky Balboa or even Sylvester Stallone's other character, Rambo. The hero in *The Matrix,* Neo, an anagram for the One, also serves as a Christ figure. Replete with cinematic nods to Jesus films, *The Matrix* adds to the mix the world of technology and even a dash of Eastern religious traditions in its setting forth of a Christ figure.

Then there's the ultimate and time-tested hero, Superman. Recently, the new Superman, *Superman Returns* (2006), also fits the part. As Jacob Adelman notes, "As one of society's most enduring pop-culture icons, Superman has often been observed as more than just a man in tights." The new Superman movie, however, takes the messianic overtones to new heights. Superman is sent by his father to Earth. Their names are "Kal-El" and "Jor-El," El opaquely representing the Hebrew word *El,* which means God. Search the blogs and you will find many, many more examples. Stephenson Humphries-Brooks argues that films depicting the epic hero, beginning in the 1950s and especially including the Westerns, have merged the story lines of the Messiah with the American hero, creating what he terms an "American Christ." Lloyd Baugh concurs, noting, "The western, a most American *genre* of cinema, provides a remarkably apt and increasing context for the development of the cinematic Christ-figure." The more you watch, the more you will likely find Christ figures in American film.[25]

A third category could be added to Jesus figures and Christ figures: films that explore rich theological themes, such as alienation and reconciliation, loss and redemption—redemptive films. Sometimes these films have a Christ figure, other times the role of the Christ figure is played off camera. But in all, the characters are confronted with their limitations, their losses, their alienation from their fellow human beings, or even from their own selves. Some characters remain in that state, though such films tend to be more popular with critics than with audiences. We have been conditioned to like a happy ending—imagine the expression on your kid's face if Wilbur the pig in *Charlotte's Web* "bought it" in the end instead of returning to the farm. Other characters, however, make it through the conflict, out of the night and into the dawn of day. They find redemption and reconciliation. David Dark, William Romanowski and others have made a compelling case for a theological reading of films. Dark especially focuses on films by Joel and Ethan Coen, including *O Brother, Where Art Thou?* (2000), *Barton Fink* (1991), *Fargo* (1996) and *The Man Who Wasn't There* (2001), among others. As with finding Christ figures, the more we watch, the more we see these redemptive themes.

---

[25]Peter Malone, *Movie Christs and Antichrists* (New York: Crossroad, 1990), pp. 17-19; Jacob Adelman, "Superman as Messiah?" Associated Press, June 16, 2006; Stephenson Humphries-Brooks, *Cinematic Savior: Hollywood's Making of the American Christ* (Westport, Conn.: Praeger, 2006), pp. 115, 127-32; and Baugh, *Imaging the Divine,* p. 157.

What is a good story without confronting the human condition and holding out hope and salvation?[26]

In chapter five I referred to Andrew Greeley's labeling of popular culture as the *"locus theologicus."* While that's certainly true of music, it's also true of film, perhaps more so. This means that we don't need a full-fledged Jesus film to launch an evangelistic campaign. In fact, given some of the problems with putting Jesus on the big screen, Christ-figure films and redemptive films might actually be the better way for telling the story of the good news.

CONCLUSION

Just in time for the Christmas movie season in December 2006, New Line Cinema released *The Nativity Story*. Unlike *The Passion*, this movie opened to none of the controversy and a fraction of the box office, just under one-tenth of the take in the first week, to be exact. The reviewers, not at all missing its lackluster performance next to that of Gibson's movie, spoke of it as "low on passion," "dull" and "unimaginative." The reviewers continue, noting that the movie lacks special effects, which produces a yawn from the audience, nothing akin to Gibson's work and the reactions of Gibson's viewers. One of the few favorable reviews came, not surprisingly, from the U.S. Conference of Catholic Bishops. "Hollywood," the Bishops' Office for Film and Broadcasting declares, "finally gets it right." Getting it right, however, simply doesn't sell. The review, however, is forced to admit that screenwriter Mike Rich, described as both "thoughtful" and a "practicing Christian," fleshes out the sparse details of the New Testament accounts. Even so the collective yawn of the movie shows the difficulty in putting Christ on the silver screen. Movies that are less risk-averse tend to fare much better. In fact, the Jesus films, as mentioned in this chapter, have done so well that Stephenson Humphries-Brooks speaks of the "Cinematic Savior," while others speak of the "Celluloid Savior."[27]

Jesus films bring together two things Americans love, Jesus and movies. The significant question seems to be, Do they mix well? Whether they mix

[26]David Dark, *Everyday Apocalypse: The Sacred Revealed in Radiohead, the Simpsons and other Pop Culture Icons* (Grand Rapids: Brazos, 2002). See also William D. Romanowski, *Eyes Wide Open: Looking for God in Popular Culture*, 2nd ed. (Grand Rapids: Brazos, 2007).

[27]Scott Foundas, review of *The Nativity Story, SFWeekly.com*, May 29, 2006; United States Conference of Catholic Bishops, Office for Film and Broadcasting, review of *The Nativity Story*, n.d.; Jeffrey H. Mahan, "Celluloid Savior: Jesus in the Movies," *Journal of Religion and Film* 6, no. 1 (April 2002).

well or not, they become the way many understand Jesus. William R. Telford points out, "Given its popularity, the Christ film is arguably the most significant medium through which popular culture this century has absorbed its knowledge of the gospel story and formed its impression of Christianity's founder." For audiences in the 1920s through the 1950s it was DeMille's Jesus they were coming to know, while today's audiences have Gibson's Jesus. This silver screen Jesus tends toward a human Jesus, though in Gibson's case a human Jesus who withstands an extraordinary amount of punishment.[28]

American Jesus films also invite us to use our imagination, even a sanctified imagination, to add to the biblical text. This furthers the trajectory that began in the nineteenth century in which the biblical accounts failed to address contemporary readers' and viewers' needs, which in turn legitimized the action of adding to the text (see chap. 3). The additions tend to have a strongly emotional appeal, embedding one's encounter with Christ in experience, an experience limited by one's cultural horizons. The Jesus of Scripture comes from outside, not from within, our cultural horizons, standing above, over and even, at times, against those horizons as the Lord and Savior.

The Jesus of American film, however, looks more like a homegrown action hero. At least that's the conclusion of Stephenson Humphries-Brooks. He sees America's fixation "to identify with, cast itself as, and become a hero in its own view" as underlying the development of Jesus as the action hero in this wave of Jesus films. Even Gibson's *The Passion* speaks to "America's preferred view of itself as a suffering hero." This leads Humphries-Brooks to pose the question, "Where is the real Jesus? For Hollywood he is no longer to be found in the gospel tradition." He continues with an explanation of why the Jesus of the Gospels no longer suffices, "We seem to desire a new kind of more heroic and more reassuring Savior," adding, "Hollywood certainly seems willing to create and to market him to us." In the turning from the Christ of Scripture to the cinematic savior, "we have lost those limits and questions posed by the individual Gospel portraits of Jesus that have from time to time ameliorated the tendency of all readers, the faithful and the not-

---

[28]William R. Telford, "Jesus Christ Movie Star: The Depiction of Jesus in the Cinema," in *Explorations in Theology and Film,* ed. Clive Marsh and Gay Ortiz (Oxford: Blackwell, 1997), p. 122.

so faithful, to see in him what they want to see." We have made Jesus a celluloid version of our own image. Maybe, at the end of the day, that is the true
controversy of Jesus films.[29]

[29]Humphries-Brooks, *Cinematic Savior,* p. 138

JESUS ON A BRACELET

Christ, Commodification and Consumer Culture

Jesus Christ—He's the Real Thing!

FROM A T-SHIRT

Christianity is becoming more of a currency than a belief.

MADONNA

For we are not, like so many, peddlers of God's word,
but as men of sincerity, as commissioned by God,
in the sight of God we speak in Christ.

2 COR 2:17

In 1996 the mammoth Anaheim Convention Center played host to one of the largest trade shows in American retail, the annual show of the Christian Booksellers Association. These were the days before Amazon, which is to say these were the days when people bought their books from local stores. And the store owners were there en masse at the trade show, housed in the convention center, to stock up on the latest bestsellers and to return home with giveaway tote bags, signed books, bumper stickers and enough pens, notepads, and key chains to withstand a long siege.[1]

Just about all of the convention center's 80,000 square feet was filled with stuff beyond your imagination. I attended that year, and the show, coupled

---

[1] CBA no longer calls itself the Christian Booksellers Association but the Association for Christian Retail. And CBA's annual trade show is the International Christian Retail Show (ICRS).

with my first pilgrimage to California, had such a dizzying effect that I only recall a bit of the spectacle. First, not only was I staying in the same hotel, but I
was on the same floor as the hottest ticket in Christian music at that time, dc
Talk. I confess I timed my departures from the hotel at the same time as dc
Talk, walking behind them so as to appear to be part of their entourage. As
for the convention itself, I remember one company hawking jewelry made
with tiny pieces of stone from the tomb of Christ. The three or four entrepreneurs who owned the company hoped to hook passersby with a taped and relentlessly repeating infomercial hosted by Ricardo Montalban. Fantasy Is-
land's former host and the unforgettable voice extolling the virtues of the
Chrysler Cordoba's "rich Corinthian leather" now rapturously lured buyers
with hopes of feeling Christ's presence as the stone, hewn from the tomb of
Christ, gently hung on their customer's neck or encircled their wrists and fin-
gers. Then there was the not-so-subtle promotion of Jim Bakker's tell-all account of his fall from grace, *I Was Wrong*. His publisher had made sure this
landmark book would not be missed. Four-foot by six-foot posters of the
cover, with a forlorn-looking Bakker, flanked the perimeter of the three-story
framed "booth." A spiral staircase took would-be music buyers from this particular publisher's music label to its third floor. Jars of Clay had released
Flood earlier that year. Their music label was giving away a truck. One final
memory concerns the legendary Charlton Heston. I stood in the long line to
get his autograph on a poster promoting his dramatic recording of the Bible.
As he signed it, I told him how much I liked his Bud Light commercials, which
had been airing ever since they were unveiled during the Super Bowl that January. He didn't seem amused. Perhaps for him too the Christian Booksellers
Association trade show had taken its toll. He could withstand chariots in *Ben
Hur,* Pharaoh in *Moses* and even the evil assembly in *Planet of the Apes.* But
at the CBA show, had Charlton Heston met his match?[2]

What would Jesus do? I pondered, as I walked the aisles of CBA. He certainly was there, ubiquitously in fact. Paintings, note cards, bumper stickers,
bracelets, ties, pins, and all sorts of jewelry, puppets, and more bore the image
and likeness of Jesus. Jesus was for sale, and sales were brisk. Commodifying
Christ, turning him into a commodity, is nothing new. As we saw in chapter

---

[2]The CBA annual show and convention in 2003 filled 350,000 square feet of convention center
space when it returned to a significantly enlarged Anaheim Convention Center.

three, such marketing of Jesus and Christianity flourished in the nineteenth century. In the early years of the sixteenth century, Martin Luther thought the church was hawking Christ, causing him to launch a protest that changed the world. While selling Jesus is not unique to our present age, it might be safe to say there is a heightened element to it that far outstrips previous ages. Our culture as a whole has increasingly become commodified, and advertising has increasingly pervaded all of life. Indeed, some creative college students went so far as to offer themselves as living billboards to any corporations in order to pay tuition. "The United States," writes economist and social analyst Juliet Schor, "is the most consumer-oriented society in the world." And in our consumer culture Christianity is not lagging behind. In fact, Colleen McDannell and R. Laurence Moore have argued that it might very well be Christians desirous of spreading the good news who have led the vanguard in the marketplace.[3]

From the outset of this chapter on consumerism and Christianity, it might be said that such cynical views ignore or downplay the sincere efforts of many who are not selling these goods simply to make a buck but are earnestly trying to do something that they believe is contributing to the church and spreading the gospel, while also making a living in the process. If people need to wear T-shirts and people need to make T-shirts, then why not wear and make T-shirts that serve higher purposes in addition to economic ones? It might be difficult to argue against that. However, I wish to pose the question from the angle of what happens to the message of the gospel in the process of this buying and selling. What happens to Christ in this culture of consumerism? This question becomes all the more urgent when the negative influence of the commercialization and marketing of Christ gets noticed by a watching and increasingly more cynical public.

Such marketing of Christianity hasn't escaped the ever-sardonic, animated show *The Simpsons*. In an episode titled "She of Little Faith," disaster has come to Springfield as a rocket, launched by Homer Simpson, crashes into the church. Left without resources to repair the church, the congregation consents to allow Mr. Burns, looking rather devilish, to rebuild the

---

[3]Juliet B. Schor, *Born to Buy* (New York: Scribner, 2005), p. 9. See Colleen McDannell, *Material Christianity: Religion and Popular Culture in America* (New Haven, Conn.: Yale University Press, 1995); and R. Laurence Moore, *Selling God: American Religion in the Marketplace of Culture* (New York: Oxford University Press, 1994).

church on the condition that he operate it as a business. The church will now be sponsored, like a NASCAR team, complete with banners and commercial announcements by the pastor during the sermons. Pews are replaced with theater seats, and kiosks surround the interior of the church auditorium, along with concession stands and JumboTrons. The congregation filters in, ecstatic over their new church. Amidst the gaping mouths and wide eyes, the sagacious character Lisa is dumbfounded. She asks, "What are they doing to the church?" only to be met with the reply, "We're rebranding it. The old church was skewing pious. We prefer a faith-based emporium teeming with impulse-buy items." The new church is also rebranding Jesus. Throughout the building, the sacred and secular mix, as religious icons appear alongside corporate logos. One such icon is a prominently placed statue of Jesus, complete with a lasso. When Lisa skeptically asks about it, Homer replies that Jesus looks like a cowboy "because he's all man." Disgusted, Lisa leaves the church, embracing Buddhism through the help of Richard Gere, playing a caricature of himself. By the end of the episode she realizes that leaving Christianity means leaving Christmas, which means leaving presents. The siren call lures her back.

Escaping consumer culture indeed is tricky business. Materialism, since the time the golden calf hopped out of the fire for the Israelites in the wilderness, seduces and draws us in. The seduction becomes all the more entangling when these commodities and products, their makers tell us, aid in the task of evangelizing. Why wouldn't you buy the T-shirt, bumper sticker or wall plaque if, as an added bonus, someone might come to Christ because of your bold and unashamed witness? In a culture with such pressures, commodifying Christ becomes all too easy. Equally, such selling of Jesus becomes all too problematic, if not lethal, for the church and the gospel. The truth is, to many in the watching world, consumer Christianity is sacrilegious, not to mention that it just plain looks silly, which is precisely the lesson taught in this parable of *The Simpson's* episode. This chapter explores this world of consumer Christianity, asking what it all means for evangelical Christology.

VALUES ORIENTED

Again Juliet Schor describes our consumer culture: "There are more than 46,000 shopping centers in the country, a nearly two-thirds increase since 1986. Despite fewer people per household, the size of houses continues to

expand rapidly, with new construction featuring walk-in-closets and three-
and four-car garages to store record quantities of stuff." She also notes the increase in TV viewing, which has "resulted in historically unprecedented exposure to commercials. And ads have proliferated far beyond the television
screen to virtually every social institution and type of public space." Schor's
book is primarily aimed at consumer culture's focus on children. Alarmed at
the "commercialization of childhood," she sets out to assess "the impact of a
new consumer environment as a whole" on children. Christians in the marketplace have always seemed to know what Schor so carefully studied, that children are a powerful market. Big Idea's VeggieTales might just provide a salient example.[4]

Hillary Warren's study of VeggieTales reveals how the "all-encompassing
media and peripheral product universe" have led to Big Idea's outgrowing the
niche of Christian retail to catch the eyes and aisle space of megaretailers
Wal-Mart, Target and Sears. These markets, however, have their own sorts of
demands on the products; they, in fact, "shape the message." Warren notes
that such markets as Wal-Mart are bent solely on maximizing profits, which
only come about by stocking products that have wide appeal, leading to the
corollary that "Developers of more exclusively constructed merchandise intended to challenge the majority culture or to spur the evangelical to action
may not find a home for their product on the shelves if it is seen as potentially
offensive, or worse, as a poor seller." Admittedly, all publishers and media
companies face the realities of market forces, and most authors and producers would like to see their work well received. But something transformative
occurs when market forces take precedence. And that transformation, sociologists like Schor and Warren, not to mention the likes of Neil Postman, have
pointed out, is for ill. Warren relates her own personal experience, likening
her son's attraction to VeggieTales characters Bob and Larry to Elmo: "he
loves Elmo but has no actual interest in anything Elmo says or does . . . and
Bob and Larry are loved for being Bob and Larry, not because they tell Bible
Stories." She also concludes, based on consumer reviews and promotional
materials, that parents buy VeggieTales products because they are fun and, in

---

[4]Schor, *Born to Buy*, pp. 9, 14, 213. Schor's study found that this new consumer environment is one
of the most significant social factors in children's development. She also concludes that this pervasive
consumer culture damages the moral and psychological well-being of children and of the families in
which they live.

accord with the new value in the post 9/11 world, they are safe.[5]

VeggieTales products do not come in two lines, one for the Christian and one for the secular marketplace, which is to say that secular viewers and buyers are merely getting a values-oriented product as are Christian viewers and buyers. As these children consumers become adult consumers, their expectations of the market will likely be already shaped, and the market will likely not disappoint their tastes. This calls to mind the words of the curmudgeonly H. L. Mencken, "Religion, if it is to retain any genuine significance, can never be reduced to a series of sweet attitudes, possible to anyone not actually in jail for felony."[6]

How ironic it would be if American evangelicalism reduces its message to such a saccharin-sweet package, not to keep up with religious pluralism or because of some philosophical or theological shift but merely because it falls victim to its own commercial success. The gospel runs deeper than a values-oriented message. In fact, a values-oriented message trivializes the most profound and significant message of all time. Chapter seven references a quote in the *New Republic* concerning how the confiscation of Christ for political ends can only serve to trivialize him. It is equally true that the commodification of Christ also only serves to trivialize him. A salient example of this is a line of products aimed at the kid in all of us: Precious Moments.

BUDDY CHRIST

Samuel Butcher ranks as one of America's most successful artists. He turned his drawings of teardrop-eyed children into a virtual industry of inspirational porcelain figurines, stationery, posters and other paraphernalia that comprises the Precious Moments empire. After art school in Berkeley, California, Sam began his career at Child Evangelism Fellowship, first in the shipping department and then moving up to the art department. The teardrop-eyed children first filled posters and drawings for friends and family, then they appeared on the children's show *Tree Top House.* In the 1970s, again when Christian retailing was taking off, Sam joined forces with a partner, Bill Biel.

---

[5]Hillary Warren, *There's Never Been a Show Like Veggie Tales: Sacred Messages in a Secular Market* (Lanham, Md.: Rowman & Littlefield, 2005), pp. 95-96, 110. For Neil Postman, see his chapter "Shuffle Off to Bethlehem," in *Amusing Ourselves to Death: Public Discourse in the Age of Show Business*, 20th anniversary edition (New York: Penguin, 2005).

[6]H. L. Mencken cited in Darryl Hart, *A Secular Faith: Why Christianity Favors the Separation of Church and State* (Chicago: Ivan R. Dee, 2006), p. 13.

They took Sam's artwork, at the time filling stationery and greeting cards, to the CBA trade show. The rest is history. In 1978 the first Precious Moments figurine came off the production line. Next came Bibles, "Precious Moments for Little Hands" and "Precious Moments Collectors" Bibles, in all colors and styles. But it wasn't until 1989 that Sam's true dream came true, when the Precious Moments Chapel in Carthage, Missouri, opened to the public. The Precious Moments Inspiration Park, in addition to the chapel, includes a visitor's center, complete with a massive gift shop and a buffet restaurant, with grounds replete with life-size statues of Precious Moments characters.

The chapel features paintings of various biblical scenes, with angels as characters, inspired by Michelangelo's Sistine Chapel. The only adult in any of the images is Christ, prominently featured in the mural Hallelujah Square, a mural that also features Timmy Angel welcoming dead children, as angels, into heaven, as they ride cars and play. Michael Horton once visited the chapel, which he describes as "part Spanish-baroque, part Anaheim-funeral parlor." Horton, like many pilgrims to the Precious Moments chapel, experienced an epiphany, though Horton's might be unique among Precious Moments pilgrims. He puts it this way, "I had my own precious moment, an epiphany. . . . Like the exaggerated features of the Precious Moment Angels—calculated to evoke particular emotions of intimacy and sweetness—popular American religion in general has become increasingly captive to false gods." Harsh words for such inspirational images. Yet Horton argues rather persuasively that Precious Moments represents a "cult of sentimentality" that eschews real worship. He likens it to Aaron and the golden calf. Horton then intones, "It was not that Aaron was willing to have Israel worship a false God, but that he was willing to let them worship the true God falsely." Horton further makes his case by noting the irony that all of the angels at the chapel, as well as those substantiated as porcelain figurines, are cuddly, cute, winsome, tepid. "One would be hard-pressed to have Michael the Archangel in mind when gazing on one of these benign figurines," writes Horton. And why was Mary "filled with terror" when angels appeared to her, Horton asks. It's not just angels that come under this purview. So does Christ.[7]

Collectors of Precious Moments could have any number of figurines with

---

[7]Michael Horton, "Precious Moments in American Religion," *Modern Reformation*, January-February, 1997.

Precious Jesus figures. These include "Jesus Is the Answer," "Jesus Is Coming Soon," "Jesus Is the Light," not to mention a host of figures related to nativity scenes. As with the angels on the rest of the statues, Precious Jesuses are cute and cuddly, looking a lot like orphans, only chubby. And they are always portrayed as children. Those who find Precious Moments figurines, well, precious, will take issue with the interpretation offered here. They might even find an ally in Timothy K. Beal. He recalls his visit to Precious Moments Inspiration Park in his book *Roadside Religion*, a travelogue of American religious attractions. What struck Beal most was the suffering and pain and loss that the pastel paints and cute expressions gloss over. Beal refers to various Precious Moments figurines that deal with loss and death, such as the figurine of a fireman (as a child) holding a baby wrapped in a blanket, a memorial to the Oklahoma City bombing in 1995. At the chapel, this pain may be seen in the room designed as a memorial to Sam Butcher's twenty-seven-year-old son, Philip, who was killed by a drunk driver. Yet even consenting to this realization of suffering beneath the surface of the cute expressions, Beal concedes that in the end, Precious Moments idealizes faith and childhood, not to mention that it thrives on healthy doses of commercialism. On one level it may be comforting to relate to a Jesus somehow stuck in a time warp of infancy and childhood. But that child grew up. He is also the Lord of the universe—a message that somehow gets lost in the personalized, sentimentalized and trivialized Precious Jesus.[8]

Such trivializing of Jesus by presumably sincere people has sparked a rash of products that step beyond the trivial and verge closely into blasphemy, which might be a good description of some of the products of the good-humored folks at Accoutrements. They market the "Jesus Action Figure." The deluxe model comes with loaves, fishes, a jug to turn water into wine and "glow-in-the-dark miracle hands." Additionally, Accoutrements sells a Jesus bobblehead, which they call a nodder. They also sell "Jesus Pencil Toppers," which come five to a package. I keep a set in my office at the college. It amazes me how many ask if they are erasers. Imagine? I am equally amazed at how many ask where they can get their own set. The move to blasphemy becomes complete at Jay and Silent Bob's website, where the

---

[8]Timothy K. Beal, *Roadside Religion: In Search of the Sacred, the Strange, and the Substance of Faith* (Boston: Beacon Press, 2005), pp. 135-58.

"Buddy Christ Dashboard Statue" is sold. This figure has a smiling Jesus with hands at ten and two o'clock, pointing at the viewer and giving a thumbs up. The figure is inspired by Kevin Smith's film *Dogma*. Forget the girl in the hula skirt, this figurine can be yours for $14.95. While intended as a spoof, sincere Christians purchase it just the same. There may be a case to be made that for the sincere all things are sincere. But something, in the immortal words of Shakespeare's Prince Hamlet, does not quite smell right in Denmark. American evangelicals, it seems, have a hard time recognizing the comic caricature that they have become. More tragic, American evangelicals have allowed Christ to become a comic caricature. And even more tragic still, American evangelicals can't even seem to realize that Christ has become a comic caricature.[9]

A scholarly article in *Culture and Religion* explores this line of merchandise, specifically analyzing Buddy Christ and the Jesus Action Figure, "which seem intended as postmodern antichrists to offend Christian sensibilities and mock the image of Christ." The article's author, Steve Nolan, however, looks beyond the surface, seeing these artifacts as reflecting "a residual respect for Christ as a spiritual guide." The sentiments expressed in these action and dashboard figures are not mocking Christ per se, as much as they mock "religious hypocrisy" and particular camps within the Christian establishment, such as the religious right—presumably included in this particular article because they are always an easy target. Hence the real sentiments of the manufacturers of these products and, I assume, the consumers who buy them, is to rescue Jesus the spiritual guide from the Jesus of religion. Nolan contends that it would be wrong "to superficially regard *Buddy Christ* or *Jesus Christ Action Figure* as irreverent parodies." Instead, there is a "juxtaposition of the reverential with the subversive." These action figures, Nolan argues, provide a means to reclaim Jesus for the masses from the institutional church's lock on him. Of course, to free Jesus in this way is to also free him from the confines of the Gospels and the biblical text. Indeed, this liberated Jesus becomes a buddy, a sort of spiritual guru to lead one along life's path. This exigent life in the modern world, es-

[9]"Jesus Action Figure," Accoutrements.com <www.accoutrements.com/products/11537.html>, and "Jesus Pencil Toppers," Accoutrements.com <www.accoutrements.com/products/11543.html>. "Buddy Christ Dashboard Statue," JayandSilentBob.com <jayandsilentbob.com/budchrisdass1.html>.

pecially given the complexities of this new millennium, however, cries out for such a guru. Fortunately, some have come to our rescue.[10]

JESUS THE BUSINESSMAN

It may be recalled from chapter four that Bruce Barton's *The Man Nobody Knows* portrayed Jesus as "the founder of modern business" and an advertising guru. Entrepreneurs of the 2000s can now turn to Laurie Beth Jones. In the introduction to her book *Jesus, Entrepreneur,* previously published as *Jesus, Inc.,* she insightfully muses, "Let's look for a moment at Jesus of Nazareth. He had a good job. A solid job. He had taken over his father's business after his death, and he enjoyed what he did." Based on these insights, Laurie Beth Jones poses as the consultant to an ever-expanding world of spiritually minded entrepreneurs, whom she terms "spiritreneurs." In this book, she transforms Jesus into a model businessman and the Gospels into a textbook for spiritreneurship 101. Consider her take on the episode of paying taxes from the Gospels:

> In the sudden rush of customer demand, a small matter of paying Jesus' taxes was overlooked. Matthew, who had been a tax collector before he became a spiritreneur, knew how serious an offense that was. Yet Jesus simply told his team to go get the money from his offshore account—which at the time consisted of a coin in a fish's mouth.[11]

Of course, Jones is attempting a humorous, catchy read of the text. She's also, however, appropriating a reading that subjects the text to contemporary sensibilities, framed in what matters to her, the language of American corporate culture. Such reading of the biblical text continues on through her other books, *Jesus, CEO* and *Jesus in Blue Jeans.* Keeping up with marketplace terminology and cognizant that CEOs recently have fallen on hard times, Jones also published *Jesus, Life Coach: Learn from the Best.* In *Jesus, Life Coach* she plays off of Jesus's words in John 21:6: "Cast the net on the right side of the boat," to offer the advice to "swim upstream." She then turns to the example of Sam Walton, Wal-Mart's famous founder who "swam upstream" by

---

[10]Steve Nolan, "Buddy Christ and Jesus Action Figure, Contemporary (Ab)use of the Christ Image(?): Thoughts on the Political Meanings of Two Postmodern Anti-Christs," *Religion and Culture* 7, no. 3 (2006): 311-27.

[11]Laurie Beth Jones, *Jesus, Entrepreneur: Using Ancient Wisdom to Launch and Live Your Dreams* (New York: Three Rivers Press, 2001), pp. xiv-xv.

founding retail centers in rural areas. Since I live in a rural area and have lived through a couple of lost battles on behalf of locals to keep Wal-Marts out, I was especially intrigued at how Sam Walton functions not only positively in her scheme but also as a model disciple of Christ. She seems to be impressed, however, only with the 3,400-plus stores his company has established and with its status as "the largest corporation in America."[12]

Laurie Beth Jones's *Jesus in Blue Jeans* also met a market niche, coming out as it did during a downsizing and simplifying trend of the late 1990s once the excesses of the 1980s caught up. In this book too she brings Jesus right into the world of the twentieth century. Using the text of John 15:16, "You did not choose me but I have chosen you and *appointed you* to do great works," she remarks that Jesus honors appointments. She then makes the application, "Yet too many of us fail to keep even simple appointments. We show up late or not at all." Drawing from the fact that "Jesus conducted his first miracle at a wedding," she concludes that "Jesus was *event* oriented." She adds that she herself, "as an advertising specialist . . . was trained early on to recognize the outreach value of 'events.'" Consequently, her advice to entrepreneurs launching a new business consists of following Jesus by hosting an event. He was, after all, "event oriented."[13]

This string of examples and the book titles themselves illustrate the malleability of Jesus in conforming to ever-shifting trends. To a world infatuated with and envious of CEOs, Jesus becomes the model CEO. For a more casual, downsized climate he becomes Jesus in blue jeans, the symbol of comfort. And in a world where the newly labeled "life coach" is much sought-after, Jesus can become that too. Yet all of these come at a cost of stretching, if not distorting, the biblical text and the true mission of Jesus as the God-man on Earth. I wonder if such book titles aren't merely pandering to consumer tastes. To put the matter more directly, at what point do catchy titles, selling books and packing out seminars notwithstanding, do an injustice to the second person of the Trinity? Portraying Jesus as the model businessman or "spiritreneur" moves beyond the selling of the gospel or the selling of Christianity. It's the selling of Jesus himself.

---

[12]Laurie Beth Jones, *Jesus, Life Coach: Learn from the Best* (Nashville: Thomas Nelson, 2004), p. 199.
[13]Laurie Beth Jones, *Jesus in Blue Jeans: A Practical Guide to Everyday Spirituality* (New York: Hyperion, 1997), pp. 261, 272.

There are also ample cases of using Jesus to sell, or at least the use of one's commitment to Jesus to sell. For those Christians nervous about allowing a secular plumber into their house, there's *The Shepherd's Guide: The Christians' Choice of Yellow Pages,* hailed by its publisher as "America's Premier Christian Business Directory." Christians in the area where I live may avail themselves of the South Central Pennsylvania edition, while other regions have their own editions. Travelers and the peripatetic may take advantage of the national online directory. Such directories advertise for Christian bus and travel tours, Christian book and gift stores, ministries, churches, and Christian camps and conference centers. But these directories also offer so much more, such as Christian lawyers, insurance agents, dentists, engineers, auto mechanics and plumbers. As for Christian lawyers, one law firm includes a biblical verse in their ad: "Where no counsel is, the people fall: but in the multitude of counsellors there is safety" (Prov 11:14 KJV). An electrical contractor uses Genesis 1:3-4, "And God said, Let there be light. . . . And God saw the light, that it was good" (KJV). Christian insurance agents appeal to our desire to be good stewards. If you happen to need a mortgage, you're likely safe in the hands of the "Dedicated Christian Servants" at Covenant Mortgage & Investment. For those needing some pampering, A Heavenly Touch offers hair and nail services, massage and electrolysis. Why not, as the ad invites, "Treat Yourself to a Christian Oasis"?[14]

Bible verses and original Christian artwork, as well as two plans of salvation and a Christian business person's credo, intermingle with the ads. The ads themselves are peppered with symbols of the cross and, of course, the ubiquitous fish. In addition, the reader also sees a number of American flags splashed on the pages. Patriotism, piety and products all coalesce, providing convenience for Christian consumers, the perfect convergence of Christ and commerce. As with many of the cases in this chapter, no doubt many of the advertisers in *The Shepherd's Guide* are sincere in both their faith and their business. In the process, however, the cross, the place on which the God-man suffered and died for us and for our salvation, is reduced to an advertising logo.

The Shepherd's Guide also reveals the discomfort many Christians have in living in the world, or the confusion they have over the sacred and the secular. In fact, many of the examples used in this book highlight this problem. It's not

---

[14]*The Shepherd's Guide: South Central Pennsylvania,* spring 2005-spring 2006, pp. 2, 9, 47, 63, 43.

enough to be a plumber who happens to be a Christian. One has to be a Christian plumber. Musicians and artists, and even writers and scholars, face this problem acutely. Being a *Christian* musician legitimizes the musical product and the musician. Evangelism has a totalizing effect on one's work. It's not kingdom work to be a good steward as an electrical engineer as much as if you witness while you work. *The Shepherd's Guide* ironically, however, dulls the edge to such a Christian witness, since it primarily serves the Christian community. *The Shepherd's Guide,* not to mention CCM and even the union of Christian insurance agents, creates an insular world for Christians. By simply sticking with the businesses in the book, you can keep yourself and your family safe from the tentacles of non-Christians. And when all these Christian plumbers come calling they find that they're witnessing to the already evangelized. They're plumbing, so to speak, for the choir. Some of these juxtapositions of Christian symbols with business can also be downright strange, such as the symbol of a cross and an empty tomb emblazoned on a sign for a septic service.

In his 1922 work *Babbitt,* Sinclair Lewis used the phrase *Christianity Incorporated* to capture the ethos of his fictional small town overrun by a blending of consumerism and religion. Lewis could find easy fodder for his book in the writings of the likes of Barton, who rather brazenly brought business into Christianity. What was good for 1922, however, may be good for today. Recently, Michael Budde and Robert Brimlow have used Lewis's phrase as the title for their exposé of the church's unholy matrimony with consumer and capitalist culture, a church full of those more schooled on Adam Smith, they quip, than the Sermon on the Mount. Whether taking Jesus as everybody's favorite CEO for book titles or whether using the cross for advertising logos, the co-opting of Christ for business hijacks the Gospels and Christ himself. Capitalist and consumerist culture becomes the context into which the gospel is made to fit, into which Christ conforms, rather than the reverse.[15]

GOLFING FOR JESUS

Of course, those engaged in such activities will contest my conclusions, opting instead to see such activities as geared toward evangelism or toward bring-

---

[15]Michael Budde and Robert Brimlow, *Christianity Incorporated: How Big Business Is Buying the Church* (Grand Rapids: Brazos, 2002), p. 177.

ing one's Christian faith to bear upon daily life in the marketplace. Church historian Sean Lucas likes to recall an incident from his days clerking in a Christian bookstore while in high school. A customer came into the store to purchase a fish sticker for her new car. When he told her that they were currently out of stock, she exclaimed in a great deal of exasperation and even a little bit of anger, "How am I going to witness?"

The extent of my golfing consists of hitting a few golf balls around in the back yard, using a used set of golf clubs purchased at a yard sale for ten dollars. I was, nevertheless, once invited to speak at an evangelistic golf outing where the foursome plays from the best-positioned ball. I was told by the host that my not being a golfer wouldn't be a problem since it was a best-ball tournament. This was quite fortunate for me, since the balls I hit ended up in the river, the ponds, nearby fields and all manner of woods. I soon exhausted my supply. One of the foursome, long on patience and well-stocked with golf balls, came to my aid. He handed over his favorite golf balls for such golfers as I, witnessing golf balls, embossed with a fish advising to read John 3:16-17 and a copyrighted saying, "I once was lost, but now am found"—words I thought to be written some time ago by John Newton. Use these, he told me, that way when you lose them someone might find them and get saved.

The Holy Spirit is indeed omnipotent, omnicompetent and endlessly resourceful, which is to say perhaps he does use fish bumper stickers and witnessing golf balls. It just seems that doing such things isn't quite on par, pardon the pun, with following the Great Commission and being committed to evangelize. But don't tell that to the makers of "The Power of the Christ" T-shirts. They fuse the universal symbol for power, an incomplete circle with a line at the top, with the symbol of the cross, cleverly arriving at the "power of the cross." Not only does the wearer get a "nice power surge by thinking of Jesus Christ" but those passersby will also be exposed to such power. This is, the designers of this particular line of Christian apparel tell us, "The Future Fashion of Faith." Christian T-shirts, while having an apparently bright future, also have a past. Coming in vogue in the 1970s, Colleen McDannell attributes their ascendancy, along with the rest of Christian retailing, to the Jesus movement. An advertisement for Christian T-shirts by The Idea Machine, self-described as "The T-Shirt People," in the May 1978 edition of *Bookstore Journal*, ran the heading, "If It's Worth Sharing, It's Worth Wearing." Folks were turned on to Jesus and ready to wear their faith on their sleeves, literally.[16]

One of the favorite themes of Christian T-shirt designers is, of course, Jesus, as in images of Jesus, sayings of Jesus and, perhaps the all-time favorite, manipulations of Jesus's image or name or biblical titles as a knockoff of well-established logos and advertising jingles. The supreme example of the latter is using "Jesus Christ" in the Coca-Cola script with a slight twist on the world renowned slogan "He's the Real Thing." Recent additions in this genre include "Got Jesus?" playing off the milk campaign, "Jesus Inside," playing off of the logo that alerts computer users that Intel is inside their computers, and the words "The Deal" over the horizontal bar of a cross while the word 'Take" splashes across the vertical bar, playing off of the popular TV show *Deal or No Deal.* The particular company that makes these T-shirts proudly tells its customers to "Be a fisher of men," which in this case presumably means to purchase and wear their T-shirts. Jeffrey Wendland, publisher of the *Online Christian Shopper,* similarly advises would-be consumers. "Almost every vestige of Christianity has been stripped from the culture," he notes before adding, "But one place they can't strip it is off your back." In other words, a foolproof way to fight America's anti-Christian culture is to wear Christian T-shirts (or sweatshirts and hoodies). By wearing these shirts Christians can reach millions—the average T-shirt apparently is seen by three thousand people in its lifetime. But not every situation allows for a T-shirt. "That's where Christian jewelry comes in," notes Wendland.[17]

John Kavanaugh raises a crucial question against such reasoning. He sees a rather stark contrast between what he broadly calls "consumer values" with "Christian values." Consumer values emphasize the "commodity form of life," which reduces people to things, minimizes personal communication and sees relationships as transactions. Kavanaugh further speaks of the commodity form of life creating an "empty interior," in which we lose our sense of our self and which leads to "broken relationships," with advertisements telling us that cars and clothes can do more for us than people. Such a dehumanized form of life results in the "degradation of justice" and a "flight from the wounded." This commodity form of life also affects more than our shopping. Kavanaugh

---

[16]See "The Power of the Christ," <ThePoweroftheChrist.com>, accessed on 12/21/2006. McDannell, *Material Christianity,* pp. 251-59.

[17]These shirts are all available at ChristianShirts.net, the website for "Christian and Pro-Life Apparel." Jeffrey Wendland, "Countering the Anti-Christian Culture," <ezinearticles.com>, March 11, 2007.

observes, "It affects the way we think and feel, the way we love and pray, the way we evaluate our enemies, the way we relate to our spouses and children. It is 'systematic.' " Christian values, on the other hand, emphasize the "personal form of life," which counters the commodity form in every way. This personal form finds its fullest revelation in Jesus Christ. The personal form of life also speaks to the deepest "identity, needs, and capacities of human nature." Given how Kavanaugh frames it, capitulating to consumer culture as the means for evangelism means adapting to a commodity form of life, a form that seemingly runs counter to Christ's rather personal call and commission of the original fishers of people. Commodifying evangelism turns persons who relate into customers who buy, a rather alien approach to that of Christ's.[18]

Such apparel and trinkets do not merely impact evangelism but also the perception of Christ. Apart from knockoffs of logos and advertising jingles, Christian T-shirts tend to portray all manner of sayings and images of Jesus. These include T-shirts manufactured by the company Christian Gear, promoting itself as marketing "Fun. Hip. Christian Merchandise," with such selections as "Rebel with a Cause," and "Christian Outfitters: Jesus Christ, Tough as Nails." You can get "Jesus Is My Homeboy" T-shirts from the company Teenage Millionaire, or you can purchase their companion offering "Mary Is My Homegirl." Many of these T-shirts blend Christianity with patriotism, American patriotism that is. A rather popular design plays off the convenient yield of USA once the words *Jesus* and *saves* are combined: JesUSAves. One company even takes patriotism to levels of statehood, offering a T-shirt sporting the fish symbol filled with the Texas flag hovering over the words, "Proud to be a Christian from Texas." In the wake of 9/11 and the war on terror, any assortment of T-shirts and posters combine, if not equate, Christianity with American patriotism. One such patriotic shirt design goes so far as to juxtapose a soldier's helmet, an M16 with bayonet attached, and the cross of Christ, with the words, "Onward Christian Soldier."

Reporting for the *Los Angeles Times,* Stephanie Simon recalls her visit to the 2006 International Christian Retailers Show. One new product caught her eye, or perhaps her nose:

Virtuous Woman perfume comes packaged with a passage from Proverbs. But

---

[18]John Kavanaugh, *Following Christ in a Consumer Society: The Spirituality of Cultural Resistance* (Maryknoll, N.Y.: Orbis, 1991), pp. 3-19, 31, 71.

what makes the floral fragrance distinctly Christian, Hobbs [the retailer] said, is that it's supposed to be a tool for evangelism. "It should be enticing enough to provoke questions: 'What's that you're wearing?' " Hobbs said. "Then you take the opportunity to speak of your faith. They've opened the door, and now they're going to get it."[19]

None of this hawking of all things Christian has escaped the eyes of a watching public. CNN's *AndersonCooper360°* ran a story introduced as "Faith for Sale," which explored "how companies use religion to sell their goods." *The Osgood File* on CBS radio network ran a story on "how faith based products are hot," though the underlying message was that "not everyone thinks that's so hot." Even bloggers get in on the action. Jesusoftheweek.com offers a platform for submissions for such commercialization of Christ as the Buddy Christ and Jesus Action Figure. This site may be offensive to most Christians as a mockery of Christ. But most of the submissions to the site are of products by Christians. And those products give non-Christians plenty to gawk at. Christian retailing has accomplished its goal of getting the word out: enlisting consumers to wear T-shirts and jewelry as fishers of people, and enlisting golfers to use witnessing golf balls. The message being heard, however, might not be the one intended. The true message of the cross, it seems, is getting lost in a sea of commerce. The commercials are too loud.[20]

The threat of losing the gospel message even within the Christian community itself looms large given that this consumer culture is so freely embraced and participated in by evangelicals. Vincent J. Miller takes us one step further in analyzing the impact of consumer culture on the Christian message. He turns to Disney, which he wryly notes is "obligatory for anyone writing on religion and consumer culture." He dives beneath the typical criticism of Disney to make a significant point concerning the merchandising that dwarfs in sales the box office take of the movies, arguing, "This use of narrative to sell merchandise gives rise to the most profound cultural impact of Disney and other producers of commercial popular culture: the formation of our habits of interpretation and appropriation." "Children," having been conditioned in their habits of interpretation and appropriation,

[19]Stephanie Simon, "Christian Retailers Put Their Print on Products," *Los Angeles Times*, July 21, 2006.

[20]Anderson Cooper, *AndersonCooper360°*, July 25, 2005; Charles Osgood, *The Osgood File*, March 9, 2005.

"learn to quickly accept narratives, to enjoy the roles and symbol systems of the stories, to locate themselves within the tales, and to consider their heroes, conflicts, and ideologies." Then Miller adds, "While children are learning to do all of this, they are simultaneously learning to treat these narratives, roles, and symbols as disposable commodities: things to be played with, explored, tried on, and, in the end, discarded." What concerns Miller the most is that while children are learning of the narratives of Disney, they're also learning of the narrative of Jesus. In fact, more often than not, they're learning both from the same DVD player, and their Christian-symbol emblazoned T-shirts are folded side by side with clothes of their favorite Disney characters in their closets and dressers.[21]

CONSUMPTION

Consumption was the term used in past centuries to refer to the disease today known as tuberculosis. It had been called "consumption" due to the way the tubercle bacillus or bacteria, lodged in the lungs, consumed the life of those fallen by the disease. Consumption, not in a bacterial but in a material form, continues to drain the life out of those caught in its grasp. Consumerism is parasitic, threatening our well-being. Colleen McDannell traces the beginnings of Christian retailing to Victorian days, noting that "Victorian domestic religion encouraged the production and use of religious objects." Once let into the home, Christian marketing had its beginnings. Popular items included sentimental figurines and mottoes. McDannell spotlights David Sydney Warner's *The Gospel Trumpet,* which was originally founded in 1881 as a newspaper but soon became a major producer and distributor of all sorts of Christian products. When the postcard craze hit America in the first decade of the 1900s, the *Gospel Trumpet* catalog from 1909 offered its customers no fewer than fifty choices. Later decades would see the addition of Scripture-embossed pencils, bookends and even "Spread-the-Light Reading Lamps." The latter included "beautiful pictures of the Savior" and were billed as "The 'Ideal' Home Lamp[,] A Testimony of Your Christian Faith." Other companies joined *The Gospel Trumpet* in making such Christian products available to an eager public through both catalogs and door-to-door sales, one of the most

---

[21]Vincent J. Miller, *Consuming Religion: Christian Faith and Practice in a Consumer Culture* (London: Continuum, 2005), pp. 5-6.

popular being the door-to-door Bible salesperson.[22]

Post-World War II American buying habits trended away from door-to-door and even catalog sales, as neighborhoods began giving way to subdivisions, developments and the beginnings of suburban America. And to meet this new buying public, Christian retail stores began appearing. The Christian Booksellers Association, founded in 1950, came to the aid of these new stores. McDannell notes how such stores prospered modestly through the 1950s and 1960s, but in the 1970s the increase in annual revenue from these stores nearly doubled national retail averages. She credits this largely to the Jesus People movement, which with its emphasis on Christianity as a "lifestyle," was anxious to read, hear and wear its faith. The 1970s saw blockbuster books like Hal Lindsey's *The Late Great Planet Earth* and Ken Taylor's paraphrase *The Living Bible*. Both dominated bestseller lists. Companies like World Wide Publications made stickers and buttons, replete with Jesus movement sayings and symbols, by the boxload in order to fill acrylic stands in the new bookstores. Shirts and jewelry, "holy hardware," came next.

One of these jewelers, Bob Siemon, began his company in the 1970s. Turned off by the "kitsch" that passed as Christian merchandise, a Tuxedo-clad Bob Siemon appeared in his own advertisements touting the quality of his merchandise. These would be decorative clocks, watches, photo frames and even potpourri jars that one could be proud of, if not admire for their beauty and elegance. After McDannell published her book, however, the company Bob Siemon created moved from being a major force to a veritable institution by producing all manner of bracelets and other trinkets emblazoned with four letters, WWJD (What Would Jesus Do)? This ubiquitous four-letter question moves millions of pieces annually and extends beyond the reach of Bob Siemon designs. There are even WWJD? boxer shorts. Propelled by the success of his company's WWJD? merchandise, Bob Siemon and Mel Gibson teamed up to launch a whole line of "Passion" merchandise. In the official press release, Siemon declares, "We distributed millions of WWJD? bracelets. . . . This is going to be so much bigger." Billions, perhaps? The Passion line of products includes trading-card style "Witnessing Cards,"

---

[22]McDannell, *Material Christianity*, p. 223. For her extended discussion of *The Gospel Trumpet*, see pp. 229-46. Spread-The-Light Reading Lamps were marketed in the *Gospel Trumpet's* 1935 catalog, reproduced in ibid., p. 238. I am indebted to McDannell, pp. 246-69, for the next few paragraphs.

which feature "images from the movie on the front and scriptures that explain the plan of salvation on the back" and the Nail, a 2 1/2-inch pewter pendant replica of the crucifixion nails. When the movie was in theaters, bookstores couldn't keep these products in stock.[23]

Dell deChant offers an explanation for the empty shelves when he speaks of the consumptive imperative. He notes, "Personal consumption becomes less of a socially constructed behavior and a much more elemental imperative." The activity of consuming isn't so much "conformity to social demands or even psychological motivations." Instead, consumptive behavior "becomes a binding obligation." Consumptive activities become "hard-wired, instinctual behaviors—ritual activities performed without reflection and without doubt." We acquire and consume, in consumer culture, as automatons, induced by nothing more than a fifteen-second advertising spot. Saying "I have to have X," comes as naturally as breathing. DeChant's point is that this is the culture in which we live, which is to say this does affect us.[24]

R. Laurence Moore, who has had a few less-than-savory things to say about Christian forays into politics and American history—he's the coauthor of *The Godless Constitution*—also has some biting criticism of these forays into the marketplace. He wryly notes that, given the "fast, friendly, and guiltless consumption" of the American marketplace, "would-be religious prophets have to learn the ways of Disneyland in order to find their audience." But the doing is their undoing, for these prophets will be so accommodated as to lose their prophetic voice. Moore wonders even how such prophets can speak to consumer culture, asking how these prophets can make consumers sold on Disneyland and McDonald's "understand that when Adam and Eve broke a commandment against a forbidden consumption in the Garden of Eden, forbidden because it was needless, they were pointing humankind towards its final agony?" Moore answers his own question by lamenting, "Probably they cannot." Christians so immersed in con-

[23]"Bob Siemon Designs Helps Share Mel Gibson's 'Passion of the Christ,'" January 20, 2004, press release, signed by Dwight Robinson of Bob Siemon Designs. See also "The Passion," *Bob Siemon Designs* <www.bobsiemon.com/bobsiemondesigns/default.aspx?DepartmentID=4&DepartmentIndex=5& CategoryID=13&CategoryIndex=0>. For the success of the campaign, see the Associated Press article, "Film Boosts Christian Merchandise: 'The Passion of the Christ' has Bookstores Scrambling to Keep Up," March 1, 2004.
[24]Dell deChant, *The Sacred Santa: Religious Dimensions of Consumer Culture* (Cleveland: Pilgrim Press, 2002), p. 94.

sumer culture and the wanton indulgence of needless consumption simply can't offer a remedy. In Moore's telling observation, Moore himself assumes the role of prophet for American evangelicals, who unwittingly, through their capitulation to consumer culture, vainly fall prey to consumption in the treating of those who are dying from it.[25]

One particular episode of VeggieTales has Madame Blueberry acquiring so much stuff that her tree house eventually collapses. She has become a slave to her stuff, to the accumulation of things. She has forsaken people, her friends, in the process. She even almost loses herself to consumption—as the collapsing house nearly takes her life. The episode bravely proclaims a counter-consumer-culture message, bravely because "Stuff-Mart," the almost hypnotically powerful source of all Madame Blueberry's stuff, functions as a rather obvious symbol of the megaretailer that stocks so much VeggieTales merchandise on it shelves. The creators of the episode were moving dangerously close to biting the hand that feeds them. But, alas, the counter-consumer-culture message gets muddled. After the episode concludes, the credits roll and the theme song reverberates from the speakers, commercials follow for VeggieTales stuff, all forms of the characters, sheets and pillow sets, more DVDs and sing-along CDs. More needless stuff, which all can be purchased at a "Stuff-Mart" near you. The prophetic voice of the episode loses a bit of its edge by being, in the end, too enmeshed in the culture against which it protests. Larry Moore might just be right.

CONCLUSION

Christian scholars and theologians rarely venture into the waters navigated in this chapter; they rarely offer a critique of Christian T-shirt websites. Yet it is precisely in these places that popular evangelical expression may be found. This is where evangelicals live. Further, more often than not, American evangelicals reflexively accept the tenets of consumer culture and adapt their faith and its expression to them. As American evangelicals we have been well-trained as consumers through countless acts of consumption. We have been taught to buy, and we're quick learners. We have come to view our faith as a commodity, and at times we make Christ into one too. It would be naive to

---

[25]Moore, *Selling God*, p. 276. Moore makes a similar "prophetic observation" regarding American evangelicals and politics, as will be seen in chap. 8.

attempt escaping consumer culture altogether. Merely having an awareness of it will likely help. Ignoring consumer culture's impact on evangelicalism and our Christology, however, comes at a cost we cannot afford.

While it may be challenging for Christianity and for individual Christians to escape consumer culture, some responses may still be in order. Rodney Clapp once called for cynicism as the answer. I'm "often happy to be cynical," he said, "Not least because it seems that cynicism is the only faithful response to hypercommercialized Christianity." Such cynicism leads to action, the action of cultural resistance, the action of difference.[26]

In the brief time between the publication of the hardback in 2004 and the paperback edition in 2005, Juliet Schor's book *Born to Buy* launched a veritable movement to decommercialize childhood. One wonders what it would take to launch a similar campaign to decommercialize Christ and the gospel. There is no doubt that the many marketing campaigns and product lines discussed in this chapter have been used to bring people to Christ and to strengthen faith. It also might pass without doubt that such marketing campaigns and product lines have injured Christ and the gospel. The televangelist scandals of the 1980s led to a public distaste for Christianity. Many onlookers had long suspected that the televangelists were exploiting the faith for their own financial windfall. Jim Bakker told audiences, "We have a better product than soap or automobiles. We have eternal life." The worldly wise among his audience knew that in Bakker's hands such a product wasn't being hawked for free. Once the scandals broke, such suspicions proved true. Many onlookers continue to harbor such suspicions of Christianity, finding all of this Christian kitsch, "holy hardware" and "Jesus junk" to be the mere exploitation of Christianity. Those outside of Christianity are readily cynical of such Christian endeavors.[27]

Even Billy Graham, while free from financial scandal, still expressed his work in evangelism as selling the gospel. In his autobiography he recalls the time, as an eighteen-year-old, going door to door taking orders for Fuller brushes. He was motivated, because he believed in the product. Every home

[26]Rodney Clapp, *A Peculiar People: The Church as Culture in a Post-Christian Society* (Downers Grove, Ill.: InterVarsity Press, 1996), p. 13. See also his chapters on Christianity and consumerism in *Border Crossings: Christian Trespasses on Popular Culture and Public Affairs* (Grand Rapids: Brazos, 2000).

[27]Schor, *Born to Buy*, p. 213. Jim Bakker, cited in Ben Armstrong, *The Electric Church* (Nashville: Thomas Nelson, 1979), p. 173.

should have a Fuller brush he would tell himself as he marched along. He, by
his own accounts, learned many things from those days of selling Fuller
brushes when he would later turn his attention to the greatest product, the
gospel and eternal life.[28]

In light of these appropriations of consumer culture, perhaps we need cynical responses from within the Christian community too, such cynical responses that refuse to be indifferent to the adaptation of market forces and
consumer practices in the task of making disciples. We need, hearkening
back to John Cavanaugh's categories, to drive our discipleship deep in the
personal form of life, eschewing the commodity form of life. To embrace the
commodity form, even in the name of evangelizing, exploits the faith and ab-
dicates our calling.

Such cultural resistance is not easy. Benjamin R. Barber speaks of the difficulty, if not near impossibility, of escaping the totalizing and insistent consumptive cultural ethos, which he refers to as the "McWorld" we all live in.
Barber is speaking to American culture in general, not the church. He proceeds, however, to think of a solution, "the only road of resistance," which he
finds to be "dogmatic religious critiques" of the "McWorld" culture. He even
speaks specifically of "Christian resistors," those who are skeptical of consumer culture and consequently avoid getting entangled in it. Barber may be
on to something. Charles A. McDaniel in *God and Money* spends a great deal
of time castigating the church for its assumptive adaptation of capitalist structures. At one point he indicts the church for its growing consensus of conformity to market ethics and market practices, claiming, "It's not capitalism per
se but rather the intensely individualistic and rationalistic character of modern capitalism that threatens Christianity's moral system and its conception
of the person." He not only tears down, he also seeks to build up by pointing
to an alternative, what McDaniel calls a "redemptive economy." David Fitch
also speaks of "redeemed economics," which requires a "Christian community to be *in* but not *of* the world." Katherine Turpin similarly speaks of the
church as a community providing a "lifelong or ongoing conversion" that
helps "branded" adolescents escape from "the dominant life script provided
by their consumerist context." A decade earlier Jim Wallis spoke of "commu-

---

[28]Billy Graham, *Just as I Am: The Autobiography of Billy Graham* (New York: Harper Collins, 1997),
pp. 37-38. It's interesting to compare this testimony of his with 2 Corinthians 2:17.

nity economics," cutting against Western capitalism and "market economics," which have damaged individuals, people groups and races, and the environment. In other words, it's quite noble for individual Christians to live as strangers and aliens, cultural resisters in consumer culture. It's another thing altogether for the church to take on the larger task of asking how it can respond to consumer culture and its dehumanizing and oppressive effects on both people and ecology. A very large task and a difficult one to be sure. But one that is worth some attention nevertheless.[29]

The commodification of Christianity not only exploits and subjects the faith to the cultural form of consumer capitalism, but it also sentimentalizes and trivializes faith. In "Inspirations: A Celebration of Faith," a catalog aimed at a Christian market by the Oriental Trading Company, parents, Christian school teachers and Sunday school teachers can avail themselves of all sorts of products for Christmas, home décor, and gifts for the whole year. On page 14 of the Holiday 2006 edition of the catalog, among the "affordable and inspirational gifts," would-be buyers could even treat themselves to "Vinyl Nativity Rubber Duckies." At $5.95 a dozen, who wouldn't want rubber ducky versions of Joseph, Mary, baby Jesus and the rest of the nativity cast? This is taking the doctrine of the incarnation to an all-time low.

One of the chapters in Timothy Beal's *Roadside Religion* recalls his family trip to Golgotha Fun Park in Cave City, Kentucky, and Biblical Mini Golf in Lexington. Golgotha Fun Park is a miniature golf course of eighteen holes that tell the biblical tale that runs from creation to resurrection. Beal, however, couldn't get over the cognitive dissonance caused by the name, "Golgatha Fun Park." The word *Golgatha* literally means the place of the skull. As Beal intones, it "doesn't exactly go with 'fun.' " The miniature golf at Lexington Ice Center and Sports Complex, however, sports fifty-four holes, with one course devoted to the Old Testament, one to the New and one to miracles. Beal finds further cognitive dissonance in the bringing together of the pro-

---

[29]Benjamin R. Barber, *Consumed: How Markets Corrupt Children, Infantalize Adults, and Swallow Citizens Whole* (New York: Norton, 2007), pp. 259, 204; Charles A. McDaniel, *God & Money: The Moral Challenge of Capitalism* (Lanham, Md.: Rowman & Littlefield, 2007), p. 310; David F. Fitch, *The Great Giveaway: Reclaiming the Mission of the Church from Big Business, Parachurch Organizations, Psychotherapy, Consumer Capitalism, and Other Modern Maladies* (Grand Rapids: Baker, 2005), pp. 153-79; Katherine Turpin, *Branded: Adolescents Converting from Consumer Faith* (Cleveland: Pilgrim Press, 2006), pp. 72-76; and Jim Wallis, *The Soul of Politics: Beyond "Religious Right" and "Secular Left"* (San Diego: Harcourt, Brace, 1995), pp. 197-209.

found and the trivial, observing, "With biblical mini-golf, then, the sacred narrative, The Greatest Story Ever Told, meets one of the most trivial of all American amusements." He illustrates his point with a run-down of these biblical mini-golf courses, "Here biblical narrative is reduced to a series of green-carpeted putting greens with Noah instead of Tom Thumb, a burning bush instead of a windmill, and an empty tomb instead of a bottomless hole." This leaves Beal to make a final, rather compelling, observation and to ask some final, rather urgent questions: "American evangelical Christianity . . . tends to be the most liberal of Christianities when it comes to its appropriating and adapting tradition to the popular interests and consumer demands of the secular mainstream. . . . What keeps it from becoming a complete carnivalization of tradition? Does it ultimately sacrifice the sacred, so to speak, in the name of spreading its Gospel?" Beal leaves these questions unanswered.[30]

American evangelicals, immersed in consumer culture, rarely even ask such questions. The spreading of the gospel at all costs, literally at times, trumps any such self-reflection and self-criticism that questions like Beal's raise. American evangelicals, however, should be asking such questions. They also need, unlike Beal, to offer answers. In those answers we may find that Jesus, the second person of the Trinity, doesn't belong as a vinyl rubber ducky, and neither does he belong on a bracelet.

[30]Beale, *Roadside Religion*, pp. 72, 76, 84, 87.

8

JESUS ON THE RIGHT WING

Christ and Politics in America

Christ, because he changed my heart.

GEORGE W. BUSH,
ON HIS MOST SIGNIFICANT INFLUENCE
IN POLITICAL PHILOSOPHY

God talk is nothing new in the realm of American politics. The founders capitalized on religious language as have their children since. "Every [presidential] inaugural address, except George Washington's very brief second one, acknowledged God and invoked his blessing on the nation," writes Scott Smith in his monumental study of the presidency and faith. But in the 1970s, American religio-political rhetoric took a decisive evangelical turn, punctuated by Jimmy Carter's declaration of being born again. Journalists scrambled to understand the meaning of this new-to-their-ears moniker, and Jody Powell, Carter's campaign press secretary, quite unexpectedly found himself schooling the press pool on the finer points of Southern Baptist theology.[1]

The four presidents since Carter have been sure to follow suit with such born-again talk, with the Episcopalian among them doing so without all that much bravado. Then, in a debate among Republican presidential candidates in Iowa in 1999, American religio-political rhetoric took yet another decisive turn in the evangelical direction as it moved from God talk to born-again talk to Jesus talk. Then-Governor George Bush responded to a question concerning which political philosopher or thinker each candidate most identified by declaring, "Christ, because he changed my heart." Pundits

---

[1] Gary Scott Smith, *Faith & the Presidency: From George Washington to George W. Bush* (New York: Oxford University Press, 2006), p. 5. William Martin, *With God on Our Side: The Rise of the Religious Right in America* (New York: Broadway Books, 1996), p. 149.

speculated that Bush knew of no alternatives, political philosophy not being his strong suit. Others saw within his answer the shrewd political calculations of one who knew he could win the White House on the basis of the evangelical vote—something he had learned in vetting the memos prepared by Doug Mead concerning the evangelical voting block as George W. worked on his father's first and only successful bid for the presidency. Others still took his words at face value, seeing Bush as not only one who indeed was born again but also as one who would take his faith commitment in all of its particulars seriously. He wouldn't, to use biblical terminology, be hiding his light under a bushel.[2]

Regardless of how Bush's statement is interpreted, one thing stands clear, Bush tilted the previously dominant but generic religious rhetoric in American politics to a specific religious rhetoric. In other words, *God* had always made appearances in American political rhetoric, but now there would be many sightings of *Jesus.* No less than *Newsweek,* in its coverage of the 2006 midterm elections, had an American-flag-wrapped cross next to the headline "The Politics of Jesus" on its cover. The pages between the magazine's cover were not discussing Christianity in general. The stories were all centered on evangelicals and "their long path to political power." If politicians are talking about Jesus more than ever before, so too are pastors talking about politics in an unprecedented fashion. De Tocqueville might have said that "American priests keep their distance from public affairs" in 1835, but no one could legitimately make such a claim today.[3]

This move from a more generic or broadly conceived God talk to a narrower Jesus talk is but representative of many shifts from the broad to the narrow in the religious rhetoric in politics. We may add to the list a shift from more generic goodness versus sin to more of a "God is on our side" versus the evildoer. We may also add a shift from "Judeo-Christian values"—left largely undefined—to a listing of specific Christian values and defined Christian virtues. Given that this shift to Jesus talk occurred alongside of the Republican Party's ascendancy, Jesus has been firmly planted on the "right wing"—and he

---

[2]Smith notes that while faith is evident throughout the tenures of the presidents, both a heightening and Christianizing of religious rhetoric occurs with George W. Bush (*Faith & the Presidency,* pp. 365-67).
[3]Lisa Miller, "An Evangelical Identity Crisis," *Newsweek,* November 13, 2006, p. 32; Alexis De Tocqueville, *Democracy in America* (London: Folio Society, 2002), 2:423.

can be seen there quite often. Yet, and likely because of such sightings, Jesus may also be seen on the left.[4]

This chapter offers some examples of these sightings, first of Jesus on the right wing and then of Jesus on the left. After which comes some concluding observations on evangelicalism and politics in America. In developing a taxonomy of those on the right and the left, certain issues obviously come into play. These include abortion; the death penalty and larger issues of criminal justice; gun control; homosexuality and gay marriage; war and peace, specifically the current "War on Terror" and the Iraq War; globalism versus nationalism, which raises the Christian Nation or Chosen Nation thesis or view, as well as the concomitant "demonizing" of our enemies; poverty, taxation, trade, and economic policy, both domestic and foreign; the environment and ecology; and technology and human identity/bioengineering, read the stem-cell debate. The right, of course, takes its stand on pro-life, pro-death penalty, pro-gun, antigay marriage, pro-war, antitax and pro-business. The right further tends to be for nationalism versus globalism, cautious in stressing the environment or ecological concerns and against stem-cell research. In general, the right also tends to favor politics of personal responsibility and social and fiscal conservatism. The left in its milder forms tends to favor a politics of social conservatism and fiscal liberalism. In its more radical manifestations, it favors both social and fiscal liberalism. (Many, though, have accused the Bush administration of abandoning fiscal restraints, while the Clinton administration was critiqued for its fiscal conservatism.) These manifestations tend to be less of an evangelical variety and more of a self-described theological liberal variety. The left further tends to, at the least, balance national concerns with global ones, which results in a different view of trade and economic policy and of the war, both on terror and in Iraq.

JESUS ON THE RIGHT WING

Among those persons and movements on the right, perhaps none has a longer or more colorful track record than Pat Robertson and his former associate Ralph Reed, their combined efforts resulting in the Christian Coalition.

---

[4]Of course, not all evangelicals are comfortable with this polarizing rhetoric trumping all religious discourse in the political arena. For example, Brendan Sweetman makes the case for using what he terms "lower-order rational beliefs" in the public square (*Why Politics Needs Religion: The Place of Arguments in the Public Square* [Downers Grove, Ill.: IVP Academic, 2006], pp. 187-216).

On his *700 Club* show, on November 10, 2005, Robertson warned that a divine strike might just be in order for Dover, Pennsylvania, adding that if it were to come, then they had better not turn to God for help. Robertson spoke of such judgments because of the ruling of the court case Kitzmiller et al. *v. Dover Area School District*, concerning the use of a textbook that advocated intelligent design. The case was hailed as "Scopes II," hearkening back to the showdown between William Jennings Bryan and Clarence Darrow in a courtroom in Dayton, Tennessee, in 1925. In Dover the court ruled against the school board and then, adding insult to injury, voters ousted the members at the polls. So Robertson thundered down invectives on the whole town. On hearing it, one of the newly minted school board members said cleverly that he'd pray for Robertson, another flat-out called him a clown. Robertson has made similar imprecatory pronouncements regarding America's impending judgment for its immoral practices, including abortion and tolerating, if not promoting, homosexuality and the "gay agenda." Reed tends to be more circumspect than his former boss. In fact, Reed ironically extols the virtues of the Christian Coalition as a group not made up of the clergy-related guard, but it rather takes its board members from the ranks of "business men and women, political operatives, physicians and attorneys." It may very well be that this new coalition of nonclergy religious conservatives have also added a heavy dose of economic issues, meaning taxes and tort reform, as well as politics of personal responsibility, to the religious right's platform.[5]

Rivaling Robertson and Reed is Jerry Falwell and his Moral Majority, a grass-roots movement that catapulted religious conservatives into the political arena and likely resulted in Reagan's terms in the White House. Falwell, before his death in 2007, promoted nationalism as a significant feature in the religious right's platform. His comments on the war on terror on CNN's *Late Edition with Wolf Blitzer* on October 24, 2004: "You've got to kill the terrorists before the killing stops. And I'm for the president to chase them all over the world. If it takes ten years, blow them all away in the name of the Lord." Richard Land, when asked by Terrie Gross (the host of National Public Radio's *Fresh Air*) for a Christian response to the "collateral" casualties of Iraqi civilians due to the war on terror played out in their country, replied, "I'm glad

---

[5]Ralph Reed, *Active Faith: How Christians Are Changing the Soul of American Politics* (New York: Free Press, 1996).

it's there and not here." It should be stressed that Land, who is the president of the Ethics and Religious Liberty Commission of the Southern Baptist Convention, was asked to give the *Christian* response, not the American, political or military response.

Also situated on the right politically is James Dobson and his Focus on the Family empire with a 2006 budget of 151.5 million dollars, including the Family Research Council and Focus on the Family Action—which does not have tax-exempt status, freeing it for its explicit political function. Dobson has been dubbed a Republican Party power broker. He has largely focused on issues revolving around the family. He sees activist courts as one of the nation's leading problems. "Right now," he told *U.S. News & World Report*'s religion editor Jeffery L. Sheler, "the courts are determined to redesign the family." Dobson also sees evangelical politicians as the solution. While he has repeatedly spoken of the limits of politics to accomplish righteous ends, he also has spent a lot of time and money doing just that. Focus on the Family Action, which is self-described as not a political action committee (PAC), claims to not actually endorse or oppose candidates. However, its website immediately, after the recent mid-term elections, noted, in its attempt to make lemonade from the bag of lemons the voters handed it, that the Republicans who were social conservatives fared well, while the moderates were the more easy targets—not congruous to my state's ousted senator's (Rick Santorum's) ears. All this to say, Dobson and the Focus on the Family empire put a lot of stock in elections.[6]

Jeffery Sheler closes his discussion of Dobson and the Focus on the Family empire by telling a parable of sorts. As he leaves the Focus headquarters in Colorado Springs, he meets up with the Groff family from Lancaster, Pennsylvania, who stopped by the Focus complex while on vacation. "We think the world of Dr. Dobson," the Groffs freely told Sheler, recalling how Dobson's advice came to their aid again and again as they raised their family. As Sheler prodded a bit concerning the seemingly political turn Dobson has taken, they confessed that they have listened to him and followed his advice less. "When a preacher or some other Christian leader I admire really gets going on the political aspects," Sheler cites Mrs. Groff, "they cross a line, and it really turns me off." I mention this because some reading my critique of Dobson may object. (Not something I have to guess at, since readers of drafts of this chapter

---

[6]Jeffery L. Sheler, *Believers: A Journey into Evangelical America* (New York: Viking, 2006), p. 78.

already did.) They may object because it appears to dismiss Dobson's contribution over the decades as evangelicalism's family and marriage counselor. Others may object that I have him hanging on the same line, so to speak, as Robertson or Reed. Others may object because they still see Dobson and his political efforts as stemming the tide of evil and secularism in America. Instead of criticizing him, many in the evangelical camp applaud his courage in publicly proclaiming virtue and the law of God. I think, however, that Sheler's encounter with the Groffs in the Focus on the Family parking lot helps here. The Groffs were not dismissive, just uncomfortable with the turn (and the tenor perhaps) that Dobson has taken. Regardless of how Dobson's political turn gets interpreted, the fact remains, Dobson has situated himself as a Republican Party (until he bolts, at least) power broker, espousing a political agenda that, while stressing family values, appears to some to be too closely connected to fiscal conservatism. While some in the evangelical camp applaud Dobson, others are leery of his platform and his politics. One could also argue that while Dobson has been successful in the election of conservative candidates, he may have been less successful in accomplishing his conservative agenda. His disillusionment with the candidates he helped get elected can be seen in, again, his threat to leave the Party.[7]

As one final example of Jesus on the right wing, let me venture outside of those whose primary profession is in the church or parachurch. This would be General William Boykin, Undersecretary of Defense for Intelligence, and a leader among the so-called hawks in the Bush administration. Boykin appeared in churches and before religious organizations in uniform declaring the Iraq War a virtual Christian jihad. He also famously interpreted the divine hand of providence when he said that George W. Bush is "in the White House because God put him there for such a time as this." Boykin's appearances and rhetoric recall the patriotic sermons emanating from the American colonies' pulpits during the Revolution or from both Northern and Southern pulpits during the Civil War. Then, our present allies, the British, or even our fellow citizens were the Philistines and the Amalekites.[8]

---

[7]Sheler, *Believers*, pp. 82-83. Ray Suarez argues that the religious right as a whole, not just Dobson, has been more successful in winning elections than accomplishing a political agenda.

[8]See "Rumsfeld Defends General Who Commented on War and Satan," CNN.com/U.S., October 17, 2003 <www.cnn.com/2003/US/10/16/rumsfeld.boykin.ap>. See also Ellis Sandoz, ed., *Political Sermons of the American Founding Era, 1730-1805* (Indianapolis: Liberty Fund, 1998).

In our current cultural climate of the red state/blue state divide, such rhetoric intensifies the polarizing effect. Just as there are discernable divides in American culture, so too there is a growing divide among evangelicals. In other words, the right wing isn't the only place where Jesus makes appearances in American politics. He may also be spotted on the left. When one widens the net beyond evangelicalism to include broader camps of American Christianity or American religion, the divide becomes sharper, deeper and wider.

JESUS ON THE LEFT WING

Rod Dreher, author of the surprisingly well-selling *Crunchy Cons: The New Conservative Counter-Culture and Its Return to Roots* (2006) sums up the criticism aimed at those on the right who have laid claim to Jesus when he notes how odd it is that the religious right limits its political concerns vis-à-vis the teachings of Jesus. The crunchy con, Dreher counters, sees a more holistic politics. Typically, that "something more" relates to poverty issues. David Callahan, author of *The Moral Center* concurs. He draws attention to the noble efforts by some evangelicals, particularly referring to a group of evangelicals who were arrested for civil disobedience while holding a prayer vigil for a "moral budget." The police played the part of Scrooge, as the *New York Times* ran the headline, during Christmas 2005. He also cites Marvin Olasky, author of the phrase "compassionate conservatism." Yet Callahan remains less than convinced that, on the whole, evangelicals take poverty issues seriously.[9]

Economic issues also literally drive Jim Wallis's criticism of the religious right. He has lent his support to the campaign started by Jim Ball, the president of the Evangelical Environmental Network, which offers a twist on the WWJD? asking instead What Would Jesus Drive? This was a clear signal that Jesus would be welcomed on the left, in terms of environmental issues. Wallis's approach takes the big-picture look at a Christian economics that would address poverty, corporate abuse, issues of business and the environment, and also the economics of race relations. He makes a profound observation concerning some on the right who view poverty not as a result of structural issues but as a direct result of morally deviant behavior. Wallace intones, "To blame all of them"—which would include single mothers, gays and lesbians—

---

[9]Rod Dreher, *Crunchy Cons,* 2nd ed. (New York: Three Rivers Press, 2006), p. 181.

"for the breakdown of the family is not only mean, but also, frankly, stupid."
Wallis, though, may not like being associated with the left. He's quick to point
out that the left has its flaws too. Further, in his books *The Soul of Politics* and
God's Politics, he argues for a middle way between the liberal left and the religious right. Nevertheless, his stance on economics, the environment and
race—issues of structural sin—certainly looks to those on the right like he's
on the left. The right further takes Wallace to be on the left when he talks
about the full culture of life versus the right's focus on abortion. The truth
may be that Wallis has forged a complex social outlook that is simply uncomfortable to those on the right. At any rate, Wallis is not alone; he is joined by
a host of others who find the right's insistence on abortion incongruous with
the right's gusto in commending the war on terror. On top of this, along with
many others on the evangelical left, Wallis opposes in principle the death penalty. Wallis, however, maintains his commitment—however unpopular with his
left-leaning friends as it may be—to the pro-life, anti-abortion stance.[10]

Wallis has difficulty, putting the matter differently, finding a home. In fact,
he would go so far as to say he has difficulty finding a home in both religion
and politics. He speaks of his own untimeliness, like the prophets. As an alternative to either an entrenched conservative or liberal religion, he holds to
a prophetic spirituality, which in turn provides him with plenty of fodder for
political engagement, which in turn he aims at greed, injustice, violence and
poverty.[11]

Randall Balmer has recently put Jesus on the left in his ode from a "jilted
lover," that is, his book *Thy Kingdom Come.* Balmer chastises evangelicals, especially Baptists, for deserting their heritage of a strong sense of separation of
church and state—it was in a reply to correspondence from Baptists that Jefferson, attempting to quell their fears, spoke of the notorious "wall of separation"
between church and state. Balmer even calls Roy Moore, Rick Scarborough,
Richard Land and Jerry Falwell "counterfeit Baptists." As for Balmer's own
take on the religiously charged political issues, he draws attention to the ambi-
guities concerning abortion—"the biblical case against abortion appears to be
somewhat less than obvious." What Balmer is really after is the so-called abor-

---

[10]Jim Wallis, *God's Politics: Why the Right Gets It Wrong and the Left Doesn't Get It* (New York: Harper-
SanFrancisco, 2005), p. 227.

[11]Jim Wallis, *The Soul of Politics: Beyond "Religious Right" and "Secular Left"* (San Diego: Harcourt,
Brace, 1995), pp. 47-53.

tion myth. Balmer contends that the religious right finds its genesis in the Bob Jones University tax case, stemming from its alleged discriminatory practices, and that later, only when a more noble cause was needed for the movement to rally around, did the leaders settle on abortion. Balmer then contends that when pro-life issues stalled in the 1990s, the right then turned to homosexuality as its rallying center. Balmer himself contends for a "radical notion of love" in the face of the religious right's politics of hate. In a later chapter, he castigates the right for ignoring environmental concerns. Balmer's thesis is surely to be contended by scholars and will undoubtedly generate a whole cottage industry of literature back and forth on its merits and demerits.[12]

The debate over greenhouse gas emissions has driven the wedge further between evangelicals on the left and right. The 2005 annual meeting program of the Evangelical Theological Society, a professional society of conservative theologians, biblical scholars and pastors, listed a number of papers on the global warming debate—this from a group that rarely enters the political arena. The papers sprang from an internecine debate between theologians and scientists, mostly within conservative evangelicalism, that were at odds over whether global warming was junk science or reality, and they were at odds over what to do about it. Some tried to argue that the Kyoto Protocol would be injurious to not only the American economy but to the economies of developing nations, while others pointed out that the ecological cost would be too great to not follow the Kyoto Protocol and that Christians have a responsibility for creation care. Again, Jim Wallis's question came to the foreground: What Would Jesus Drive?

The real firestorm came, even garnering national headlines and media coverage, when Richard Cizik, vice president for governmental affairs for the National Association of Evangelicals (NAE), backed the Evangelical Climate Initiative, written in January 2006 and unveiled in the next month. This proposal is the tangible result of Cizik's commitment to "Creation Care." The proposal also prompted James Dobson to call for Cizik's rather unceremonial ouster. Dobson felt the initiative distracted valuable resources and attention

[12]Randall Balmer, *Thy Kingdom Come: How the Religious Right Distorts the Faith and Threatens America, An Evangelical's Lament* (New York: Basic Books, 2006), pp. 68, 8, 14, 25, 144. The Bob Jones University tax case began with Bob Jones University *v.* Schultz in 1971. The case went before the U.S. Supreme Court in 1975, only to set off more disputes with the IRS and return to the U.S. Supreme Court in 1983.

from the true moral crises of our day. Dan Gilgoff adds, "Dobson wrote to NAE's Colorado Springs headquarters calling for Cizik's firing. . . . The NAE expressed its surprise at Dobson's request," seeing as Dobson "is a member neither of the organization's board of directors nor its executive committee." Jerry Falwell joined in as well, declaring from his Lynchburg pulpit in the same month the initiative was unveiled, "1 am raising a flag of opposition to this alarmism about global warming and urging all believers to refuse to be duped by these 'earthism' worshippers." Evangelical scholars, theologians, lawyers and scientists also weighed in, forming the Interfaith Stewardship Alliance, which in turn issued responses to the Evangelical Climate Initiative. Amidst the ruckus, Paul De Vries, a board member of the NAE, said, "It ought to be God's agenda, not the Republican party agenda that drives us," before making an opaque reference to Dobson's empire, "We're actually tired of being represented by people with a very narrow focus. We want to have a focus as big as God's focus." Cizik, like Wallis, articulates a complex social agenda for evangelicals, perhaps simply too complex for some.[13]

Beyond those self-described evangelicals, other broadly defined Christians are putting Jesus on the left (the far left, if you like). Here the pro-life position is called into question. Falwell's nemesis, Barry Lynn, author of *Piety and Politics: The Right Wing Assault on Religious Freedom,* argues that the view that abortion is murder is a "theological accretion, not something derived from the interpretation of scripture." He also adds, by the way, Scripture does not "denounce condoms by name."[14]

Linda Seger agrees. Her book *Jesus Rode a Donkey: Why Republicans Don't Have a Corner on Christ* extols the liberal values of Jesus versus the conservative politics of the "dominionists"—which she defines as those who wish to "reclaim America for Christ, whatever the cost," counting among their number Jerry Falwell, D. James Kennedy and David Limbaugh. Jesus, Seger

[13]"Climate Change: An Evangelical Call to Action," Evangelical Climate Initiative, January 2006; Adelle Banks, "Dobson, Others Seek Ouster of NAE Vice President," Religion News Service, posted on ChristianityToday.com, March 2, 2007 <www.christianitytoday.com/ct/2007/marchweb-only/109-53.0.html>; Dan Gilgoff, *The Jesus Machine: How Dobson, Focus on the Family, and Evangelical America Are Winning the Culture War* (New York: St. Martin's Press, 2007), pp. 268-74; E. Calvin Beisner et al. "A Call to Truth, Prudence, and Protection of the Poor: An Evangelical Response to Global Warming," Interfaith Stewardship Alliance, 2006; and Paul De Vries, cited in "Global Warming Gap Among Evangelicals Widens," CNN.com, March 14, 2007 <www.cnn.com/2007/POLITICS/03/14/evangelical.rift/index.html>.
[14]Barry Lynn, *Piety & Politics* (New York: Harmony Books, 2006), p. 181.

declares, opposed the death penalty (as seen in the woman taken in adultery episode), and therefore he lines up squarely with the Democratic Party. As for abortion, this issue is much more complex than the right makes it out to be, she argues, adding that the prophets, Jesus, Paul and the rest of the New Testament writers fall silent on the issue.[15]

The near silence of the biblical authors also extends to the issue of homosexuality, contends Seger. Jesus is entirely silent on it, and Paul, while he may talk of homosexuality, is silent on the issue of gay marriage. Out of the entire Bible, she contends, fewer than ten verses address homosexuality. She apparently finds the social science research not to be silent on the issue, which she seems to be affected by when she muses, "We don't know why some people are homosexuals."[16]

Kathleen Kennedy Townsend, devout Roman Catholic and member of America's most entrenched family on the political left, also gives attention to the biblical silence on issues near to the heart of the right. She begins by castigating the church for neglecting to fight for social justice, throwing a wide net that encompasses both Roman Catholics and evangelical Protestants. "What kind of Christianity," she asks, "blinds us to the needs of the homeless, the hungry, the stranger—the least among us?" She proceeds to chastise the church for privatizing religion and consequently reducing the church's prophetic voice merely to issues of personal sexual behavior. Then she indicts both evangelicals and her "own Catholic Church" for "allow[ing] its social agenda to be trumped by an all-consuming focus on contraception, abortion, same-sex marriage, and embryonic cell research—none of which are mentioned in the Bible." Indeed, how amazing that Paul neglected to speak of embryonic cell research. Even high school composition teachers warn their students about the fault of arguing from silence.[17]

Robin Myers also chastises the church for not living as resident aliens; they have become too comfortable with a narrow understanding of political engagement. He sees the Sermon on the Mount "missing in action" in the way the church relates to social issues, which ones they engage and which ones they ignore. "What Jesus did talk about," Myers advances, "was the failure of public pi-

---

[15]Linda Seger, *Jesus Rode a Donkey* (Avon, Mass.: Adams Media, 2006), pp. 15, 28, 113.
[16]Ibid., p. 138.
[17]Kathleen Kennedy Townsend, *Failing America's Faithful: How Today's Churches Are Mixing God with Politics and Losing Their Way* (New York: Warner Books, 2007), pp. 18-19.

ety to manifest itself in meaningful private compassion." His read on the religious right is that such compassion is missing. Not only are compassion and the Sermon on the Mount missing but, Myers contends, based on stacks of correspondence he receives from the religious and not-so-religious alike, Jesus is missing too: "The amazing thing to me about this diverse group of people, churched and unchurched alike, was how much they *miss Jesus!* How much they want him back." Myers proceeds to align Jesus with a left-leaning agenda.[18]

And then there is the very angry Clint Willis, whose books are titled *The I Hate Republicans Reader; The I Hate Corporate America Reader; The I Hate George W. Bush Reader* and the declaratively stated *Jesus Is Not a Republican: The Religious Right's War on America.* Willis concludes the latter's preface by explaining, "What do I mean when I say that Jesus is not a Republican? I mean that Jesus as I imagine and know him would not support policies that profit the strong at the expense of the weak." If the selections in the book are any indicator, however, Willis means far more than simply issues of economic justice. In fact, his reader is a definitive survey of Jesus on the left, ranging from economics and poverty issues to issues of nationalism, the death penalty, abortion, homosexuality and gay marriage. Willis isn't the only one who's angry. Dan Wakefield comes out with both guns blazing as he intones that Jesus has been hijacked by the right. "Millions of Christians like me," writes Wakefield, "are appalled by this distortion of our faith which only three decades ago stood for peace, equality, healing, and compassion for society's outcasts—the issues that comprised the ministry of Jesus." He describes his book as telling the story of how the Christian faith "has been turned upside down to become a cultish kind of Christianity as dangerous as it is distorted, co-opted in the service of a right-wing political agenda that it serves." And like the others on the left, Wakefield sets out "to reclaim the Jesus of the Sermon on the Mount."[19]

TO SEE OURSELVES AS OTHERS SEE US

It was Robert Burns who famously and poetically put it best:

---

[18]Robin Myers, *Why the Christian Right Is Wrong* (San Francisco: Jossey-Bass, 2006), pp. 17, 183.

[19]Clint Willis and Nate Hardcastle, eds., *Jesus Is Not a Republican: The Religious Right's War on America* (New York: Avalon, 2005); Dan Wakefield, *The Hijacking of Jesus: How the Religious Right Distorts Christianity and Promotes Prejudice and Hate* (New York: Nation Books, 2006), pp. 1-3.

O would some Power the gift to give us,

To see ourselves as others see us.

To apply the matter directly: What have we gained from all of this political involvement since American God talk took its decisive evangelical and Jesus-centered turn? There are indeed plenty of answers. For, just as there is no shortage of appearances of Jesus on the right or the left, there is no lack of observations by a watching public. Recent books on the matter include Jeffery Sheler's *Believers*, Monique El-Faizy's *God and Country* and Ray Suarez's *The Holy Vote*, among others. These three authors are of interest since all of them claim to have an evangelical past but would not identify themselves as an evangelical in the present. These three also, while being straightforward and critical, tend to be sympathetic and fair.[20]

In his chapter on "God's Country," exploring the various evangelical institutions housed in Colorado and spotlighting Dobson's Focus on the Family, Jeffery Sheler makes a rather curious point. For all of his apparent cultural engagement, Dobson is portrayed as rather unengaged in culture. Sheler's conversation with Dobson also reveals the level of Dobson's political rhetoric and argument. In commenting on the lack of a lobbying voice for family values, Dobson says, "The possum growers of America have a lobbying voice, and everyone else who is trying to promote something, but the family is just ignored. Well we're not going to let that continue." Such rhetoric may play well for the radio audience but is likely to have little affect on people like Sheler, who was sitting across the table at the time, and is likely to have even less affect on someone who is poised to disagree with Dobson and Christianity.[21]

Sheler has Dobson sequestered in his Colorado Springs enclave—a city unto itself. "In Dobson's world," versus the real world, "ambiguity is error and

---

[20]Robert Burns, "To a Louse" (1786). I think the work of Michelle Goldberg, *Kingdom Coming: The Rise of Christian Nationalism* (New York: Norton, 2006), deserves mention. She looks for a "bellicose fundamentalism" that is asserting itself in American culture. She finds it at the 2005 Christian Home Educators of Colorado Conference. Her tour of the parking lot reveals that it "teem[s] with SUVs bearing Bush/Cheney decals, metallic Jesus fish, and magnetic Support Our Troops ribbons." She further positions that the American culture on which the right is asserting itself is precariously placed between two fundamentalisms, the religious right in the West and Islam in the East. She also sees a culture war in contemporary America, between medieval (the right) and modern (everyone else in America) values (ibid., pp. 91, 210). Also consider Gregory Boyd's *The Myth of a Christian Nation: How the Quest for Political Power Is Destroying the Church* (Grand Rapids: Zondervan, 2006) and Balmer's *Thy Kingdom Come*.

[21]Sheler, *Believers*, p. 79. See also Rodney Clapp's critique of the "family values campaign" in *Border Crossings* (Grand Rapids: Brazos, 2000), pp. 110-25.

compromise is defeat. There are no," alluding to the view out Dobson's office window, "hazy horizons in God's country—only stark snow-tipped mountains and azure skies that clearly define the boundaries of heaven and earth." Sheler also notes how pervasive Dobson's products are in the lives of his followers. For all of their speaking to America, Sheler concludes, they are essentially speaking to themselves, establishing the parallel institutionalism that James Davison Hunter describes. For all of the professed cultural engagement, Sheler contends that Dobson and Focus on the Family are ironically rather insular.[22]

Dan Gilgoff offers another angle of criticism of Dobson and those on the right who focus on family issues and on individual sexual morality, avoiding entering larger humanitarian discussions. Gilgoff chides Dobson, or at least he stands back to let others chide Dobson, when it comes to issues of climate control and environmental ethics. Gilgoff also observes a similar stance by Dobson on issues of international human rights. Gilgoff lets Michael Horowitz, whose job as general counsel in the Reagan White House Office of Management and Budget Dobson helped to save through a letter-writing campaign, offer the criticism. Horowitz notes that Dobson would have him on the show to talk of the persecution of Christian communities around the world, while "avoiding broader human rights issues." "I would say," recalls Horowitz, "wait a minute—what about discussing Christian involvement in stopping the trafficking of women or ending prison rape or taking on the North Korean regime—why only focus on ending religious and anti-Christian persecution?" Horowitz concludes, "He tends to be into a much more parochial set of issues." Horowitz further muses that Dobson's reluctance to join in the fight regarding broader human rights issues would require alliances with those on the left, alliances Dobson would just as soon not make.[23]

Monique El Faizy, a self-described former evangelical, makes another ironic observation, namely that, while evangelicals have indeed influenced the nation, "so, too, has America made its mark on evangelicals. They now look, sound, and in many areas—though obviously not all—think like the rest of us." She's talking about our economics, our use of power, our nationalism and our methodology,

---

[22]Sheler, *Believers*, p. 84.
[23]Michael Horowitz, quoted in Dan Gilgoff, *The Jesus Machine: How Dobson, Focus on the Family, and Evangelical America Are Winning the Culture War* (New York: St. Martin's Press, 2007), pp. 280-82.

political and otherwise. Perhaps that is to say that the (mostly right) evangelical political and cultural engagement has been somewhat akin to straining out gnats while swallowing camels. To be sure, evangelicals, through fighting for their distinctives, have "redefined the mainstream." Yet evangelicals also have, in her view, donned the trappings of the mainstream, coming to resemble a secular America. Hers is a complex but not contradictory thesis.[24]

Ray Suarez also has an evangelical past. His final thoughts on the matter at hand are instructive:

> Religion has turned out to be a potent tool in rousing people and driving them to join winning electoral alliances. Religion has been less successful in helping us create the blessed community, the [community that] people on all sides of the hottest debates in our common life hope and pray for.

Again, as Burns put it, it is a great gift to see ourselves as others see us. Listening to the critics of evangelicalism, both sympathetic and not, may go a long way to helping see blind spots. Perhaps evangelicals especially have such blind spots because of putting Jesus, whether it's on the left or the right, in the wrong place.[25]

LIVING WITH THE MONSTER

Like Dr. Frankenstein, the church now has to live with the monster of political entanglement that it has created. In fact, some contend that not only American evangelicals have to do so but Americans in general will have to as well. Kevin Phillips, in his bestselling *American Theocracy*, notes, "Few questions will be more important to the twenty-first century United States than whether the renascent religion and its accompanying political hubris will be carried on the nation's books as an asset or as a liability." The question might be a bit too hyped; it is, after all, only the beginning of what promises to be a long century. Nevertheless, his question is still a good one. And we can turn it toward the twenty-first-century church in America: What will the renascent religion and political coalition and engagement be on the church's books? An asset, or a liability?[26]

---

[24]Monique El-Faizy, *God and Country: How Evangelicals Have Become America's New Mainstream* (New York: Bloomsbury, 2006), pp. 238-40.

[25]Ray Suarez, *The Holy Vote: The Politics of Faith in America* (New York: HarperCollins, 2006), p. 299.

[26]Kevin Phillips, *American Theocracy: The Peril and Politics of Radical Religion, Oil, and Borrowed Money in the 21st Century* (New York: Viking, 2006), p. 99.

The following four observations are an attempt to decipher this dilemma.

The first observation concerns the need of evangelicals to avoid the seductive siren of power. Cal Thomas and Ed Dobson leveled this charge in their book *Blinded By Might*, where they (the particular chapter in view is by Thomas) make the point that evangelical and Christian leaders have compromised their spiritual integrity due to the seduction of power. They reference Henri Nouwen's comment that power functions as an easy substitute for the harder task of love. And they cite Pat Robertson and the Moral Majority as examples of those seduced by power who then themselves abuse power. Later Dobson and his organization also come into the purview.[27]

Consider also David Kuo's controversial kiss-and-tell *Tempting Faith*, which is about his days in the White House's Office of Faith-Based and Community Initiatives. In it Kuo makes a point that may largely go unnoticed by those for whom it is intended. "All too often," Kuo observes, "when put before power, Christian leaders wilt." They are, he argues, seduced by power. Kuo falls back on the experiences of a pre-born-again Chuck Colson for support, as Colson remembered how easily religious leaders were won over by merely being ushered into the Roosevelt Room and then into the Oval Office. He then concludes, "On the whole, of all the groups I dealt with, I found religious leaders the most naive about politics." Colson takes a stab at explaining such naiveté before he offers one final possible reason, "Or, most worrisome of all, they may simply like to be around power." Kuo then makes the connection to today's evangelical leaders, mostly the religious right, who have so enjoyed their seat at the table that they either are incredibly forgiving of politicians' failure to deliver on their promises, or they wield their power as a threat. As for the latter, consider Dobson's rather bold and public threat to "bolt" from the Republican Party, to which Dobson added, "And if I go, I will do everything I can to take as many people with me as possible." He certainly would not have joined the Democrats, doubtful he would have given his list over to Ralph Nader, either. So what would he have done?[28]

[27]Cal Thomas and Ed Dobson, *Blinded by Might* (Grand Rapids: Zondervan, 1999), pp. 49-83.

[28]David Kuo, *Tempting Faith: An Inside Story of Political Seduction* (New York: Free Press, 2006), pp. 172. Colson is quoted in ibid.; James Dobson, quoted in Michael Gerson, "A Righteous Indignation: James Dobson—Psychologist, Radio Host, Family Values Crusader—Is Set to Topple the Political Establishment," *U.S. News & World Report*, May 4, 1998, pp. 20-24, 29.

Not only can evangelicals be seduced by power, we can also be seduced by speech, by rhetoric. This is true not only of the present but also of the past. The advocates of "return to the Christian America" fall in here. I once heard a speech by a very conservative, evangelical congressman, delivered at a Christian organization's banquet. He said, "I know there are some who denounce Thomas Jefferson as not being a Christian." But, he informed us, "I have read some of his prayers"—indicating that he had access to documents a largely ignorant public did not—"and I can tell you for certain that he is a Christian." (My first thought was sheer anxiety, because he was also in the middle of reading an omnibus appropriations bill and by now I was quite suspicious of his hermeneutical ability.) Lost are the words and the days of Woodrow Wilson, "The silent gospel reaches further than the grandest rhetoric."

One of the ways to avoid both the seduction of power and the seduction of speech is to remember the spiritual nature of the kingdom as well as the limitations of government. It would be a good day for American evangelicals if parts of Augustine's classic text *City of God* were compulsory reading. Also it might not hurt for those outside of Anabaptist traditions to read a little John Howard Yoder. I'm not advocating all of Yoder (or all of *City of God* for that matter). But, especially since most American evangelicals are not likely to instinctively agree with Yoder and the Anabaptists, evangelicals should listen to what they have to say and seriously consider some of it. Having been seduced by power, evangelicals have unwittingly, perhaps, succumbed to the wrong agenda. They have consequently blended in a little too much, losing their distinctive, prophetic voice in the process. John Howard Yoder called the church to its role to "witness to the world" as "resident aliens" and not as the "established power." P. Travis Kroeker put Yoder's view this way: "The witness of the church . . . is precisely to witness to the flaws in Babel-like unity, rooted in coercive, centralized, sacral authority, the idolatrous politics of empire that substitutes human for divine kingship and that tries to take charge of human history via external conquest." Arne Rasmusson calls this Yoder's "politics of diaspora." This isn't a politics of surrender. It's just a different way of looking at how to bring the truth that Jesus Christ is Lord of the universe to bear on the reality of things seen. It's the subversion and not the adoption of power politics. Stanley Hauerwas well summarizes Yoder's contribution: "Prior to Yoder the subject of Christian ethics in America was always America."[29]

Standing outside as a witness and a prophetic voice can be valuable for the church as it follows its mission. D. G. Hart has recently argued for such an approach in his *A Secular Faith: Why Christianity Favors the Separation of Church and State.* Hart extols the "otherworldly" nature of Christianity, criticizing those Christians who "have tried to use their faith for political engagement," noting that such attempts "have generally distorted Christianity." Hart provides the example of the *New Republic's* coverage of then Texas Governor George W. Bush's declaration of June 11, 2000, as "Jesus Day." The magazine's editorial, in the words of Hart, "suggested that Bush did not glorify but 'cheapened Jesus,' because the reason for Christ's specialness is not simply his contribution to social service but his status as second person of the Trinity." Hart concludes, "Attempts to employ the sacred and eternal for the common and temporal end up trivializing faith, which is 'the certain fate of religion in the public sphere.' " Co-opting Christianity for the cause of politics does not serve to elevate but reduce Christianity, to relegate it to a place it does not deserve.[30]

Of course, there are those who disagree with Hart and Yoder, and even with Augustine for that matter. These dissenting voices would contend that evangelicals are not to be faulted for engaging in politics, they're just guilty of too selective of an application of their Christianity to politics. Obery M. Hendricks, who would likely put Jesus on the left, has made some observations of his own worth noting. His interpretations of the biblical text are helpful to me, in my context as a rural and formerly suburbanite, middle-class, white male. I don't agree with all of his conclusions, but he raises a significant point largely lost on those putting Jesus on the right. He contends that poverty serves significantly as the backdrop for the Gospels, as do the social factors of oppression and marginalization. For those weaned on interpreting Luke's "Blessed are you who are poor" (Lk 6:20) by harmonizing it with Matthew's "Blessed

---

[29]John Howard Yoder, *The Politics of Jesus: Vicit Agnus Noster,* 2nd ed. (Grand Rapids: Eerdmans, 1994); Arne Rasmussen, "The Politics of Diaspora: The Post-Christendom Theologies of Karl Barth and John Howard Yoder," *God, Truth, and Witness: Engaging Stanley Hauerwas,* ed. L. Gregory Jones, Reinhard Hutter and C. Rosalee Velloso Ewell (Grand Rapids: Brazos, 2005), pp. 88-111; and Stanley Hauerwas, *A Better Hope: Resources for a Church Confronting Capitalism, Democracy, and Postmodernity* (Grand Rapids: Brazos, 2000), p. 129.

[30]Darryl Hart, *A Secular Faith: Why Christianity Favors the Separation of Church and State* (Chicago: Ivan R. Dee, 2006), pp. 11-12.

are the poor *in spirit"* (Mt 5:3), Hendricks wants us to deal solely with Luke.
He further argues that bringing Jesus into the political conversation necessarily entails talking about poverty and structural or social sins. Hendricks even
proceeds to grade Ronald Reagan and George W. Bush against the politics of
Jesus. Neither receives a passing grade. For those evangelicals accustomed to
viewing Jesus as a Republican, Hendricks offers, at the least, a moment of
pause and a challenge to those who would identify him with a political and
economic ideology.[31]

Due to reasons of race, Hendricks may also approach the politics of Jesus
differently than those who see Jesus on the right wing. As an African American, Hendricks might be more sensitive to issues of social oppression, marginalization and poverty than white evangelicals. In fact, since the era of Reagan, though perhaps not as true since the Kerry-Bush presidential race, white
evangelicals have been perplexed by why many African American evangelicals are so wedded to the Democratic Party, given the party's platform of advocating the woman's right to choose on the abortion issue. Yet African
American evangelicals are as equally perplexed by the virtual identification
of white evangelicals with the Republican Party, given the GOP's economic
and social justice policies. The two sides are coming at the political issues
from the 1970s to today from two entirely different contexts. Allen Dwight
Callahan has recently argued for a distinctive reading of the Bible by African
Americans, arguing that the past context of slavery and Jim Crow segregation
have resulted in a fundamentally distinct African American hermeneutic.
This may very well account for the uniqueness of Hendricks's reading of the
Gospels. White American evangelicals, having been conditioned by a different set of cultural circumstances, naturally have a different hermeneutic. Obviously culture and cultural conditioning play a role in how we read the text,
how we interpret Jesus and how we employ Jesus.[32]

It might also serve well to mention the observation of Alan Storkey, speaking as a biblical scholar, on the matter. He notes, "Jesus has been portrayed
as a revolutionary, an independence fighter, a socialist, or a conservative. . . .
The Nazis asserted that Jesus was Aryan rather than Jew. . . . He was [further]

---

[31] Obery M. Hendricks, *The Politics of Jesus: Rediscovering the True Revolutionary Nature of Jesus'
Teachings and How They Have Been Corrupted* (New York: Doubleday, 2006).
[32] Allen Dwight Callahan, *The Talking Book: African Americans and the Bible* (New Haven, Conn.:
Yale University Press, 2006).

identified as a Marxist, a hippie, or a Thatcherite." Then Storkey notes, "From our vantage point it is sobering to see the way in which ideological contamination of the understanding of Jesus takes place." Indeed, these Jesus sightings are sobering. Evangelicals, however, should not assume that they somehow escape being guilty of the same things. As mentioned in previous chapters, Jesus comes to us in the biblical narratives as a rather full and complex character. Those who wish to enlist him in politics should take care that they allow for the full-orbed character of Jesus' own politics to speak.[33]

Further caution is in order when Jesus is appropriated by a particular political cause. History tends to be messy, ambiguous, which does not always sit well with those who like things clear and distinct. To avoid such messiness and ambiguity, we are often tempted to enlist Christ or God for our side—the temptation of the Christian nation impulse. In the Christian nation view, the lines between "us" and "them" become the lines of good versus evil. That may be a convenient place in which to stand; it certainly makes interpreting events easy. It is, however, a rather dangerous place to stand. Again, this hearkens back to the Christian America/chosen nation thesis. We forget that, unlike biblical history, we do not have accompanying revelation as a guide for our interpretation of current events. This does not deny providence—one of the favorite doctrines of the Christian-nation thesis. But it does deny the right to say, "Thus says the Lord of Hosts" about the affairs of our nation. Allowing for history to be messy and ambiguous doesn't always make for the best history, but it does serve well to keep us humble and humane. Demonizing our enemies, on the other hand, can lead to arrogance and abuse. Both are certainly not the order for the church or even for the Old Testament's theocratic nation.

A final observation is a bit of an alternative to such Jesus-charged politics, whether of the right or the left. Here the politics of Jonathan Edwards might help. Among other things, Edwards forged in my view (and this is shared by other interpreters of Edwards, such as Gerald McDermott, Roland Delattre and Paul Ramsey) a quite helpful distinction between true virtue and common morality. True virtue is that which pleases God, is produced by those regenerated by the Spirit and is tantamount to fulfilling the Law and the Prophets. Common morality is yet another thing. In the more typical language of theology, Edwards's common morality goes by the name common grace. Ed-

---

[33]Alan Storkey, *Jesus and Politics: Confronting the Powers* (Grand Rapids: Baker Academic, 2005), p. 9.

wards, the best of theologians who write on common grace, did not intend
common pejoratively when he spoke of common morality. That is, he did not
mean *common* as in vulgar or lesser. By *common,* he meant universal. As Paul
Ramsey declares, in Edwards's hands common morality is "a rather splendid
thing." Edwards also said something good about the word *morality.* He would
not agree with the expression "You can't legislate morality." Edwards would
counter that such a position denies the fabric of the universe. God in his common grace did not leave his creation without a moral compass.

Following Edwards's lead, perhaps we are better served to enter politics
from the basis of "common morality" than "true virtue," that is, from the politics of common grace rather than, with apologies to the likes of Obery Hendricks and John Howard Yoder, from the politics of Jesus. For one, politics is
the world of the public square, and our public square, whether we like it or
not, is a pluralistic one. This does not mean we cannot appeal to particularly
Christian notions. But it does mean that we look for those impulses of justice
and fairness that are universal as the basis of our political appeals and political
work. Brendan Sweetman has recently spoken of a similar approach that appeals to "lower-order rational beliefs." The opposite approach, the politics of
Jesus and higher-order beliefs, tends too easily to suffer from either manipu-
lating the gospel or allowing it to be manipulated. Again Hart observes, "Efforts to use Christianity for public or political ends fundamentally distort the
Christian religion."[34]

Hart dedicates his book "To the memory and legacy of J. Gresham Machen,"
due mostly to the fact that Machen espoused the exact sort of approach to
politics that Hart's book promotes. Machen had a profound space for politics
and political engagement, so long as such engagement occurred on the level
of the individual and not on the level of the church. For Machen, the type of
politicizing of the church that was going on in the 1910s and 1920s was dangerous. It wasn't only due to the fact that Machen liked his alcohol when virtually all of Protestantism vigorously supported prohibition. His overriding
fear was that the church would lose its message in the wake of political engagement. Machen also happened to espouse libertarianism, so he tended to
look to local and personal solutions for problems, keeping government at bay
and to a minimum. When it came to his own personal engagement in politics,

[34]Hart, *Secular Faith,* p. 16.

however, Machen by both exhortation and example made a case for intense involvement. He wrote letters in attempts to preserve the mountainous coasts of Maine. He appeared before the U.S. Congress to argue against the move from a Bureau of Education to the Department of Education. He even appeared before the Philadelphia City Council to argue against traffic signals. (I told you he was a libertarian.)[35]

Not all American evangelicals are comfortable with Machen's view of the church's role in politics, neither may they be comfortable with Edwards's "true virtue"-"common morality" distinction that I am advocating, but I think that American evangelicals, especially those "anxious about the empire," would do well to pause and consider these approaches. Our life of proclaiming the gospel and true virtue very well may be related to our obligations to live and proclaim "common morality," but they are not identical. It has been a longstanding tradition for United States presidents to choose the text that the Bible is opened to when they are sworn into office. Ronald Reagan, who before George W. Bush was the symbol of the religious right's success, chose 2 Chronicles 7:14: "If my people who are called by name, humble themselves, . . . " as his choice. This text plays perfectly into the Christian-nation thesis, and is typically employed by American evangelicals in a variety of pleas for God's direct blessing. That Reagan chose this text only further convinced the religious right that he was indeed God's choice for the post. Jimmy Carter, on the other hand, never really enjoyed the support of evangelicals, especially after he took office. Carter chose Micah 6:8:

> He has told you, O man, what is good;
> and what does the Lord require of you
> but to do justice and to love kindness,
> and to walk humbly with your God.

In other words, Jonathan Edwards, were he alive at the time, may very well have voted for Jimmy Carter (at least once).[36]

Thinking of our political engagement from a platform of common morality

---

[35]See D. G. Hart, *Defending the Faith: J. Gresham Machen and the Crisis of Conservative Protestantism in America* (Baltimore: Johns Hopkins University Press, 1994); and also Stephen J. Nichols, *J. Gresham Machen: A Guided Tour of His Life and Thought* (Phillipsburg, N.J.: P & R, 2004), pp. 137-52.

[36]To set the inaugural speeches of Carter and Reagan in a larger context, see Smith, *Faith & the Presidency*.

stresses justice and fairness, which went by the term *equity* in the history of political philosophy. It also stresses the underlying dignity of humanity as well as principles of stewardship and the cultivation of creation. It should be noted that the cultural mandate, Genesis 1:26-28, was given in a garden, which necessitates an ethic of cultivation, not consumption. All of these issues adumbrate the theological term "common grace." They also provide a rather substantial base for political activism. Calvin, in his discussion of civil government near the end of his *Institutes of the Christian Religion,* makes the point that the gospel can flourishes in a context of civil order, saying famously that it provides a sustaining environment for the religion of the Christian and upholds "humanity among men."[37]

CONCLUSION

The approach to evangelical political engagement, to living with the monster we created, outlined in these few pages dodges the question as to which wing of American politics Jesus belongs. Such dodging is purposeful. For in the end, he likely doesn't belong on either one. To be sure there are particular issues that are identified with the political left that would be a stretch to see Jesus advocating. Jim Wallis, Obery Hendricks and others have also made a fairly good case that there are issues on the right that would be difficult to connect to Jesus as well. No political party platform is nearly large enough to contain Christ and the full complement of his teachings. Even in Christ's own day attempts were made to enlist him into the services of political parties, or of religio-political parties. Christ resisted all such attempts, instead espousing a party that those consumed with the affairs of the present age had forgotten about, had ignored and had eclipsed. My kingdom, Christ said, is not of this world.

That Christ may have been apolitical does not suggest that Christ was unengaged in the issues of poverty, social justice, the upholding of human dignity and stewardship of creation. Again, Obery Hendricks's reading of the Gospels argues for poverty and oppression as factoring significantly into Jesus' teaching. If we were to remove all of the biblical teaching on caring for the marginalized and the significance of social justice, we would be left with a rather slim book. If we took away the role of stewardship of creation and of

---

[37]John Calvin *Institutes of the Christian Religion* 4.20.3.

cultivating natural resources, Adam and Eve would have been left with very little to do in the Garden. It would be too easy to simply identify Jesus with a political party, to simply put him on the left or on the right. The ethic of the new community demands humble participation, maybe even realizing that the solutions to complex social issues and problems transcend party platforms. The ethic of the new community may demand that—like all things for its members—we recognize that we now see dimly, and not so clearly as those who have put Jesus on the left or on the right would like us to think.

EPILOGUE

Jesus and the Gospel in the Twenty-First Century

We believe in one Lord, Jesus Christ,
the only Son of God,
eternally begotten of the Father,
God from God, Light from Light,
true God from true God. . . .
For us and for our salvation
he came down from heaven:
by the power of the Holy Spirit
he became incarnate from the Virgin Mary,
and was made man.

THE NICENE CREED

All of these historical appearances and cultural sightings of Jesus in America mean that he shows up just about everywhere and that he becomes all things to all people. The non-Christian punk band Bad Religion captured this almost too perfectly in their song "American Jesus." He's in the corporations, on the Interstate, lurking in the halls of power, on TV through the televangelists. "We've got the American Jesus," they belt out the recurring lyric, "overwhelming millions every day." The song, from 1993, was intended as a critique of George H. W. Bush's Persian Gulf War with Iraq (1991). They wrote it after they heard then-President Bush speak of assured victory since Jesus was on our side. When George W. Bush returned for more war in Iraq, the song took on whole new life through YouTube and other Internet venues. We know things are bad for Jesus when he shows up not only in songs like this but also on a twenty-five-dollar poker chip, in the sacred heart pose, available on eBay. Jesus, welcome to twenty-first-century America.[1]

This book, however, hasn't been primarily about Jesus in the broader scope of American culture. Instead, attention has been on the Jesus of American evangelicalism. But ferreting out the difference between the broader contours of culture and the specific contours of the subculture of evangelicalism isn't always that easy. To put the matter directly, Jesus hasn't fared too well in American evangelicalism either. I'm not so sure that we are, therefore, necessarily doomed to reap the harvest from the sins sown in the past. For one thing, we have our own sins to contend with. And I think there is something that can be done positively and constructively for American evangelical Christology. In fact, I think there has to be, for the gospel depends on it.

So where does that leave American evangelicalism in looking for a Christology that it can and should hold to, in the words of Jude 3, "once for all"? Perhaps the analysis of the Jesus People by Martin Marty, dean of American church historians, can help. After revealing that the secret to the success of the Jesus People concerned their ability to boil everything down to their focus on the personal experience of Jesus, Marty quickly points out, "Of course, there are problems ahead on all fronts." One such front, Marty contends, is theology. He then parlays the problem: "After the Jesus experience, there occurs at least a minimal measure of interpretation. Who or what did I experience? At this stage the issues of Chalcedon arise." He explains why this ancient council and its creed have a way of popping up: "Is Jesus God?" he would ask of the Jesus People converts, answering for them, "If they want to take their Bible seriously, they have to struggle with ambiguous and complex texts and to qualify the assertion as the church fathers did." Marty also probes on the other side of the Chalcedonian formula, "Is he man?" He then tackles the tough one, how the two natures come together, observing, "Sooner or later they have to relate the divine and the human, and they are back to or have caught up with the Christological and Trinitarian problems that have always haunted Christians." These are haunting challenges indeed.[2]

Marty's questions of the Jesus People actually apply to a great deal of the terrain covered in this book. I think they especially apply to today. I think of his questions when I hear book titles, such as the one by Anne Graham Lotz,

---

[1] I will forever be grateful to Randy Weir, one of my graduate students, for giving me the poker chip.
[2] Martin E. Marty, "Jesus: The Media and the Message," *Theology Today* 28, no. 4 (1972): 475.

Just Give Me Jesus. My question is exactly the same as Marty's. Which Jesus? One could, however, deconstruct the entire title. The word *just* in the title tells us that we need to keep things simple, undefined, focused. The word *me* plays right into the sensibilities of individualism, the privatization of faith and the subjective personal experience—all of the hallmarks of American evangelicalism. And then there's *Jesus.* Of course, she means the God-man, the second person of the Trinity, the one who was born, made human and took on flesh, the one who died and rose again, the Lord and Savior of the universe. No one would expect all of that to be in the title, but one would at least hope to find it in the pages of the book.

American evangelicals have sterling proficiency in the realm of the subjective and experiential. But not all of the answers to life's questions come from within or come from our own time. If American evangelicalism will ever land on that crucial, life-giving Christology it will have to deal with the fifth-century council at Chalcedon as well as that fourth-century one at Nicaea. Behind these councils of course lay the holy Scriptures, the Gospels and Paul, the Old Testament prophets and the other New Testament writers, and their concrete discussion of who Jesus is, what he did and what those two things mean. The Bible and these councils save us from our limited perspectives and our cultural static. In one sense, then, we can answer the question concerning how we construct our deposit of faith in the twenty-first century by telling ourselves that we don't have to start from scratch.

Some might argue that this view fails to see the cultural static at work at Nicaea and at Chalcedon. They were, after all, historically situated events. It's not prudent to argue that the bishops at Nicaea or at Chalcedon were some type of objective and neutral, epistemologically perfect automatons, devoid of individual biases or cultural perspectives. It may very well be prudent, however, to ask, How can the church improve on declaring, as those bishops did, that Christ is fully God and fully human, with two natures united perfectly in one person? And when we add the words from the Nicene Creed that Jesus, who, as God, became human "for us and for our salvation," how can we not see that this view of Jesus as the God-man is imperative for any right understanding of the gospel? These creeds and the biblical texts they are fashioned from provide the church with its perennial theology, which the church in any country in any century simply cannot afford to live without.

From the vantage point of the past, we can cast a more critical eye on the present. Even from the vantage point of the future, we can cast a more critical eye on the present. Looking both backward and forward, in other words, serves to make us a little more mindful of our task in understanding, expressing and even contending for the faith, which has been delivered, entrusted over the centuries, to the saints (Jude 3; 2 Tim 2:2). When it comes to the person and work of Christ, there can be no more crucial task for the church than doing this well. Why wouldn't we seek help from the past?

When we look at and listen to the present, this task becomes all the more urgent. Listening to the present, we hear voices with American accents using Christ for political agendas, and we hear the almost incessant chant of "Just give me my own personal Jesus." When we look, we see Christ reduced to slogans on T-shirts or to moralistic musings on selflessness in a selfish world on a DVD or CD. Rather than develop increasingly cynical eyes and ears to these things, we need to develop discerning eyes and ears that will see through the fog and hear past the din and chatter. Like the Old Testament prophets, we also need to build up, in addition to tearing down. In order to do this, some practical steps may be in order.

To start, it may be helpful to listen to Scripture first, then to tradition (our own church, denominational or confessional tradition), then to experience, rather than the more typical reversal of that order. Listening to tradition means not relying on our own resources to solve all of our problems or answer all of our questions. It takes humility to look to the past. And it takes humility to submit to Scripture.[3]

Second, it also might help to challenge the idea that because something is, it is acceptable. A case in point, we should challenge the idea that because we live in such a consumer-driven culture, the commodification of Christ and Christianity may be given a pass. At times our call to be Christ's disciples means challenging ideas and even whole systems that are presented to us. Often our cultural critique doesn't go deep enough. We have a great deal to say about pornography on the Internet, but we might not be saying enough to how Internet technologies are subtly changing our conceptions of being human and our understandings of human limitations. Again, looking to the past

---

[3]It seems that currently much more attention is given to the voices of the past. InterVarsity Press's ambitious undertaking in publishing the Ancient Christian Commentary on Scripture and the Reformation Commentary on Scripture series are cases in point. This attention bodes well for the church as it moves into the twenty-first century.

helps us gain some perspective on the ways in which we have capitulated to our culture and have subjected Christ to our cultural predilections. Cultural discernment will guard against the acculturation of Jesus that we find so humorous and alarming in others. Along these lines too, exposure to cultures other than American can also be helpful in the development of cultural discernment. Our age is increasingly becoming global, and so is the church. If Philip Jenkins is right, and many think he is, then Christianity is going south—the global South, that is. American and Western evangelicals have long assumed the role of teacher to the global church. We may very well find ourselves to be the students, and we might very well find that we have a great deal to learn.[4]

Third, we must build up and not just tear down. This book has largely been one of criticism. (In my defense, I also recently wrote a book that sought to relay the history of the doctrine of Christ in the early church.) Amidst all of the criticism, which is one of the roles of the theologian in the life of the church, there also needs to be constructive work. We cannot simply assume that those who claim Christ know that he is the God-man, divine and human natures conjoined in one person. It is the task of the church in every age to teach, and teaching the cardinal doctrine of the person of Christ lies at the center of that task.

Finally, and this is especially true in the area of Christology, we need not shrink back from complexity. Jesus comes to us primarily in complexity. He is the God-man, fully human and fully divine in one person. That's a statement packed with tension. And the temptation is to release the tension. This tension is not restricted to theological statements but extends to the actions of Jesus. He is both friend of sinners and righteous Judge, extending both mercy and wrath. Jesus is surprising and unpredictable; he is faithful, demanding, chastising and rebuking, yet loving. In his person and his actions, Jesus is complex; reducing him does not help but harms. In fact, the snapshots of the acculturated Jesus presented in this book, by and large, derive from attempts to reduce Christ, from attempts to relax the tension. But a reduced Christ is less than the Christ of Scripture.

Looking to Scripture and tradition, developing a discerning engagement of

---

[4]Philip Jenkins, *The Next Christendom: The Coming of Global Christianity* (Oxford: Oxford University Press, 2002).

culture, building up by explicitly teaching about and accepting Christ in his complexity all go quite far in preventing us from being overtaken by culture. Of course, they offer no guarantee. Jesus has been made in America, many times over. It is highly likely that he will continue to be remade in the generations to come. This is not a note of pessimism but of realism, and a note that calls us to humility in our own understanding of Jesus. In humility, we look to the God-man, asking him to safeguard us as we safeguard "the faith that was once for all delivered to the saints" (Jude 3).

READING LIST

THE HISTORICAL JESUS AND THE GOSPELS

Bock, Darrell L. *Jesus According to Scripture: Restoring the Portrait from the Gospels*. Grand Rapids: Baker, 2007.

Catchpole, David. *Jesus People: The Historical Jesus and the Beginnings of Community*. Grand Rapids: Baker, 2006.

Evans, Craig A. *Fabricating Jesus: How Modern Scholars Distort the Gospels*. Downers Grove, Ill.: IVP Books, 2006.

McClymond, Michael J. *Familiar Stranger: An Introduction to Jesus of Nazareth*. Grand Rapids: Eerdmans, 2004.

Roberts, Mark D. *Can We Trust the Bible? Investigating the Reliability of Matthew, Mark, Luke, and John*. Wheaton, Ill.: Crossway, 2007.

Stafford, Tim. *Surprised by Jesus: His Agenda for Changing Everything in A.D. 30 and Today*. Downers Grove, Ill.: IVP Books, 2006.

Storkey, Alan. *Jesus and Politics: Confronting the Powers*. Grand Rapids: Baker, 2005.

Witherington, Ben, III. *The Jesus Quest: The Third Search for the Jew of Nazareth*. Downers Grove, Ill.: InterVarsity Press, 1997.

Wright, N. T. *The Challenge of Jesus: Rediscovering Who Jesus Was and Is*. Downers Grove, Ill.: InterVarsity Press, 1999.

———. *Following Jesus: Biblical Reflections on Discipleship*. Grand Rapids: Eerdmans, 1995.

EARLY CHURCH FATHERS

Hall, Christopher A. *Learning Theology with the Church Fathers*. Downers Grove, Ill.: InterVarsity Press, 2002.

———. *Reading Scripture with the Church Fathers*. Downers Grove, Ill.: InterVarsity Press, 1998.

Hanson, R. P. C. *The Search for the Christian Doctrine of God: The Arian Controversy, 318-381.* Grand Rapids: Baker, 2005.

Hardy, Edward Roche, ed. *Christology of the Later Fathers.* Louisville, Ky.: Westminster John Knox Press, 1977.

Hurtado, Larry W. *How on Earth Did Jesus Become God? Historical Questions About Earliest Devotion to Jesus.* Grand Rapids: Eerdmans, 2005.

Litfin, Bryan. *Getting to Know the Church Fathers: An Evangelical Introduction.* Grand Rapids: Brazos, 2007.

McKechnie, Paul. *The First Christian Centuries: Perspectives on the Early Church.* Downers Grove, Ill.: InterVarsity Press, 2001.

Nichols, Stephen J. *For Us and for Our Salvation: The Doctrine of Christ in the Early Church.* Wheaton, Ill.: Crossway, 2007.

Tanner, Kenneth, and Christopher A. Hall, eds. *Ancient & Postmodern Christianity: Paleo-Orthodoxy in the 21st Century: Essays in Honor of Thomas C. Oden.* Downers Grove, Ill.: InterVarsity Press, 2002.

Williams, D. H. *Evangelicals and Tradition: The Formative Influence of the Early Church.* Grand Rapids: Baker, 2005.

Williams, Rowan. *Arius: Heresy & Tradition.* Grand Rapids: Eerdmans, 2001.

SERIES

Ancient Christian Commentary on Scripture. 29 vols. Edited by Thomas C. Oden. Downers Grove, Ill.: InterVarsity Press, 1998- .

Early Christian Writings <www.earlychristianwritings.com>

"The Fathers of the Church," New Advent <www.newadvent.org/fathers>.

HISTORICAL AND THEOLOGICAL WORKS ON CHRISTOLOGY

Anselm. *Why the God-Man?* In *A Scholastic Miscellany: From Anselm to Ockham.* Edited by Eugene R. Fairweather. Philadelphia: Westminster Press, 1961.

Bloesch, Donald G. *Jesus Christ.* Downers Grove, Ill.: InterVarsity Press, 2005.

Bonhoeffer, Dietrich. *Meditations on the Cross.* Edited by Manfred Weber. Louisville, Ky.: Westminster John Knox Press, 1998.

Horton, Michael Scott. *Lord and Servant: A Covenant Christology.* Louisville, Ky.: Westminster John Knox Press, 2005.

Jenson, Robert. *Systematic Theology.* Vol. 1, *The Triune God.* Oxford: Oxford University Press, 1997.

Kärkkäinen, Veli-Matti. *Christology: A Global Introduction.* Grand Rapids: Baker, 2003.

Letham, Robert. *The Work of Christ.* Downers Grove, Ill.: InterVarsity Press, 1993.

MacLeod, Donald. *The Person of Christ.* Downers Grove, Ill.: InterVarsity Press, 1998.

O'Collins, Gerald. *Christology: A Biblical, Historical, and Systematic Study of Jesus Christ.* Oxford: Oxford University Press, 1995.

Stinton, Diane B. *Jesus of Africa: Voices of African Christology.* New York: Orbis, 2004.

Stott, John R. W. *The Cross of Christ.* 20th anniversary ed. Downers Grove, Ill.: IVP Books, 2006.

Wells, David F. *Above All Earthly Powers: Christ in a Postmodern World.* Grand Rapids: Eerdmans, 2005.

CHRISTIANITY AND CULTURE

Borgmann, Albert. *Power Failure: Christianity in the Culture of Technology.* Grand Rapids: Brazos, 2003.

Chung, Sung Wook, ed. *Christ the One and Only: A Global Affirmation of the Uniqueness of Jesus Christ.* Grand Rapids: Baker, 2005.

Clapp, Rodney. *Border Crossings: Christian Trespasses on Popular Culture and Public Affairs.* Grand Rapids: Brazos, 2000.

Dark, David. *Everyday Apocalypse: The Sacred Revealed in Radiohead, The Simpsons, and Other Pop Culture Icons.* Grand Rapids: Brazos, 2002.

———. *The Gospel According to America: A Meditation on a God-Blessed, Christ-Haunted Idea.* Louisville, Ky.: Westminster John Knox Press, 2005.

Edwards, James R. *Is Jesus the Only Savior?* Grand Rapids: Eerdmans, 2005.

Grant, Paul. *Blessed Are the Uncool: Living Authentically in a World of Show.* Downers Grove, Ill.: IVP Books, 2006.

Hsu, Albert Y. *The Suburban Christian: Finding Spiritual Vitality in the Land of Plenty.* Downers Grove, Ill.: IVP Books, 2006.

Kavanaugh, John F. *Following Christ in a Consumer Society: The Spirituality of Cultural Resistance.* New York: Orbis, 2006.

Metzger, Paul Louis. *Consuming Jesus: Beyond Race and Class Divisions in a Consumer Church.* Grand Rapids: Eerdmans, 2007.

Moore, R. Laurence. *Touchdown Jesus: The Mixing of Sacred and Secular in American History.* Louisville, Ky.: Westminster John Knox Press, 2003.

Niebuhr, H. Richard. *Christ and Culture.* 50th anniversary ed. New York: Harper, 2001.

Romanowski, William D. *Eyes Wide Open: Looking for God in Popular Culture.* 2nd ed. Grand Rapids: Brazos, 2007.

Sheler, Jeffery L. *Believers: A Journey into Evangelical America.* New York: Viking, 2006.

Vanhoozer, Kevin J., Charles A. Anderson and Michael J. Sleamsman. *Everyday Theology: How to Read Cultural Texts and Interpret Trends.* Grand Rapids: Baker Academic, 2007.

Index